A Civil War
Correspondent
in New Orleans

A Civil War Correspondent in New Orleans

The Journals and Reports of Albert Gaius Hills of the Boston Journal

EDITED BY GARY L. DYSON

McFarland & Company, Inc., Publishers
Jefferson, North Carolina, and London

LIBRARY OF CONGRESS CATALOGUING-IN-PUBLICATION DATA

Hills, Albert Gaius, 1829–1879.
    A Civil War correspondent in New Orleans : the journals and reports of Albert Gaius Hills of the Boston Journal / edited by Gary L. Dyson.
       p.   cm.
    Includes bibliographical references and index.

    ISBN 978-0-7864-7193-5
    softcover : acid free paper ∞

    1. Hills, Albert Gaius, 1829–1879—Diaries. 2. Hills, Albert Gaius, 1829–1879—Correspondence. 3. New Orleans (La.)—History—Capture, 1862—Personal narratives. 4. Gulf Coast (La.)—History, Naval—19th century. 5. Mississippi River—History, Naval—19th century. 6. United States—History—Civil War, 1861–1865—Naval operations. 7. War correspondents—Louisiana—New Orleans—Diaries. 8. War correspondents—Louisiana—New Orleans—Correspondence. 9. United States—History—Civil War, 1861–1865—Journalists. 10. United States—History—Civil War, 1861–1865—Press coverage. I. Dyson, Gary L., 1965– II. Title.
E472.88.H55 2013
973.7'5—dc23
                                                                           2012045769

BRITISH LIBRARY CATALOGUING DATA ARE AVAILABLE

© 2013 Gary L. Dyson. All rights reserved

No part of this book may be reproduced or transmitted in any form or by any means, electronic or mechanical, including photocopying or recording, or by any information storage and retrieval system, without permission in writing from the publisher.

Front cover images: *The Battle of New Orleans* by Kurz and Allison (Library of Congress); journal page © 2013 Shutterstock; arms permit issued to Albert G. Hills, April 29, 1864, allowing Hills to carry a rifle and revolver for self defense (author collection); Perrin Revolver, serial #755 (courtesy Tim Prince of College Hill Arsenal Civil War Antiques)

Manufactured in the United States of America

McFarland & Company, Inc., Publishers
  Box 611, Jefferson, North Carolina 28640
    www.mcfarlandpub.com

Contents

Preface	1
Introduction	2
1. The Life of Albert Gaius Hills	7
2. Taking New Orleans, 1862	23
3. Covering the Campaign	37
4. About the Journals of A.G. Hills, Reporter for the *Boston Journal*	40
5. Journal of a Military Expedition from Boston to _____	42
6. Sketches Showing the Action on the River	109
7. Memoranda of Letters Sent to the *Boston Journal*	116
8. New Orleans Under Occupation	118
9. A.G. Hills' Third Journal and His Return to New Orleans	123
10. The Reports for the *Boston Journal*	128
Bold Strategy of a Rebel Schooner Under the Guns of Fort San Louis and Confederate Soldiers Captured by the U.S. Steamer *Montgomery*	128
Recollections of the Siege of Forts Jackson and St. Phillip and the Capture of New Orleans	131
Seeking Information Under Difficulties [1]	131
U.S. Steamer *J.P. Jackson* off New Orleans April 30, 1862	132

Letter to Charles O. Rogers, April 28, 1862	149
The Mississippi and the Ram Manassas	151
Letter from the Mississippi River	152
Spectators of the Bombardment	166
How the Sabbath of the Siege Was Observed	166
A Plan for Obstructing the Mississippi at the Forts; Found Among the Papers Left in Fort Jackson and Pronounced Impenetrable by the Most Skillful Officers of Our Squadron	168
The Loss on Both Sides	169
Seeking Information under Difficulties [2]	170
The Surrender of the City	170
Albert Gaius Hills Timeline	173
Notes	175
Bibliography	188
Index	190

Preface

This book presents the wartime journals and articles of Albert Gaius Hills, a correspondent for the *Boston Journal* before, during, and after the Civil War. These journal entries have never been published until now. They present a first person account of the campaign to take New Orleans that began in November 1861. They were included in Mr. Hills' effects that have been passed down through the years.

This book is dedicated to the memory of my father-in-law, Alfred Cochrane Farrell. It was his introduction to the documents left by his ancestor Albert Gaius Hills that made this book possible. He held onto these records and used them as a means to reconnect with distant (living) family members for years. He absolutely appreciated the service of his ancestors and was proud to be part of their bloodline. Al was a student of the period and enjoyed studying the Civil War and visiting the local sites up to his passing in 1997. I wish he could have seen the complete transcriptions of these records that he started so many years ago.

I am also thankful for my wife Emily's help with the transcriptions. Although she never quite deciphered what was written on the pages it helped to have someone else try while my eyes readjusted to proper focus. I am very thankful for her unwavering support and encouragement during my obsession to get every word just right and to make twenty-first century sense out of the nineteenth century transcriptions. She also provided invaluable assistance as an editor, typist, and as a reader with not so much knowledge of the Civil War, helping me to present A.G. Hills' journals in a way that would be appreciated by those who don't consider themselves civil war buffs or history enthusiasts.

Introduction

Although history has never been my vocation, it has always been my passion. As a Maryland native I have always been surrounded by it. The western part of the state has Fort Frederick, a stone fort built for the defense of the frontier during the French and Indian War. Annapolis boasts a rich naval tradition as the home of the United States Naval Academy. Fort McHenry near Baltimore inspired our national anthem while under British bombardment in 1814. The bloodiest single day in the Civil War happened here in September 1862, and there were other important battles and numerous skirmishes in the state during the Civil War years.

The American Civil War grabbed my interest at my first exposure to it, and over time I became a student of other American and European wars as well. The first "vacation" I can remember was a trip to the Antietam Battlefield in Sharpsburg, Maryland. There was a quick visit to the visitor's center (it was free then), the auto tour, getting out at some of the numbered points, and a stop at a local antique shop to buy advertised relics of the battle. I still have a bayonet that was supposedly dug up from that battlefield. There never seemed to be much of a crowd in those days, allowing my mind to better picture what the battlefield conditions were in 1862. Living in the suburbs of Washington, DC, I was centrally located to visit all of the major battlefields of the eastern theatre: Manassas, Antietam, Gettysburg, the Wilderness, as well as the lesser known fields of Ball's Bluff, South Mountain, and the Monocacy, and many times at each site. On a few occasions I was privileged to visit some western battlefields like Murfreesboro, Chickamauga, and Lookout Mountain. All were unique in the history they told.

Over the years I have accumulated a respectable library covering American wars both near and far, and adding to my "bucket list" of battlefields I'd like to visit. One of my greatest regrets is not visiting some of the World War II Pacific battlefields when I served an enlistment in the Marine Corps in the 1980s, especially while on Okinawa. I've made it a goal not just to read the history books but to try to experience the battlefields at the ground level to the best of my ability. Learning the strategies and tactics specific to each battle is important, of course, but to me nothing can substitute for walking the ground that has become sacred. To this day a favorite pastime for me and my friends Bobby and Jim is to grab one of Harry Pfanz's Gettysburg books and pick a regiment to trace, or find the modern day location of a Civil War photograph found in one of William Frassanito's, sometimes photographing a friend mimicking a deathly pose with a stick picked up nearby. Crossing streams, fences, and dodging livestock just adds to the fun. On one trip to Appomattox we drove five hours, stayed for one hour, and then drove straight back. Not seeing everything we planned to see on a particular battlefield would just give us a good excuse to return again and again. We'd spend a lot of time at the bookstores to add to our libraries. Over the years I've collected regimental histories, and I've read newspapers, diaries, and any first person accounts I could get my hands on to learn every possible detail about the combatants.

After I was married, I learned about my wife Emily's ancestors and their connection to the Civil War through actual first hand documents and handwritten journals. Her family had kept accurate genealogical records for over a hundred years, making the tracing of family history remarkably clear. More than one of her ancestors can be traced back to the *Mayflower*. There are veterans of King Phillip's War in 1676 as well as French and Indian War and Revolutionary War veterans. Her great-great-grandfather was Frederick Calvin Hills, Assistant Paymaster serving on the USS *Isaac P. Smith* and later the USS *DeSoto* during the Civil War. He was wounded and captured when the *Isaac P. Smith* came under a murderous cross fire from hidden Confederate field batteries along the Stono River near Charleston, South Carolina, early in 1863. Grounded and unable to get free, the ship surrendered. An attempt to rescue the vessel failed, and the rebels salvaged her for their own use. F.C. Hills spent time as a prisoner of war in South Carolina before being exchanged at Libby Prison in Richmond. His total service was about two years and he was discharged at the end of 1864. We are all, of course, extremely proud of his service (and survival) that has brought us to our current place in history. Other than some period photographs and a document of his service record and maybe some documents relating to a pension there is little tangible evidence of his service. But his brother Albert Gaius Hills left so much more, and his legacy may be even more entwined in the war's events.

A.G. Hills was a reporter for the *Boston Journal* before, during and after the war, and kept records of just about everything he did. He left his journals, three of which I have transcribed for this book, but he also acquired documents of the events transpiring around him. As a reporter he found value in the newspapers printed where he was sent. He collected these papers as well as many other documents related to the conflict, especially those of the Southern Confederacy. While in New Orleans he gathered issues of the *Daily Delta, Daily Picayune, Daily True Delta, Southern Sentinel, Opelousas Courier*, and a few others. Several were Confederate editions printed on wallpaper. He also kept letters and passes related to his own movements within the theatre of war, and picked up other documents such as a Confederate Constitution, Confederate General Orders for the defense of New Orleans, troop rosters, ship crew lists, autographs, pamphlets related to southern secession, maps, and some interesting letters from other participants within the Department of the Gulf. How he acquired so many documents will remain a mystery, especially since a considerable amount either came from places he had never been or were dated at times when he was home or many miles away. All of these he kept after the war along with a journal of his postwar travels to Europe to sell the Marshall engraving of Abraham Lincoln.

A.G. and his wife Sarah had no children to inherit these documents and records, so it is likely that they became a part of Frederick Calvin's archive and were eventually passed to his children. Frederick Calvin's eldest son was Frederick Albert Hills and his eldest child was Katharine Hills, mother of Alfred Farrell, my father-in-law. Al had access to these documents at least by his undergraduate days at Middlebury College in Vermont in the late 1950s (I have one of his history term papers to prove it) and tried through the years to transcribe the journals. He had some success but wasn't able to get very far due to raising a family and working and finding the time. He came to possess much of the family archive after his mother Katharine passed away in 1986. Later as he became a brittle diabetic, his vision began to fail, making transcription of A.G.'s journals nearly impossible. Al knew that he had records of the Civil War of historical value, and I am grateful that he held on to these journals and papers as long as he did. He wanted to know all he could of this part of American history since he had a direct connection, and I was happy to take him to the nearest battlefields so he could see them as best he could. With his passing in 1997, I became the keeper of everything historical, and from time to time over the years I dipped into the journals, a page or two at a time. I knew that there were many items of historical interest, and some things that were of considerable value.

Introduction 5

Following a recent early retirement I gained the time to complete the work Al started, a task which hasn't failed to both frustrate and excite me. Having an extensive knowledge of the period in general and a substantial library to focus on specifics of the battles in Louisiana helped immensely in the transcriptions. Finding some of the actual newspaper articles from A.G. Hills in an original *Boston Journal* edition helped to verify my efforts. I could trace Hills' travels using the *Official Military Atlas of the Civil War*, discovering points on the map that are not so easy to find using a simple internet search. These along with other documents helped to trace the movements of A.G. Hills with relative certainty through April of 1864 and with probability through the first couple of months of 1865. Family legend has him as a prisoner at Libby Prison following an unsuccessful scout of the defenses of Savannah in 1864, but this has not been verified. I have my doubts. The documents he had left clues to where he had been and what he was doing even when journal entries did not. I read these documents numerous times with new bits of information making more sense each time I read them. The dates, names, and signatures helped fit the pieces together for his story. Finding his name in newspapers from 1849 through 1879 provided information the family had never known. Based on the documents he left behind I'm confident he finished the war as a correspondent covering the last of the seaborne campaigns against the Confederacy and sought opportunities in the postwar South. Regardless of any questions about his life or inconsistencies in his story, A.G. Hills had a front row seat to some of the pivotal battles and campaigns of the Civil War, especially those on the lower Mississippi and the Gulf Coast.

The journals and reports themselves were recorded in period journal books and loose paper, some very thin and translucent, and well preserved and protected. There were sketches and notes tucked in some of the pages and book entries were made from both ends; that is, the journal was flipped over and new entries made as if in a new book. A separate journal contained newspaper clippings related to secession only, a subject that seemed to be of great interest to Mr. Hills.

Hills' practice of writing down his thoughts and scenes in journals, especially during those turbulent years, has produced a valuable historical resource. I believe the journals and articles are interesting, entertaining, and informative in their own right and could stand alone as a reference for those who know about the battle. I have included histories of Hills' life and of the campaign to take New Orleans in 1862 so the reader may better understand his story. A section about New Orleans in late 1862 has also been included to coincide with Hills' return. Hills used the phrase "Up All Hammocks!" on a few occasions, indicative of the frequent alarms on ship for the crews to get up and begin firing mortars at Forts Jackson and St. Phillip or prepare to run past the forts entirely. It has stuck with me since reading his journals because it reminds me of the sound of the metal trash can being slung down the concrete floor of my barracks at Parris Island MCRD as a seventeen year old recruit. It meant it was time to get up and be ready for action, a very fitting phrase for the Union fleet as it ascended the Mississippi River on the way to New Orleans and into battle for the first time for most of the participants.

While I hope the journal entries and reports are of value to Civil War history enthusiasts, my goal has been to make an interesting read for anyone seeking a personal history of the period regardless of their knowledge of the battles and campaigns. After all, A.G. Hills was a reporter, not a soldier or a sailor. The letters he sent back to the *Boston Journal* were meant for everyone to understand and appreciate the sacrifices being made on their behalf. Regrettably I do not have an original image of Mr. Hills, just photocopies which would not reproduce well for this book. By the Civil War he was mostly bald with a long beard. He had a slight frame at about 5' 8" and 145 pounds despite eating and drinking well by all accounts. Had he lived a bit longer I have no doubt he would have compiled his own memoirs, so I hope this work does him justice describing his remarkable life.

1

The Life of Albert Gaius Hills

A.G. Hills, eldest son of Luther Hills and Mercy Eldridge, was born on August 26, 1829, in Yarmouth, Massachusetts. His parents were from Swanzey, New Hampshire, a town founded in 1733 a little north of the Massachusetts border and just a little bit south of Keene.[1] His great-great-grandfather Samuel Hills was one of the original grantees of Swanzey.[2] A.G.'s great-grandfather Ebenezer Hills was one of the first children born there, and his grandfather Gaius Hills is credited with establishing the Universalist Society[3] there. His father, Luther Hills, was a self-made man, having lost his father at the age of 4 and mother when he was 15. The children likely were placed in the custody of their uncle Ebenezer Hills, who moved to Swanzey the year of their mother's death (1815).[4] Family records suggest that Luther resided with Ebenezer's family for just a couple of years and moved to Boston at the age of seventeen, with his brother Albert and sister Clarissa following him later. Luther married Mercy in 1827. A.G. was born two years later, the eldest of seven. His brother Frederick Calvin Hills would become an officer in the Union Navy in 1862. His other siblings were Charles Cummings, Olive E., Frederick W., Almaritta, and Irene.

Luther was employed as a pattern maker and later as a painter, but he became a very successful lecturer on the subjects of natural history and phrenology, receiving numerous accolades from the social elite of Boston, and providing the necessary resources to raise a large family. The family resided in Barnstable, Dorchester, Yarmouth, and finally Chelsea, Massachusetts, by the time of the Civil War, although A.G.'s father was constantly traveling on the lecture circuit throughout Massachusetts and into adjoining states. Despite the travel the bond between father and son was very strong. A.G. had great respect for his father and appreciated his humble beginnings.[5]

Albert did not follow in his father's footsteps, at least not at first according to an 1850 census taken in Yarmouth, Massachusetts, on August 18. That census lists Albert as a sailor, a curious career choice for someone who suffered frequently and severely from seasickness according to his own journal entries. The family must have moved soon after that census because they also appear on the 1850 census for Dorchester, Massachusetts, taken on September 14 the same year. There Albert is listed as a pattern maker, just like his father, Luther. No matter his vocation, by all accounts he was extremely healthy and bright[6]; he graduated December 23, 1853, from the Mercantile Academy at 9th and Tremont Streets in Boston having mastered a program of "practical writing, bookkeeping, and arithmetic." Also in 1853 he married Sarah Kenfield, who he would often refer to as "Sallie" in his letters home during the Civil War. Sometime between 1853 and 1860 Hills decided to make the most of his education and became a reporter for the *Boston Journal*, his profession of choice for the rest of his life. Sometime in the late 1850s Hills started suburban reporting for the *Journal*, the first of the Boston papers to start that practice.[7] It is ironic that his profession as a reporter took him back to sea on so many occasions.

As war approached A.G.'s sentiments were decidedly anti-slavery and pro–Lincoln. He even attended an inaugural ball at Mount Vernon Hall[8] on March 6, 1861. He later associated with "Black Republicans"[9] in the press corps, although he was much more moderate in his political views. Still, he was an ardent Unionist and supporter of President Lincoln, and deemed the southern secessionists as traitors. He had several ancestors who had served in the Revolution, and he was motivated to travel far in the service of his country. So at the age of 32 he began his war experience as a correspondent for the *Boston Journal*, attached to Major General Benjamin Butler's campaign to capture the Confederacy's largest city, New Orleans.[10] One could speculate that he was assigned to cover the naval campaign because of his past experience as a sailor, leaving the land campaigns to others like the older Charles Coffin.[11]

The war was seven months old but there was still a sense that it wouldn't last too long if only a major victory could be achieved. Hills was very excited to be part of the expedition but still apprehensive. He was following in the footsteps of his revolutionary ancestors, albeit with a pen instead of a musket, and he was proud to be among his fellow New Englanders. Many of the regiments in the expedition were from New England, and Hills believed he had a responsibility to document the Massachusetts troop's exploits for the readers back home. As the war hadn't begun all that favorably for the Union, Hills must have thought of the possibility of not surviving, even though he was a noncombatant. Before he left he took out an insurance policy on his life just in case.

A.G. wasn't certain of the destination of the expedition until orders were open while at Fortress Monroe in Virginia at the end of November 1861. The Union army regiments under Butler and the naval forces under Flag Officer David Farragut and Commodore David Porter were to collect and train forces at newly acquired Ship Island off the Mississippi Coast. They would then force a passage of the Mississippi past Forts Jackson and St. Phillip below New Orleans, and then force the surrender of the forts and the city. A.G. kept copies of the general orders (almost every single one, and original copies were used for this book) issued by the Department of the Gulf during his stay on Ship Island and at New Orleans. These orders provide a chronological description of the buildup before the attack and of the occupation. Enduring months at sea and excursions around the gulf, he finally witnessed action and enemy fire on multiple occasions late in April 1862.

His travels took him to Key West, smaller keys (that are not generally identified on some modern maps) on the west coast of Florida, Fort Pickens, Biloxi, and his home away from home, Ship Island. His journal recorded the scarcity of rebel troops along the Gulf Coast and went into detail describing the existing conditions of Cedar Key, the defenses of Pensacola, and raids outside Fort Pickens and Biloxi as well as noting flora, fauna, and local histories. He kept a journal of his experiences from the day he left Boston on November 21, 1861, until the opening of the naval battle that led to the capture of New Orleans. After the passage of the forts he renewed his entries in a new journal and added some statistics and sketches. In the weeks following the capture he took time to write more descriptive (and legible) reports of the various engagements. While in the Gulf and on the Mississippi River he associated with others in his vocation representing papers such as the *New York Herald*, *Frank Leslie's Illustrated*, and *Harper's Weekly*. In May 1862, after the fall of New Orleans, he traveled back to his home in Chelsea, Massachusetts, to reunite with family and prepare for his next assignments. Hills' reports for the campaign found their way to other papers as well, even the *Sacramento Union*.

After the fall of New Orleans and a brief respite at home he boarded another steamer to cover the war effort. Once again he wasn't certain of his destination, but once again he ended up in New Orleans. In that city he discussed the failure of the Union attack on Galveston, Texas, with his reporter friends, perhaps as background information for reporting the next attack there early in 1863. He then followed General Nathaniel Banks' 1863 expedition to push up the Mississippi and capture Port Hudson. He began a journal of these actions but either stopped abruptly or kept his writings in other books that have been lost. (A description of his activities and those of others in his profession have been preserved in the Thomas Banks Gunn diaries.) His journal covering General Banks' campaign started almost exactly one year after he left Boston for New Orleans. He writes of meeting General McClellan in New York as the expedition begins and predicts that McClellan will run for President in the 1864 election (he was right). Some of his journal is illegible, but his last entry describes a battle scene in which Union troops suffer heavy casualties. He admits to not being able to express what he has seen, and then the journal ends in mid-sentence.

A.G. Hills spent a lot of time in New Orleans in 1863. He was privileged to reside at the St. Charles Hotel in close quarters with General Butler and his staff, and was able to view (or procure) documents related to the New Orleans Campaign specifically or the Confederacy in general, as well as several dozen Union and Confederate newspapers from the region. Some of these papers predate the Union occupation of New Orleans, so how he got them remains a mystery. He interviewed General Butler, Commander Porter, and Flag Officer Farragut. As late as 1864 he was still going about his duties in New Orleans and other parts of Louisiana. In addition to acting as a correspondent he and fellow reporter Alfred C. Hills (unrelated) became editors of the New Orleans *Daily Delta* (soon to be renamed the *Era*) newspaper, and set up shop on 94 Camp Street. A.G. Hills was frequently in the company of a group of reporters from several different northern newspapers. During the New Orleans Campaign these included Waud and Winser. On his return these were Gunn, Hills (A.C.), Hayes, Hamilton, Powers, Waud (again), and F.H. Schell. They appear to have become good friends, although they certainly embraced a highly competitive spirit.[12]

Although A.G. kept journals, documents, and "souvenirs" of his travels, his family knew little about his personality until I read portions of the Thomas Butler Gunn diaries. Gunn was from England and a correspondent like Hills, but wrote in his diary of the daily activities of a group of correspondents covering the war on the Mississippi. From New York City they departed for points unknown once again, on the steamer *North Star*. Some thought they were heading for Texas, but they seemed to hope that it wasn't Virginia. They frequently associated with officers and were fond of alcohol, a combination likely to provide needed information for their letters to their home papers. Gunn described Hills as "a good looking fair-bearded Bostonian" and "good natured and approbative," but "terribly nervous and apprehensive"[13] about his peers' getting ahead of him, being particularly jealous of a younger reporter named Hayes. Gunn described this rivalry as comical and seemed to be quite entertained by it. Competing with the New York papers, Hills was at a slight disadvantage, there being an extra mail day between New York and Boston when reports were sent home. Gunn even noted that Hills was not averse to using underhanded means to stay a step ahead of his competition, and that Hills seemed to lack confidence that he was up to the task of performing as a war correspondent. Hills seemed to always be nervous about the reception of his letters sent back to the *Journal*, as he was bent on excelling in his profession. The group had an agreement that they would share information, but Hills and other did not always honor the pact. Correspondents who struck out on their own without informing the group risked being shunned from the correspondents' activities.

Despite rivalries, the group managed to get along together rather well, frequently dining together and enjoying "whiskey-skins"[14] on numerous occasions.[15] They thrived on the "Bohemian"[16] lifestyle, consuming applejack, ale, and other spirits and often loafing between opportunities to cover stories in the field. Meals were taken at "Wibels," "the Southern Restaurant," the Richelieu and the St. Charles Hotel where they enjoyed steak, eggs, and oysters.[17] Despite the close quarters shared by this group it is interesting to note that Hills did not mention Gunn in any of his journals, and the candor with which Gunn wrote regarding his correspondent friends is mostly absent in Hills' journals. I believe that Hills shied away from such remarks because his journals had already been accessed on his first trip to New Orleans when he was on the *Constitution*.

Once in New Orleans they ventured up and down the river between New Orleans and Baton Rouge. They expected to come under fire as they neared Baton Rouge, but there was little to report since rebel forces had recently pulled back to the defenses at Port Hudson. This lack of reporting fodder sent the reports back to New Orleans where they found other diversions to pass the time, frequenting Union ships and prying information out of officers. Hills continued collecting newspapers from the region from both sides, and one of his sources for these was Union General Grover.[18] When there was something to report it had to be done quickly in order to send reports downriver to New Orleans. Gunboats transporting this news were on the navy's schedule, not theirs, so the reporters had to be ready when they were. Staying together as a group or in pairs seems to have been the rule, there being violence in the streets at times with murders all too frequent.

Movements of the correspondents required permits from the Provost Marshal. Hills kept permits and a letter that allowed him to carry weapons for personal protection within the lines. Sailing on gunboats and supply ships upriver was equally dangerous with Confederate bushwhackers eager to pick off Unionists and capture badly needed goods. On one excursion after Christmas 1862 Hills traveled to Berwick Bay to visit the encampment of a Negro regiment, the 2nd Louisiana Native Guards. It may have been during this visit that he was inspired to join the war effort as an army officer, although serving more as an editor-reporter at the *Era* for General Banks seems to have been the primary reason. On January 7, 1863, he was issued a horse, saddle and bridle in New Orleans from the Quarter Master, S.B. Holabird,[19] to accompany an expedition whenever he needed them. Whether this was for an immediate expedition or the one in March towards Port Hudson is not clear.

Although Hills spent most of the war as a correspondent, for a brief period he served as an army first lieutenant in the 4th Regiment Louisiana Native Guards. In March the unit was renamed the 76th Colored Infantry,

Arms Permit allowing Hills to carry a rifle and revolver for self defense.

a unit in the famed Corps d'Afrique, recruited from slaves and free blacks in the New Orleans area.[20] Hills was assigned to Company C. His commission was dated February 15, 1863, the same date as that of his friend Alfred C. Hills,[21] although A.C. had persuaded General Banks to give him the rank of lieutenant colonel in the same regiment.[22] Regardless of any army service Hills was still able to maintain his position as an editor of the *Era*,[23] so with two army officers as editors there can be little doubt that it was a very pro–Union paper supportive of General Banks.

There is a sense that A.G. Hills lived somewhat in the shadow of A.C. Hills while in the 4th and with the *Era*. A.G. followed A.C. into the army and the *Era* although not with an abundance of enthusiasm or braggadocio. It is probable that the Hillses' venture with the *Era* caused a rift in the cadre of correspondents since the Hillses had gained an advantage in area reporting as an extension of the army. Banks used the paper to counter the other southern-leaning or less Republican papers in New Orleans and as a political tool to help elect a free governor of Louisiana, Michael Hahn, early in 1864. While not all papers where anti–Union, they may not have been pro–Banks. A.G. Hills still managed to cover military campaigns in the state. Stories from the *Era* were picked up by other papers in New Orleans, as made evident by the June 2, 1863, edition of the *Bee*:

A Great Battle at Port Hudson
LOSS HEAVY ON BOTH SIDES
The *Era* has received the following dispatch
From Port Hudson, with authority to publish:
Headquarters 19th Army Corps
Before Port Hudson, May 28, 1863
To the Editor of the Era:
A severe battle was fought here yesterday by the forces under Major Gen. Banks and the rebel garrison in Port Hudson. The loss was considerable on both sides, but will fall short of the first estimate. Our forces advanced to the enemy's works, and hold their position to-day. A. G. H.

A.G. Hills served for only three months, however, and by May 1863 he had resigned his commission for the reasons described in this resignation letter:

New Orleans May 18th 1863

To Lieut. Col. Irwin
A.A.G.

Sir, I have the honor most respectfully to tender my resignation as First Lieutenant, Co. C. 4th Louisiana Native Guards, and to ask that the same may be accepted immediately.

My reasons for this step are, that in my connection with the publication of the Era Newspaper I can in my opinion better serve the interests of the government in a private capacity than as an officer of the service, and that the colonel commanding my regiment desires the services of First Lieutenant in my company.

>I am Colonel,
>most respectfully,
>your obt. Svt.
>Albert G. Hills
>1st Lieutenant Co. C 4th La. N.G.

Approved
  N.P. Banks
  M.G.C.

A.C. Hills resigned in July of 1863, for the same reasons as A.G. Hills (the letters are almost identical in wording).

The 4th didn't see any major action while A.G. was a member, but he may have still managed to witness some of the carnage inflicted on Union units during the assaults on Port Hudson before being commissioned. Fortunately for A.G. he was able to resign well before the mutiny in the 4th Regiment in the summer of 1863.[24] General Banks had issued a general order earlier in the year to set guidelines for officers desiring to resign their commissions, as the practice may have been getting out of hand.[25] It was also about this time that A.G.'s brother Frederick Calvin Hills, a naval officer on the USS *Isaac P. Smith*, was slightly wounded in the temple and captured in the only instance in the Civil War where Confederate field batteries captured a U.S. Navy warship. Not knowing his brother's fate may also have been a factor[26] for A.G.'s resignation, even though he didn't mention it.

Without journal entries or correspondence after early 1863, Hills' actions for the remainder of the war have been extrapolated from the artifacts he left behind and period newspapers. Passes and authorizations through the Provost Marshall's office in New Orleans place A.G. in New Orleans as a resident at least as late as April 1864, but he did get away from time to time. He made a trip to New York in June 1863 but returned to New Orleans in August. Hills also took a side trip to Havana in January 1864. He was registered as a qualified elector in New Orleans in November 1863 and had to sign a loyalty oath in January 1864 despite being a Massachusetts resident. In April he was covering the Red River campaign, moving up the river from Alexandria, Louisiana, to join General Banks' headquarters. This was not a lengthy tour since at this time the Red River Campaign was ending in failure following a defeat at Sabine Crossroads.

In late May 1864 he was granted permission to carry a double barreled shotgun to New York by the Provost Marshal, and by the end of that month he was returning to New York.

1. The Life of Albert Gaius Hills 15

The *Era* was still being published until early 1865, but Hills' association with it seems to have ended in March 1864 following a disagreement with A.C. Hills. A.C. Hills seems to have retained a connection with the *Era* until January 1865 when he joined the staff of the *New Orleans True Delta*. The disagreement resulted in the two going their separate ways, but the financial settlement of their feud was left to their widows and the United States Government. The widows' petition was described and resolved in a claim to the Senate on July 5, 1882:

[47TH CONGRESS   REPORT
1st Session.   **SENATE**   {No. 786.
IN THE SENATE OF THE UNITED STATES.
      JULY 5, 1882.—Ordered to be printed.
Mr. HOAR, from the Committee on Claims, submitted the following
         REPORT:
     [To accompany bill S. 1931.1

The Committee on Claims, to whom was referred the bill (S. 1931) *for the relief of Agnes W. and Sarah J. Hills, have considered the same, and respectfully report:*

  That the facts in this case are set forth in the annexed report from the Committee on War Claims of the House of Representatives, which your committee adopt, and recommend that the bill do pass.
Mr. RANNSEY, from the Committee on War Claims, submitted the following report (to
       accompany bill H. R. 6182):
The Committee on War Claims, to whom were referred the bills (H. R. Nos. 692 and 843) for the relief of Sarah J. Hills and Agnes W. Hills, report as follows:

  It appears from the papers in the case, which are very voluminous, that General Butler, while in command at New Orleans, suppressed and took possession of the True Delta newspaper for a violation of a proclamation, and that the property was occupied and used for printing purposes for the Army, and a paper issued publishing orders, proclamations, &c.
  General Butler was finally succeeded in command at New Orleans by General N. P. Banks, who, by special order No. 40, dated February 9, 1863, granted permission to the workmen employed on the Daily Delta to continue its publication until further orders, under the management of its foreman, one Henry Green.
  On the following day, by special order No. 41, General Banks directed:
  "Paragraph 10. The newspaper and job office of the Daily Delta, together with the presses, paper, type, ink, materials, & c., will be turned over to Lieut. Col. Alfred C. Hills, Fourth Regiment Louisiana Native Guards, and to Albert G. Hills, esq., who are charged with the publication of the Daily Delta newspaper and the management of the job office from this date."
  On March 5, 1863, by special order No. 64, General Banks directed:
  "Paragraph 6. Lieut. Col. Alfred C. Hills, Fourth Louisiana Native

Guards, and First Lieut. Albert G. Hills, Fourth Louisiana Native Guards, are detailed for special duty in this city (New Orleans) to take charge of the Era newspaper and job office, to date, the former from the 23d, and the latter from the 20th ultimo (February)."

It appears from the papers that these officers remained in the service, A.G. until May 1863, and A.C. until July 1863, at which dates they resigned their commissions. But they continued in the management and charge of the *Era*. The *Era* was the same establishment as the *Daily Delta*, the name only having been changed. A.G.'s formal association with the *Boston Journal* appears to have come to an end, but he wasn't forgotten in the Boston papers. This article appeared in the *Boston Herald* on May 21, 1863, after a report that he was arrested for allowing a questionable article to be printed in the *Era*:

AFFAIRS ABOUT HOME
PERSONAL. It was erroneously stated in this paper the other day that Capt. A.G. Hills had been placed under arrest in New Orleans. Lieut. A.G. Hills, formerly connected with the Boston press, is the business manager of the New Orleans Era. The editor of that paper is Lieut. Col. A.C. Hills, formerly of the New York press, and the similarity of the names led to the error. The friends of Lieut. Hills may be assured that he has not been interfered with in his duties.[27]

In October, 1863, under the orders of the President of the United States directing captured and abandoned property, not required for military purposes, to be turned over by the military authorities to the special agents of the Treasury Department, General Banks' quartermaster, Colonel Holabird, turned over this property to B. F. Flanders, special agent of the Treasury Department, but on the 25th of October, 1863, General Banks, by a letter to Mr. Flanders, setting forth the necessity of having a newspaper for the publication of his proclamations, orders, &c, withdrew the property from Wanders, revoking Colonel Holabird's action.

On the 16th of March, 1864, General Banks, by special order No. 67, directed:

"Paragraph 3. The editors of the Era, Messrs. Hills & Hills, being unable to continue the business of publication together, are relieved from the operations of the order issued in regard to the management of the Era. The conducting of the paper is hereby assigned to Messrs. J. W. Fairfax and T. G. Tracy, employees in the office, to be conducted under the same general regulations and instructions given to the Messrs. Hills by paragraph 10 of special order 41, of 1863, from these headquarters, and by letter dated February, 1863. Capt. Stephen Hoyt, mayor, Col. Frank E. Howe, and James T. Tucker are hereby appointed to settle the affairs of the concern, and will report their judgment to these headquarters for confirmation."

On the 7th of April, 1864, the commission named above made a report, which is as follows:

"The undersigned, appointed a commission by special order 67, Department of the Gulf, a copy of which is herewith enclosed, to settle the affairs of the Era concert, have the honor to respectfully report that after an investigation into the affairs of the Era, they recommend that the management and conducting of the paper known *as* the Era be turned over to Messrs. J. W. Fairfax and T. G. Tracy, now and for a long time past employees of the Era, it however being understood that the status of the government in regard to the management of the paper and the office is in no way changed by the action of the commission, or rather by its recommendation. We do this because we believe that it is impossible and impracticable to settle the differences between the Messrs. Hills & Hills. To do this it seems to be necessary for the government to advance to the Messrs. Hills *&* Hills, as due them at the date of the order (March 16, 1864), for stock in the office as below mentioned, exclusive of course of all the type and material in the office belonging to the government, or as left by Messrs. Clark & Brown at the time of the possession given to Hills & Hills, the sum of $7,561.80.

Material and type in the newspaper office	$2,500.00
Type and material in the job printing office	1,900.00
News printing-paper on hand	2,900.00
Sundries	261.00
	7,561.80

"Say $7,561.80, the government being held secure not only by this amount of stock now on hand, but also by deducting this amount from the bills that are first due the Era for the public printing and advertising, as was done in the case of Messrs. Hills & Hills, who thus liquidated the claims of the government against them at the time of their taking possession of the office.

"STEPHEN HOYT.
"FRANK E. HOWE.
"JAMES T. TICKER"

This newspaper establishment was carried on by the Messrs. Hills until the 16th of March, 1864, a period of about thirteen months. During the period this newspaper establishment was under the control of the Messrs. Hills — from the 10th of February, 1863, to the l6th of March, 1864 — large quantities of material necessary to the operations of the office were purchased by them, and, at the time of the transfer of the establishment to their successors under the military order above referred to, a certain quantity of this material remained on hand unexpended and unused. For the value of this material, consisting of type, material, and paper, a claim was made by the Messrs. Hills against the government, amounting to $10,779.30: and on the giving up of the newspaper establishment under the order of General Banks by the Messrs. Hills, a commission was appointed by the department commander to make an estimate of the value of the materials on hand, as had been done when they took possession, the object of the survey being to ascertain whether the then value of the materials exceeded or fell short of its amount when the establishment was turned over to them. By the report of this commission the amount of the claim of the Messrs. Hills was reduced to $7,561.80.

Subsequently, on the 23d of November, l864, an order was issued by

General Hurlbut, the department commander who succeeded General Banks, appointing a board of survey to ascertain whether the Messrs. Hills owed anything to the government for rent of material in the newspaper and job office used by them during the period they had possession. This board of survey made a report to the effect that $1,950 was due on account of rent of such material.

It may be well to remark, in this connection, that the Messrs. Hills distinctly understood that no rent was to be charged for the use of the materials to be used by them as the publication of a loyal newspaper in such a city and at such a time was deemed amply sufficient to compensate for the value of all materials so used.

General N. P. Banks makes the following statement concerning the claim of Messrs. Hills:

"During the early part of the war there were several newspapers published in New Orleans, all hostile to the government, and very free in the expression of their views when it was thought to be safe. Several of these journals were suppressed. That left upon the hands of the government a considerable quantity of printing material, presses, &c. In February, 1865, Col. A. C. Hills, formerly of the New York Evening Post, and Mr. A.G. Hills, of the Boston Journal, desired to use some of these materials for the publication of a daily journal in support of the government. Such a paper was greatly needed for the publication of proclamations, circulars, military orders, and the news from different parts of the country, of great interest to the people, and constantly misrepresented by the Southern journals. The property was rightfully in possession of the military authorities, and could not have been properly used except by their consent. The use of these materials was accorded to these gentlemen for the, purpose stated, and they published a very spirited and useful journal for more than a year. The materials they used and the building assigned to them were unoccupied and worthless to the government for any purpose whatever; they could not have been rented, except for speculative purposes, or with a view to opposition to the policy of the government, for any sum whatever. The enterprise they had undertaken was successful, and a considerable amount of printing material was added to the stock of government property during this period. The material added to the stock of type, &c., was indispensable to complete the equipment requisite for the publication of their journal; without these additions the material would have been worthless for newspaper purposes. In March, 1864, a disagreement occurring between the Messrs. Hills, I ordered them to turn the property over to Tracy and Fairfax, men employed in the office, and appointed a commission to settle their affairs. After a careful examination of all the property, the old and the new, the commission, composed of just and careful men, with a proper regard for the interests of the government, reported that the printing material added to the government stock had cost several thousand dollars: the exact amount will be shown in the report. In November, 1864, while I was in the North on leave of absence, a board of survey was appointed to ascertain what amount, if any, might be duo from the contractors of the journal to the government for rent of property and building. This board reported that the sum of $1,950 was due from them. It was never my intention that any rent, either for material or building, should be charged to them or paid by them, as at the time they took the property it would have been worth nothing to anybody except for the purposes stated above. The property added to the printing material belonging to the government was purchased by them out of their own funds, and it belonged exclusively to them; they were not expected to account for and pay it over to the government, nor was the government under any obligation to make good any claims that might exist against them. They were to have all the profits and take all the chances of loss and gain, and be responsible for all losses. They were not agents of the government, but acting as owners, and as such, with all the rights of the latter. They were under no obligations to the government, except to return in good condition the property which was intrusted to them. They had the use of the material and the rent of the building free; beyond that the government was under no obligation to them whatever. Suit was afterwards brought by the successors of Hills & Hills against the supervising agent, of the Treasury Department who dispossessed them of the property, in the court of the United States of the district of Louisiana, and decided in their favor after a full review of all the facts. This was a just decision, perfectly in conformity with the true statement of the facts. It is unnecessary for me to speak of the object had in view by the parties who pursued these men and who sought possession of this property."

General Hurlbut, in a letter dated at Washington, D. C., February 26, 1879, says:

"The board of survey was ordered by me on the official report of Mr. B. F. Flanders. The facts stated by General Banks were not presented before the board or known to me as the approving officer. Had they been presented I have no doubt the decision would have been in favor of the Hills."

The Messrs. Hills have both died, and the claim is now prosecuted by the widows of the deceased.

The committee are of opinion that the sum of $7,561.80[28] is justly due the claimants, and report a substitute for the bills (H. R. 692 and 843) appropriating that amount, and recommend its passage.[29]

There are still some holes in the story of A.G. Hills. That he continued following the Union war effort in the Department of the Gulf is known, but following his work with the *Era* he did not return to the *Boston Journal* for several years. His connections and friendships still gave him access to war news. Among his possessions was a January issue of the *Savannah Republican*[30] as well as a detailed map of the assault on Fort Fisher, North Carolina, in January of 1865, so in all likelihood he was still reporting, covering that battle at that time in some capacity. It is not known for certain if he returned again to New York or New Orleans, but by the summer of 1865 he was in North Carolina ready to invest in a postwar business opportunity.

Poor economic conditions in the southern states at the conclusion of the Civil War encouraged many northerners to head south to seek a

Pass authorizing Hills' travel to Army of the Gulf Headquarters "up Red River," April 17, 1864.

fortune. These fortune-hunters were sometimes not so affectionately called "carpet baggers." One could consider Hills a member of that group, noting possible financial opportunities during his southern travels. In July 1865 Hills and fellow Bostonians J.T. Bridge and Henry C. Barr entertained a business venture with G.W. Ferry, a planter of New Bern, intending to construct a factory to "extract turpentine, oil and prodigious acid, by the new process of destructive distillation of lightwood."[31] The area was rich in suitable resources and other factories were in the works. Whether or not this opportunity developed was not mentioned by Hills, but he seems to have had reason to stay for at least a year. The following year he was still in New Bern, even participating in a July 4th celebration. During this celebration Mayor John Washington toasted "to the President of the United States, J.W. Pigett for "North Carolina," A.G. Hills of Boston for "The Press," and Dr. Meadinzer for "The Star Spangled Banner."[32]

After his North Carolina diversion A.G. promoted the idea of touring Europe as a distributor of Lincoln memorabilia. He left home in early 1867 and spent time in England and France selling a portrait based on an engraving by William Edgar Marshall (through Ticknor and Fields) of the late president. His efforts were endorsed by the abolitionist William Lloyd Garrison and Senator Charles Sumner.[33] He also kept a diary of this time overseas and retained receipts, notes, menus, entertainment and other publications indicative of living the high life in better social circles. (This diary may be a future transcription project, especially since Hills left a considerable archive of this adventure as well.)

1. The Life of Albert Gaius Hills

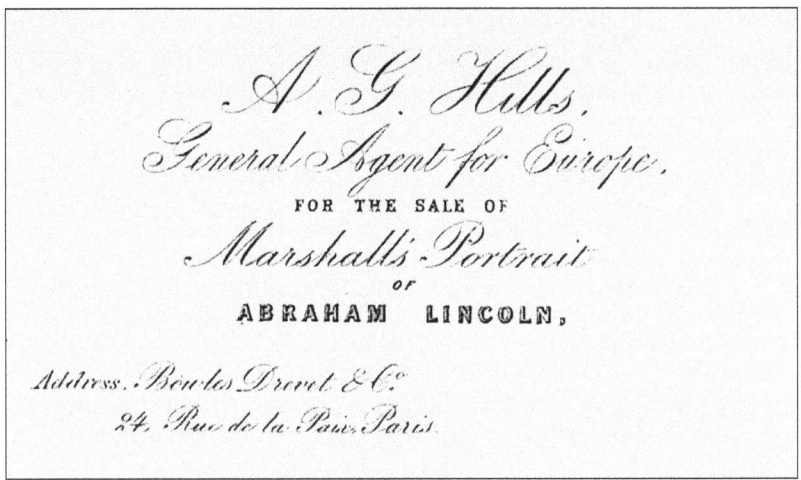

A.G. Hills' business card for his travels to Europe after the Civil War.

Upon his return to the states in August he was writing and lecturing on agricultural and natural resource topics, with a specific interest in fisheries. The influence of his father, Luther, is clearly evident in his works, and Luther's death in 1872 must have been hard to take.

By 1870 A.G. was once again a reporter for the *Boston Journal*. Agricultural topics were his trademark. His reputation as a war correspondent maintained his popular status for the rest of his life. Even a minor carriage accident he had in North Hadley, Massachusetts, with his wife Sarah in September 1870 made the news.[34] (He broke his right arm but was otherwise OK.) Hills also served as a member of the Massachusetts Legislative Committee on Railroads in 1870 and on other local governing boards. In 1875 Hills had a role in the funeral of Vice President Henry Wilson. Wilson was Ulysses S. Grant's second-term running mate who died of a stroke while in office. Hills knew Wilson when he was a U.S. Senator from Massachusetts and the two were apparently good friends. Hills was selected by Wilson's family to escort the body from Baltimore back to Massachusetts with a couple of others including the famous abolitionist Frederick Douglass.

Hills approached his later years as though they were full of promise, but he died suddenly on June 24, 1879 (not yet 50), while residing at the Hotel Dearborn. He had suffered from Bright's Disease, which causes inflammation of the kidneys. His obituary from the June 25, 1879, *Fitchburg Sentinel* read, "Mr. Albert G. Hills of the Boston Journal, well and favorably known in this vicinity, died at the Hotel Dearborn in Boston,

Tuesday. Mr. Hills' pleasant face and cheerful greeting will be greatly missed, particularly by newspaper men among whom he was a general favorite." An obituary from his own *Boston Journal* on June 24, 1879, was even more kind:

> **Albert G. Hills**
>
> It is with a sense of personal bereavement that we record the death of Mr. Albert G. Hills of The Journal reportorial force, which occurred at his rooms in the Hotel Dearborn at twenty minutes past nine o'clock this morning. The disease which caused his death was Bright's disease of the kidneys, and the first serious attach occurred on the 30th of last October, when he was suddenly prostrated in The Journal counting room. Since that attack Mr. Hills had frequently complained of not feeling in his usual health, but few of his friends apprehended any serious result, until his last brief illness. Mr. Hills was born in Yarmouth, Mass., Aug. 26, 1829, and came to Boston when he was seventeen years of age. For a time he followed mercantile pursuits, but about twenty years ago he became connected with The Journal as a reporter. During the war of the rebellion he served The Journal as a correspondent in the field, and many of our readers will probably recall the graphic and interesting letters from his pen, over the signature of "Agaius," describing military operations in the Department of the Gulf. After New Orleans was occupied by the Federal forces he published the New Orleans Era as a Union sheet, and remained for some time at the head of that paper. Returning to the North after the close of the war, he spent several months in Europe, and after his return was engaged for some time in agricultural pursuits. But his tastes were for newspaper work, and about nine years ago he resumed his connection with The Journal, and continued in active service until the 14th of the present month. Mr. Hills had a very wide circulation of acquaintances, who manifested their regard for him in many pleasant ways on the occasion of his silver wedding, May 29, 1878. He was one of the oldest reporters upon the Boston press, and his frank and cordial manner made him a general favorite, not only among those associated with him in work upon this paper, but among newspaper men generally, and, indeed, among all with whom he was brought in contact in social or business relations. As a journalist he was ready, accurate, and faithful, and capable of doing well a wide variety of reportorial work. His relations with his associates were invariably pleasant and cordial, and his unlooked for death gives them sincere sorrow. He leaves a widow but no children.

He was laid to rest in the family plot at Mount Auburn Cemetery, Cambridge, alongside his parents, Luther and Mercy, sister Almaritta, and later his brother Charles Cummings Hills. His wife Sarah lived with members of the Hills family until they passed away, eventually spending the rest of her days in Leominster, Massachusetts, in a home for the elderly. She was buried with A.G. in 1915, but her name is not on his headstone.

2

Taking New Orleans, 1862

When the war began the Federal government had no ready strategy with which to subdue the South. Most believed the war would end quickly after one major battle (like First Manassas), so long term plans were not thought out. With a sobering Union defeat at Manassas and the loss of federal installations along the Atlantic and Gulf coasts, military minds began to consider the means to restore the Union by force. These developed over time as the reality of a long and protracted war sank in. The North of course had the greatest resources of manpower and materiel, but perhaps their greatest asset when the war began was its navy. Blockading of southern ports and defending of United States forts and property commenced almost immediately, but offensive operations to take southern ports did not. Closing these ports to blockade runners to starve the South of essential imports could severely degrade the Southern war effort, and the commitment to do this was evident in the Anaconda Plan.[1] Of all the southern ports New Orleans was the largest and of the greatest strategic importance as the southern key to the Mississippi River.

In November of 1861 the plan to take (or retake)[2] New Orleans got its start. According to Commodore David Porter this was his idea, and he easily gained the support of President Lincoln who questioned why such a campaign had not begun sooner.[3] Manpower for the naval expedition had to be procured through General George B. McClellan (at this date the General in Chief of the Union Armies) who never seemed to have enough troops at his disposal. He did agree to detach some troops from his command, but not as many as desired to exploit any successes following the capture of New Orleans. Warships and transports also had to be gathered from various commands to escort the troops and destroy or neutralize rebel defenses. The Federal command had envisioned a thrust all the way to Vicksburg in conjunction with the northern river fleet coming from Cairo, Illinois, before Confederate defenses could develop and be much of a threat, but this proved to be too ambitious a venture for late 1861 and early 1862. Although the "official" kickoff for the campaign was in January of 1862, resources began heading in that direction as early as late November 1861 as described in the early entries of A.G. Hills' journal. In command of the Union army for the campaign was Major General Benjamin Butler, a man with no military experience before the war. In command of the Union navy were Flag Officer David Farragut and Commodore David Porter, both of whom already had served with distinction before the war.

The expedition that Hills accompanied left Boston in November 1861 for a destination unknown to most in his group, at least until they reached Fortress Monroe in Virginia along the way a few days later. That destination was Ship Island, a narrow island about eight miles long but less than half a mile wide at any point and about twelve or thirteen miles south of both Gulfport and Biloxi, Mississippi. The island contained a partially constructed fort at the entrance to its harbor with a few buildings still intact. There were ravines and ditches, live oaks and cedars. Storms had created a marshy area that cut the island in two. Storms continue to change the shape of the island to this day.

Ship Island was ideally located for forces planning an attack anywhere on the Gulf Coast and had been used by British forces 46 years earlier when they tried and failed to take New Orleans. Ship Island had been occupied by Confederate forces earlier in 1861 but was evacuated on September 16. Although the Confederate War Department wanted to occupy the island to deny federal use of it for offensive operations, sustaining a force here in the face of the overwhelming U.S. Navy presence simply wasn't a realistic strategy. Union troops occupied it in force in December with troops under the command of Brigadier General John Wolcott Phelps.[4] The large assembly of Union troops in a confined area naturally led to some disciplinary problems, and General Butler was none too shy about carrying out courts-martial and issuing numerous General Orders like this one which intended to curb the inevitable influence of alcohol:

> Headquarters Department of the Gulf
> Ship Island, March 28, 1862.
>
> GENERAL ORDERS No. 7.
>
> It has come to the knowledge of the Commanding General, that notwithstanding all his efforts to prevent the introduction of intoxicating liquors into the island and among his command, to be used as a beverage, we are still followed by this curse of the army.
>
> Forbidden by every regulation, prohibited by official authority, con-

demned by experience, it still clings to the soldier, although more deadly, in this climate, than the rifle.

All sales, therefore, within this Department, will be punished by instant expulsion of the party offending, if a civilian, or by court-martial, if an officer or soldier.

All intoxicating liquors kept for sale or to be used as a beverage, will be seized and destroyed, or confiscated to hospital uses.

By command of
MAJOR-GENERAL BUTLER
GEO. STRONG, A.A.G.

Leaving Fortress Monroe, the expedition sailed along the east coast past Cape Hatteras to Key West and into the Gulf of Mexico, at times under the eyes of Confederate steamers but always on the alert for enemy gunboats. The expedition arrived at Ship Island on December 3 with Hills going ashore the next day. Ship Island was to be a busy place as preparations to take New Orleans evolved. The troops that sailed with Hills were the 9th Connecticut, 26th Massachusetts, and 4th Massachusetts Battery of artillery.[5] These disembarked and began training for the assault, to be joined later by the 30th and 31st Massachusetts, 12th Connecticut, 6th Michigan, 4th Wisconsin, 6th Massachusetts and 4th Vermont Batteries, and two companies of the 2nd Massachusetts Cavalry Battalion. In all this would total about 6,000 men.[6] Training could not have been very exciting on the desolate island, and even General Phelps told the troops their training on Ship Island would be the most action they would see, that they would not face serious opposition in New Orleans. While on the island the biggest threat to the troops was in the form of accidents, and Hills himself indicated he was too close to the impact of a minie-ball that was probably (one hopes) an errant practice round. By the end of March 1862, the Department of the Gulf consisted of the following units:

Headquarters Department of the Gulf
Ship Island, March 22, 1862.

General Orders No. 3

The troops in this Department will be brigaded as follows:

First Brigade, Brig. Gen. J. W. Phelps, U.S. Volunteers, Commanding —

8th	Regiment	N.H.	Volunteers	
9th	"	Conn.		"
7th	"	Vermont		"
8th	"	"		"
12th	"	Conn.		"
13th	"	"		"
1st		Vermont	Battery	
2nd		"	"	
4th		"		

Read's Cavalry (one company)
Second Brigade, Brig. Gen. Thomas Williams, U.S. Volunteers, Commanding—

26th	Regiment	Mass.	Volunteers
31st	"	"	"
21st	"	Indiana	"
6th	Michigan	Volunteers	
4th	Wisconsin	"	
6th	Mass.	Battery	

Nim's Battery
Durivage's Cavalry (one company)
Third Brigade, Acting Brig. Gen. G.F. Shepley, Colonel 12th Maine Volunteers, Commanding—

12th	Regiment	Maine	Volunteers
13th	"	"	"
14th	"	"	"
15th	"	"	"
30th	"	Mass.	"

1st Maine Battery.
Magee's Cavalry (one company)
By command of
                    MAJOR-GENERAL BUTLER
GEO. C. STRONG, A.A.G.

Joining the troops was a considerable array of warships and transports. They did not simply stay and wait for the attack to begin, however, but continually patrolled the Gulf to intercept rebel blockade runners, probe port defenses, and prevent rebel warships from interfering with the campaign. Although it was fairly obvious that New Orleans was the intended target of the expedition, defenders of Mobile, Pensacola, and other ports had to be on their guard. Likewise, Ship Island was not immune from enemy visits, as is also described in Hills' journal. While the number of ships was impressive, no ironclads were present, and these were believed to be necessary to counter the previously engaged ram CSS *Manassas*[7] and the new iron monster CSS *Louisiana* under construction. The ships that Hills listed as being present for the campaign are as follows:

Under the command of Flag Officer D. Farragut: USS *Iroquois, Winona, Kennebec, Penola (Pinola), Sciota, Itasca, Kinio (Kineo), Katahdin, Wissahickon, Cayuga, Verona (Varuna), Montgomery, Kittatinny, Calhoun, Hartford* (flagship), *Colorado, Richmond, Pensacola,* and *Mississippi.*

Under the command of Commander D. Porter: Steamers *Harriet Lane, Miami, Westfield, Clifton, Jackson*. Mortar Flotilla, 1st Division, *Norfolk Packet, Oliver Lee, Para, C.P. Williams, Arletta, William Bacon, Sophronia*; 2nd Division, *T.A. Ward, Sydney C. Jones, Matthew Vasser, Maria*

Carlton, Orvetta, Adolph Hugel, George Mangham; 3rd Division, *Horace Beals, John Griffiths, Sarah Bruen, Racer, Sea Foam, Henry James, Dan Smith*.[8]

Other ships are mentioned in his journal, but these were not directly assigned to the New Orleans expedition and some were not warships at all.

The mortar flotilla was comprised of schooners modified to carry mortars for the purpose of bombarding Confederate forts Jackson and St. Phillip to improve the odds of federal warships' heading up the Mississippi River successfully. Many would need to be towed up the river to their firing positions due to the powerful river current. These ships were also nicknamed "bummers" (at least by Hills) or part of the "bummer fleet," probably because they were not likely to be at the head of any attack, rather staying towards the rear as they were intended.

During the buildup of federal forces Hills took advantage of the time and sailed on various ships and witnessed the attack on Biloxi, Mississippi, revisited Key West, saw the sights in Havana, Cuba, and noted rebel defenses along the west coast of Florida to Pensacola and Mobile. As a bit of a naturalist he wrote his observations of wildlife and terrain as well as the economic interests that might be exploited during more peaceful times. When he received word that the grand attack was about to begin he arranged to return to Ship Island in time. On March 31, 1862, Hills boarded the steamer *Connecticut* and headed for the Southwest Pass of the Mississippi River to join the other steamers and gunboats across the bar. Union transports from Ship Island embarked on April 10 and followed the rest of the fleet as described in the General Orders of the Department of the Gulf below.

These general orders show the intended troop distributions by troop transport. General Order 8 may have been the first troop transport assignment which was apparently overridden by General Order 9. The 9th Michigan listed in G.O. 8 was in Tennessee at the time. This order was also dated before the 9th Connecticut was sent on the expedition to Biloxi and Pass Christian.

Headquarters Department of the Gulf
Ship Island, March 29, 1862.

GENERAL ORDERS No. 8

The following named regiments and corps will embark to-morrow, commencing

At 8 A.M., and in the following order, viz:

1. On board steamer *Mississippi*—
    The Commanding General and Staff.

4th Regiment Wisconsin Volunteers.
   Durivage Cavalry (dismounted), and Manning's Battery.
   Weitzel Pioneers.
2. On board steamer *Matanzas*—
   Brig. Gen. Williams and Staff.
   21st Regiment Indiana Volunteers.
3. On board steamer *Lewis*—
   9th Regiment Connecticut Volunteers.
4. On board ship *North America*—
   26th Massachusetts Volunteers.
   Everett's Battery.
5. On board ship *Wild Gazelle*—
   9th Michigan Volunteers.
6. On board ship *E. W. Farley*—
   12th Connecticut Volunteers.

Each Regiment will take three (3) tents, and the detached companies of cavalry, artillery and pioneers one (1) tent each. The remaining tents will be left standing. The troops will carry their camp kettles, mess pans, cups, plates, knives and forks, and each soldier his knapsack, overcoat, blanket, one extra shirt, one extra pair of drawers, one extra pair of shoes, canteen, and in his haversack four days' cooked rations. They will also tale all axes, hatchets, picks, shovels and spades they may have in possession.

Officers' baggage will be limited to bedding and one valise, bag or knapsack; no trunks in any case to be taken. The remaining baggage of officers and men will be properly secured, as compactly as possible, marked and turned over to the Division Quartermaster.

Captains of companies will be held responsible that every soldier has in his cartridge box forty (40) rounds of ammunition.

The troops will be inspected at 6 P.M. to-day, to see that this order has been complied with as far as may be necessary at that hour to insure promptness in the embarkation to-morrow. One non–commissioned officer for each regiment will be left behind to turn over the baggage, tents, etc., to the Chief Quartermaster.

   By command of
                        MAJOR-GENERAL BUTLER.
GEO. C. STRONG, A.A.G.

                    Headquarters Department of the Gulf
                         Ship Island, April 10, 1862

GENERAL ORDERS NO. 9.
   The following named regiments and corps will embark, commencing at ___ M., and in the following order:
   1. On board ship *Great Republic*—

21st Regiment Indiana Volunteers.
4th Regiment Wisconsin Volunteers.
6th Regiment Michigan Volunteers.
2. On board steamer *Mississippi*—
26th Regiment Massachusetts Volunteers.
31st Regiment Massachusetts Volunteers.
Brown's Sappers and Miners.
Everett's Battery.
3. On board steamer *Matanzas*—
9th Regiment Connecticut Volunteers.
2nd Vermont Battery.
4. On board ship *North America*—
30th Regiment Massachusetts Volunteers.
Read's Cavalry
Durivage's Cavalry.
Manning's Battery.
5. On board ship *E. Wilder Farley*—
12th Regiment Connecticut Volunteers.

III. The amount of provisions, baggage, etc., to be carried by the troops will be the same as heretofore designated in General Orders No. 8, current series. No knapsack will be unslung during embarkation or disembarkation, or on board a lighter in going to or from any transport.

By command of
MAJOR-GENERAL BUTLER
GEO. C. STRONG, A. A. G.

Ascending the Mississippi River was not an easy task for the U.S. Navy. Some of the warships drafted more than would easily allow their passage across the bars that formed at the Delta. The Southwest Pass at the Delta offered the deepest draft, so that is where the largest ships of the federal fleet entered the river, or at least tried. Other ships accessed the river via the Pass à Loutre[9] to the east. Some ships struggled to pass the bar. The USS *Colorado* for one was unable to pass, but some of its cannon were made available for other ships. The *Connecticut, Brooklyn, Pensacola,* and *Mississippi* had some difficulty but were eventually forced across by lightening loads, using tow lines, and being persistent. Local pilots were not as useful as U.S. Navy skill and determination in forcing ships across. The river was shallower here than surveys had indicated despite the above normal river levels upstream.

Once across the bar the fleet moved up river to the Head of Passes.[10] The river was deep enough to allow for the drafts of the many ships, but they now had to adjust to the confines of the river. The river was high and the current very strong, a hindrance moving upriver but later a benefit when attacking the rebel shore defenses. There were scouting expeditions to the forts to observe their strength along with potential obstacles. Farragut himself participated in one of these and came under fire. There was also some skirmishing between opposing naval forces as each tried to determine the other's strengths and intentions. Union troop transports followed about two weeks later. Although Hills' journal doesn't indicate any special preparations for land forces attacking the forts, his *Boston Journal* report states that scaling ladders had been accumulated for a land assault that proved unnecessary. The fleet passed Pilot Town,[11] in more peaceful times a place to secure a pilot to navigate the treacherous turns upriver, and soon to be the location of a hospital for Union wounded. Still upriver was "The Jump," about midway between the Head of Passes and Forts Jackson and St. Phillip, a point stationed by a rebel telegraph operator.[12] There were others living along the river as well, but their loyalties and intentions could not be trusted as yet, and Hills noted the presence of fellow New Englanders living on the river. At this time there was no doubt of the impending Union navy attack.

The rebel defenses awaiting the federal fleet had some depth. First, there was the constant threat from snipers or bushwhackers from either river bank that required a vigilant watch all the way to New Orleans. Next, after passing The Jump, Forts Jackson and St. Phillip were less than ten miles away under the command of Confederate Brigadier General Johnson H. Duncan and garrisoned by about 1100 men. The forts had been taken over by rebel forces on January 10, 1861 (even before Louisiana eventually seceded on January 26), and had seen some improvements. Both were masonry structures with clear lines of sight to the river and protected gun emplacements. Fort Jackson held 78 guns and St. Phillip 44 according to Hills' journal. Just below Fort Jackson (300 yards) the rebels had placed a heavy chain across the river spaced with ship hulks[13] to block (or at least slow down) any attacking force heading up river. Confederate General Bragg believed that obstructions across the river were the most important means of defense to block the Union fleet. The original chain and raft obstruction had been weakened by spring rains, and repairs had been made but not quite to the standard of the original. According to Hills there were eight large schooners, some as large as five hundred tons, at anchor with the current. A heavy chain was stretched across the river on the decks of these ships with another one below the water line. A light chain was placed to connect one of the schooners to the shore by Fort Jackson; the chain would be lowered to allow rebel ships to pass. Hills also refers to stockpiled wood and debris in the river to be released as if bursting a dam. There was a scarcity of drift wood on the river and it was speculated that this was being accumulated to be released when the Union Navy approached. A rebel prisoner told Hills that a raft was being built out of this wood to obstruct any advance. This defense could also damage ships in their own right.

Just beyond the forts the rebels had ready numerous fire rafts to launch at an enemy. Despite growing shortages in the South there was plenty of turpentine and cotton available to create hazardous fires. These could be released in the hope they would strike a slow moving warship trying to maneuver a treacherous turn in the river. Some could even be guided to a target with unarmed vessels, increasing the likelihood of a hit.

The next line of defense was the rebel fleet led by Commander John K. Mitchell. The primary rebel warships were the ram *Manassas*, gunboats *McRae, Jackson*,[14] *Governor Moore, General Quitman*, and state river vessels *Warrior, Stonewall Jackson, Defiance, Resolute, General Lovell*, and *Breckinridge*. There were also several unarmed tugs available for towing ships and pushing fire rafts. The rebels also had the ironclad CSS *Louisiana* which (if operable) should have been more than a match for any of the federal vessels in the attacking force. Unfortunately for the rebels, she lacked the required machinery to steer herself so she needed help getting into a defensive position. Rebel crews were also mostly recruited from the army, and their lack of experience would become glaring in the river battle to come. However, the longer it took for the federals to crack the fort and chain defense the more time the rebels would have to complete the CSS *Louisiana*.

The final line of defense was a line of shore batteries on either side of the river near where British forces made their failed assault in 1815. The Chalmette line was partially protected by the river levee which obstructed the direct line of fire from enemy gunboats. The trenches also contained troops that could block any land assault, just as had happened under Andrew Jackson. Flanking these positions overland would be difficult due to the marshy terrain. Once past this line, however, there was nothing left to stop any advance.

By April 18 the Union mortar fleet was in position to begin the bombardment of the forts. Anchored 3,000 yards down river, they were hidden from the view of the forts by woods. An earlier position closer to the forts had drawn fire because it was too close to the cleared area adjacent to Fort Jackson. With deafening booms the "bummers" fired constantly for six days, lobbing thousands of explosive shells into the forts. Damage was done to the forts but not enough to silence all of their batteries. Hills and other reporters were able to view the action from the masts of federal warships waiting for their turn to enter the battle. Confederate losses were minimal, especially considering what had been thrown at them. The mortar crews experienced fatigue from their constant work, and ammunition for the mortars was nearly depleted. At this critical point the decision was made to pass the forts and to move the fleet on to New Orleans instead of continuing the bombardment, with the hope that the fort defenses had been degraded enough to get through. This still required passing through the chain obstacle below the forts. During the night of the 20th a daring move to break the chain near the left bank succeeded, creating a gap for the Union fleet to pass while under fire from the forts. According to a report by Hills, on the night of the 20th the chain across the river was cut by the crew of the gunboat USS *Itasca*, commanded by Lieutenant Caldwell of Boston, assisted by the crew of the USS *Pinola*, commanded by Lieutenant Crosby.

Early on the 24th the fleet got under way for the run by the forts. The mortar flotilla opened fire again to prevent any repairs to the damaged forts. Ships passing the chain opened fire on the forts with grape shot and canister to discourage rebel artillery crews from manning their guns. Although some ships suffered multiple hits none were sunk and casualties were few. Rebel fire rafts wreaked some havoc as they neared the fleet, even causing a fire on the *Hartford* which was quickly extinguished. Many of the fire rafts failed to even ignite and were a common sight along the riverbanks for days after the battle. The fleet successfully passed both forts and proceeded to the next obstacle, the rebel gunboats.

Leading the way was the *Varuna*, and while first driving away some rebel vessels she soon found herself too far in advance of the rest of the fleet and got into trouble. The rebel gunboat *Governor Moore* delivered well placed rounds into the *Varuna* and the *Stonewall Jackson* rammed her, causing her to sink but with surprisingly few casualties. But this was the extent of success for the rebel navy. Union fire either sank or forced aground most of the rebel fleet, including the *Governor Moore*. The ram *Manassas* was herself rammed by the USS *Mississippi* and knocked out of action. She was abandoned, filled with combustibles, and drifted down river where she blew up harmlessly. The incomplete ironclad *Louisiana*, which failed to come down river to support the forts, finally entered the battle but was ineffective, unable to steer herself. When the Union fleet passed out of her range and with her commanding officer killed, her crew abandoned her and set her on fire where she drifted down river and exploded uncomfortably close to Union warships. This did not set well with Union naval officers who were accepting the surrender of Confederate forces while this was happening. Not all rebel forces fled the area. While the steam frigate *Mississippi* was at anchor below Fort Jackson a large river boat approached loaded with a band of armed men, intent on boarding her. The *Mississippi* allowed the boat to get within a few yards before she opened fire with a broadside. The rebel boat was destroyed with a total loss of life to her occupants. Continuing toward New Orleans the Union fleet entered the English Turn[15] and faced the last line of defense, the Chalmette Line.

The Chalmette Line was manned by 90 day recruits for local defense only. Manpower was in short supply due to the need to fill the ranks of Confederate armies fighting in Tennessee and Virginia, especially following the bloody battle of Shiloh in western Tennessee earlier in April. The defense was no match against the might of the federal fleet under normal circumstances, and it was rendered even less effective by the high water in the Mississippi River. The water level was nearly to the top of the river levees, so there was no obstruction to federal guns firing over it. Brushing by this line, the fleet pressed on to New Orleans, and the ominous masts of the ships were well visible to the residents of New Orleans. Meanwhile, having been bypassed by the federal fleet and written off by the Confederate leadership, Forts Jackson and St. Phillip surrendered on April 28. Some 300 rebels at Fort Jackson mutinied soon after the fleet passed and left before their eventual surrender. Union troops occupied the forts and settled in to their quarters in the stifling heat and humidity of southern Louisiana.

Two naval officers were assigned the task of demanding the surrender of New Orleans. Captain Theodorus Bailey commanded the first division of gunboats and the *Colorado*. Lieutenant George H. Perkins was second in command on the *Cayuga*. They marched through a hostile crowd to meet the mayor, who refused to surrender at first, expecting that task to be the responsibility of the Confederate army. With the army no longer around, this tactic delayed the inevitable for a few days only. Tactfully waiting for a time to raise the U.S. flag without causing further rioting, the city was not officially surrendered right away. On April 29 Marine Corps Captain John L. Broome with all available Marines from the fleet occupied New Orleans until they were relieved by Union Army troops.[16] General Butler landed his troops and the surrender became official on May 1.[17] The May 2 edition of the *New Orleans Bee* reported the scene of the Federal fleet:

> THE FEDERAL FLEET AND TROOPS
> The U. States fleet now lying in our river comprises the following vessels:
> The flag steamship Hartford, bearing the blue pennant of Com. Farragut; the Steamships Brooklyn, Pensacola, Mississippi and Pocahontas;[18] and nine gun boats, numbered from 1 to 9. The Steamship Tennessee, the Towboat St. Charles, and the Steamboats Diana and Sallie Robinson, were seized by the enemy, since their arrival in this port.
> The Steamer DeSoto, which formerly ran between New Orleans and New

York, is also in port. Some of the prisoners brought from the forts and released on parole — came up in this vessel. The Steamboat W. Burton, the tow boat Landis, and a large side-wheel, two-masted steamship, full of troops, arrived on Wednesday. They were joined yesterday by ten transports among which are the following: Steam war ship Mississippi, lying in the First District, Post 16, with a large number of troops, which came on shore. Sailing ship E. Wilder Farley, lying in the First District, Post 18, with a swarm of troops. Ship Idaho, lying off the Point, filled with troops. The balance of the transports are small steamers or tug boats, as far as we could judge. They have landed from four to five thousand men.

Most residents of New Orleans felt betrayed by the inadequate defense provided by the rebel army and navy. Showing contempt toward their unwanted occupiers was commonplace. Not every citizen felt this way, but their support for the Union was muted until the occupation was well established. The population contained a number of residents from Free states as well as foreign nationals who didn't embrace the southern cause. There was a total failure of Confederate land and naval forces to cooperate and coordinate their defenses. Each seemed to operate independently. Federal strategy to take New Orleans may have taken some time to develop, but Confederate forces did not take advantage of that time to prepare an adequate defense. New Orleans now would be under the rule of Major General Butler. During the upcoming months Butler earned his nickname "the Beast" by his actions to crush the rebellious spirit displayed by the citizens of New Orleans.

Other area forts were included as part of the surrender deal, such as batteries above New Orleans, Proctorville just to the east, and Fort Livingston in Barataria Bay which surrendered on its own accord. Forts Pike and Wood guarding New Orleans at the entrance to Lake Pontchartrain were abandoned with the guns spiked and other damages inflicted on the forts.[19] Remaining rebel forces nearby made their way to other commands. News of the surrender was printed in the *Boston Journal* on April 29th, but the reports couldn't have traveled by steamer that quickly. Southern telegraphers tipped off the news when they were unable to return to New Orleans due to the surrender, so the rebel telegraph service gets the credit for the breaking news:

> FORTRESS MONROE, April 28. A flag of truce today took dispatches and letters for the Union prisoners. No newspapers were received, or at least none came into the hands of the reporters of the press.
> The city of New Orleans has been taken by the Union forces. The telegraph operators having left, as previously reported, no particulars have been received. It is stated however, that the operator subsequently attempted to return, but found the city in possession of the Union troops. It is probable

the city surrendered without resistance after the fleet made its appearance. There is a report that the enemy's much boasted iron gunboat, built there as a second Merrimac, was, while on its way, destroyed by the United States steamer Pensacola.

The surrender was reported locally through the Soldier's Newsletter printed on Ship Island on May 10:

GLORIOUS NEWS!
NEW ORLEANS IN OUR POSSESSION
FORTS JACKSON AND PHILLIP CAPTURED!!!

Forts Jackson and Phillip are in our possession. We are informed, on Monday last, to our naval authorities in command of the Blockading Squadron. Finding themselves cut off from communication with New Orleans, with Gun Boats above and below, they had little else they could do but surrender.

New Orleans is occupied by our troops, making no resistance to their entrance into the City,— yet they can hardly be said to have voluntarily surrendered, as they utterly refused, it appears, to haul down the flag of Louisiana, which in her present relations to the Federal Government, represents the cause of Treason to that Government, the Constitution and the Union. Until the people of Louisiana publicly recede from their present position, they must, by virtue of the past action of the State, be held and deemed to be traitors to the General Government — at least in their present capacity.

The surrender of New Orleans cost the Confederacy its largest city and port. The Mississippi River was closed to imports of war materiel and the South had to rely on other ports for exporting cotton and other resources to help pay for the war effort. Rebel forces would be strained to man defenses of other river cities up the Mississippi and Red Rivers. For the moment Federal officials took advantage of any goods left at docks and warehouses and confiscated them for their own gain. Rumors of rebel reinforcements returning to retake New Orleans never materialized. Union forces consolidated their gains, manned the existing rebel defenses, and prepared for their next move.

For Flag Officer Farragut the immediate next move was to test rebel defenses as far upriver as Vicksburg, although the mortar flotilla had been sent back to Ship Island for an anticipated move against Mobile. With no army support at the time, taking the city was not possible, and would in fact take more than a year and many bloody battles to force its surrender. Other Confederate Gulf ports were also in the cross hairs, such as Mobile and Pensacola. Mobile proved to be better defended than New Orleans and wouldn't fall until early 1865, but Pensacola was not, so shortly after the surrender of New Orleans Union forces regained control of the navy yard there. To build on the gains of New Orleans more federal forces would be needed to advance both up the river from New Orleans and down the river from Memphis.

A.G. Hills took a bit of a respite from the war. Gaining passage to New York on the USS *Rhode Island* was his opportunity to reunite with his wife and family until the *Journal* saw fit to reacquaint him with the war effort. This came at the end of 1862 with a return to New Orleans to report on the push up the Mississippi River and one of its tributaries, the Red River. His sense of excitement was diminished from months of seeing the war up close, but not enough to prevent him from returning to New Orleans almost exactly one year later.

3

Covering the Campaign

Although the assignment to cover the New Orleans Campaign was certainly a new one to A.G. Hills, he immediately started laying the framework for good communications, introducing himself to and making friends with Union army officers and their wives as soon as he boarded the transport *Constitution*. He made a habit of making connections whenever possible, and this included other members of the press who covered the campaign from competing newspapers. Despite being competitors they established a camaraderie that benefited them all. This became especially evident in the "press gig" while on the Mississippi River during the battle when cooperation was essential. It also made it easier to keep aware of all the other activities taking place from Key West to Galveston during the same time period. Hills shared the "press gig" with Henry Winser of the *New York Times*[1] even though there was at least one other *Journal* reporter there, who went by the name of "Foretop." Stories of New Orleans appear from both reporters in the April 29, 1862, edition of the *Journal*, but Hills makes no mention of him. This may be due to his competitive streak against other reporters. He might share information with a paper from a region other than Boston but certainly not one from his own city. He was also careful what he wrote in his journals. In his first journal a couple of pages were written on by some of his shipmates to form a "medical diagnosis" of Hills. It was obviously meant in jest with descriptions such as "skin dry and crusty, inclined to drink whenever asked, double parenthesis in good condition, bath recommended." Others were "tongue in abundance and cheek in same proportion," "eye inclined to the amorous, barefooted on the top of his head." Afterwards Hills seems to have been a bit more protective of his journals.

All through his trips to Ship Island, the Gulf, and eventually up the

Mississippi he composed letters for the family back home as well as his employer, the *Journal*. Usually these were sent via the pursers of the ships he passed heading north, and other times they would be sent with friends that were leaving the area. Although he trusted these carriers there was always some anxiety about his letters' falling into the hands of competitors or being lost altogether. On one occasion Hills and his correspondent friends trusted their letters to a "friend" who was later arrested by Federal authorities and needed assistance from General Banks to retrieve them.

Hills also had the foresight to take some meticulous notes of his observations from each ship he sailed on as well as Ship Island and the passage up the Mississippi River. Some of these were observations of flora and fauna that were useful in his reporting and lecturing after the war, but most enabled him to gain a more intimate knowledge of the Gulf of Mexico and the importance of various sites as they related to the war effort. He also took every opportunity to board as many naval vessels as possible and note the arrivals and departures of them as well as noting where they had come from and where they were going. It seemed as if he had a meal on just about every ship that arrived at Key West or Ship Island when he was there, learning about and gaining the approval of the officers on board. He also traveled around the Gulf on various ships as they tested rebel defenses and chased after blockade runners.

There was no free ride for reporters in the Gulf. Hills had to pay for rations and board while on Ship Island. At the Russell House in Key West he paid $20 for his two week stay and another $30 for cigars from Havana. He was evidently paid by the *Journal* while on the campaign, but he did borrow money from some ships' officers to tie him over.[2] This was another reason to maintain good relations with the officers.

By the time the Union navy was ready to ascend the Mississippi River to New Orleans, Hills had gained a good understanding of the plan of attack and the expectations of what lay ahead. He also experienced the caution and even fear as the fleet entered enemy territory and wondered what might be lurking behind the dense cover along the river banks. The opening bombardment of the mortar fleet was deafening to Hills as he and other members of the press struggled against the current to gain news of the effects. As exciting as the moment was he still rowed the "press gig" between the ships for information and better viewing points. As the battle progressed upriver he relied on those previous connections he had developed throughout the Gulf to learn what was happening beyond the view of the mast tops in the mortar fleet.

As it was apparent that the Union navy had accomplished a stunning victory, Hills concentrated on reporting his observations on the Confed-

3. Covering the Campaign 39

erate defenses and the damage inflicted on them by the bombardment of the mortar fleet. He also interviewed the combatants of both sides, something not so common in more modern times but not hindered by any language barrier other than accents. When he eventually sailed toward New Orleans he continued to make observations all along the river. What he saw was a bit of a cultural shock to say the least, not at all reminiscent of his native Massachusetts. Arriving in Algiers opposite New Orleans he couldn't help but notice the unrest of the inhabitants, and that may have contributed to his sense of being the "conqueror." He conveys a sense of contempt for the rowdy populace with their approval of the slavery institution, but perhaps even more so for their efforts to leave the Union. Although journals of his stay beyond early 1863 haven't been found, one might assume that his attitude mellowed as his stay extended into 1863 and 1864, since the war settled into more of a routine for him as a newspaper editor.

4

About the Journals of A.G. Hills, Reporter for the *Boston Journal*

In the following chapters are transcriptions of the original journals of A.G. Hills, along with some related materials. In the transcription, a few words are my best efforts at interpretation. Places marked "[illegible]" are words I couldn't interpret after too many hours of trying. Areas left blank were left blank by Hills for reasons unknown, excepting areas where he wanted to add an expletive or simply forgot a name. Mr. Hills used ellipses in several journal entries. While these may be difficult for the reader to understand, I have made every effort to transcribe the journals as they appear. One exception to this is the presence of italics. All underlined text and strike-throughs were as they appear in the journal, however italics were added by me for consistency. Abbreviations have been spelled out when necessary to help with understanding. Obvious spelling errors have been corrected. I have made no effort to edit what may be considered "politically incorrect" today. Hills also had a penchant for using commas and creating two word sentences. I have cut down on the commas to make the entries more understandable.

Some portions of the journal covering late April and early May 1862 have been omitted entirely because they simply proved indecipherable. When Hills had time, his writing was for the most part legible, but when he was in a hurry was clearly evident in his pages. To say the least, transcribing these journals has been difficult. Progress has been painfully slow at times, in some instances requiring several days of research to understand the meaning or intent of a single word. In some extremely difficult cases I was able only to summarize the passages.

Mr. Hills wrote in this first journal until a few days after the occupation of New Orleans in May 1862, and then wrote a series of articles and letters depicting specific events or points of interest of the battle. The war was still in its early stages, and the victory at New Orleans led Hills and others to believe that the war would soon end, that "secesh"[1] was dead, even as the casualty reports from the battle of Shiloh in Tennessee were still coming in. At this point in the war I believe A.G. and many others were still not aware of the horrors of war and the inevitable multiple year course of the war. The New Orleans Campaign had been relatively bloodless compared to the great battles yet to come. As he has time to make lengthy reflections he almost seems to describe the war as a crusade, and does get a bit verbose and flowery in his descriptions of battle scenes and their aftermath. At times you can sense his excitement as on a great adventure. I can't fault him at all for this. I don't think he really understood what he was getting himself into. It was only at this time that photographs were about to bring the graphic images of war to the American public en masse to give more meaning to the casualty numbers alone. I just wish I could have found journals describing the war as it intensified and dragged on. Still, Hills wrote what he saw and had an eye for detail. Some entries may seem to express random thoughts, but I believe these cases to be more a result of poor penmanship than anything else. Some words I thought were nonsense were actually terms used in the nineteenth century. Hills mentions a multitude of ships in his entries, many of which were contracted by the U.S. Navy to transport troops or supplies. I have attempted to identify as many as possible using U.S. Navy records. There are a few that I could not identify and some others that might be misidentified by Mr. Hills. His entries show attention to detail when describing the forces massing for attack. These provided the framework for his letters to the *Journal*. But he also shows his humorous side as he relates his experiences. The numbers shown in brackets correspond to page numbers in the journal. Near the end of his stay near New Orleans he jumps back and forth describing the action on the river. It is evident that he was trying to recollect his thoughts and experiences as well as the words of those he interviewed while they were still fresh in his memory. With some entries I have added his articles that were published for the subscribers back home.

The journals were written in books made for that purpose. Some articles were written on what appears to be a kind of tracing paper, very thin and fragile. Other articles were written on period letter stock. All have been preserved from generation to generation.

5

Journal of a Military Expedition from Boston to _____

Hills ended the title of this journal with a blank line (as shown) because, like many others on the expedition, he did not know the destination until the opening of orders at Fortress Monroe.[1]

Thursday November 21, 1861

Joined the Pacific Mail Steamship *Constitution*,[2] Capt. Fletcher in Boston Harbor. Had on board 26th Reg. Mass. Vol. and 9th Reg. Conn. Vol., 5th Mass. Battery Capt. Manning.

Introduced to Dr. Bradt, Asst. Surgeon 26th as my companion du voyage. Occupy aft state room on starboard side. Consider self exceedingly

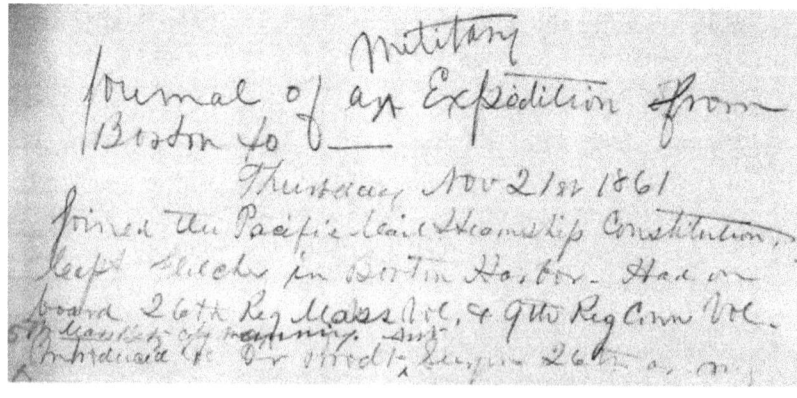

First page of Hills' journals.

5. Journal of a Military Expedition from Boston to _____ 43

fortunate in quarters and chum. Took breakfast on board. First impressions and bust joak. Army worm in biscuit. Ladies on board Mrs. Col. Jones, Mrs. Maj. Sawtell, Mrs. Lt. Col. Farr, Mrs. Dr. Horker, all of 26th, Mrs. Major Frye, Conn. 9th. Whose presence will shed a homelike influence over voyage.

Thanksgiving Day. Turkeys gobble in the country. "Old hens look forsaken when young ones are taken." To fill earthen plator so crusty. Crowds on Long and Tea Wharves all forenoon. Boats plying between steamer and shore,

[2]

boxes and packages for Jones. Sloop and tugs took off freight. [illegible] left to fill ship *Kingfisher*.[3] Chartered for purpose. Ship hauled into wharf as we left.

At 12.30 P.M. weighed anchor. Heavy walking beam worked up and down. Bands of the 26th and 9th on hurricane deck united skillfully, and voices harmony joined in singing "Dixie." Cheers from crowd on wharf. Hearts of 2000 men lighten load lifted with anchor from the hearts of all. Passed Fort Independence. Engineer Corps saluted us. Cheers exchanged.

Fort Warren garrison on parapet. Rebels prisoners hovering near shore and side fort looked moody and sullen at troops going to chastise their brothers. Much sickness on passage to Portland. Anchored Case Bay off Cape Elizabeth.[4] 1–5 o'clock. Sle....

Friday Nov 22.

Went ashore with Smith, Capts.Clerk and Pubter N.Y. Herald. Returned to steamer and tried to sleep, then to write — no go — went on shore at

[3]

daylight. Breakfast U.S. Hotel with Cushing and Gen. Butler's[5] Staff. Wrote letter to Journal and returned on board steamer.12th Ill, Reg. came off but returned to land. Learned from Maj. S. steamer would touch at Fortress Monroe. Telegraph to Maj. C.O.K. he said "come home." Went to Boston to office. 15 minutes late and should be off same night for Fortress. Major came in. Made fun of me. Told me to go home and sleep with my wife. Did so for her sake. Left next morning — good spts.[6] I and few (not at) quarters. Had to explain. Left town 5½ o'clock P. M. via Worcester and Norwich. Stopped in New York (5th Ave.) Sunday. Wrote letter home and drifted about generally. Tried to find Stewart failed. Left New York on Sunday evening in company Major Rogers and party got some sleep in all night, next to Baltimore. Went in ferry boat (can on top) from Perryville per Harve de Grace, Md. Snow in Philadelphia. Cold north

wind in Baltimore over to Barnum's and went to bed. Got a nap disturbed by lunular season. Met father somehow.
[4]
Can't tell under what circumstances. At nine per niger called me and blacked my boots. Took breakfast and walked out to look for Billy Brigham. He was in Wash.—saw his cuz—Cole who took me in tow and went to Wash Monument. Had good view of all of Balto. Federal Hill heavy fortified by Duryee Zouaves. Gen D. reviewed 1st regt. of Maj. Harris cavalry on Eutaw Street. Wrote letter home and to journal and took colored boy to pack valise to steamer. Left Balto at 6 o'clock. Stopped Fort McHenry. Took arms for 76 Penn Regt at Fort Monroe. Went to bed early and slept well all night and woke up.

> *For the days the expedition spent sailing from Boston to New York to Baltimore, Hills did not separate each daily journal entry. It doesn't appear that he needed to go to Portland since his ship returned to Boston. Instead of re-boarding in Boston he took a train to New York and later a ferry across the Susquehanna on his way to Baltimore. Here he saw some sights and later rejoined the expedition. During this time he was able to spend one last night with his wife Sarah. The description of a disturbed nap is unclear. There was no full moon that night but it could have been bright nonetheless. I doubt he met his father Luther in person. He may have been having a dream, and these he would write about during his journal.*

Tuesday Morning Nov 26th—in Chesapeake Bay. Wild fowl plenty—flew near steamer. Soldiers shoot three with revolvers. No boats allowed to go off from shore. Canvas back ducks in Balto Market—Gen. great man
[5]
for ducks. Arrived Fortress Monroe 8 o'clock. Met Capt. Davis P. M., invited by Acting Asst. P. M. on steamer. Met W. H. Stiner N.Y. Herald. Took up quarters with him outside fort. Monroe big place—*Minnesota*[7] and *Colorado*[8] in stream. Rip Raps look rough place. Had interview with General Wool.[9] Nice old gentleman. Week side vanity. Likes Davis. Saw Frank Baten. Firm hand. Barely escaped with life from excess of cordiality. *Constitution* arrived 10 o'clock. Boarded in Co. Capt. Millwood and Davis—got items and went ashore. Wrote story for Journal and letter home. Evening went to quarters of Richardson Light Infantry. Off. present Dr. Bradt, Capts. Blood, Annable, Adj. Davis and others. Home outside

5. Journal of a Military Expedition from Boston to _____   45

fort 11 o'clock. Challenged by sentinel. Divoll last P.M., gave word and passed out.
　　Wednesday Morning—Went to Hampton. 16th. Regt. Faller. Sharp. North. Sentry boxes. Hampton Village.
[6]

Wednesday Nov 27th—Left Hampton Roads 2.50 P.M. Tug with officers of Conn. 9th late and putback. Steamer hauled up shut off. Duleavy aft returned. 2 guns fired "*Colorado.*" Manned rigging—dipped colors and Regt. salutes. Cheers both vessels. Detainer ½ broken. Paron light boat Willoughby Spit. Capt. Chas. H. Dennison of U.S. gunboat *Daylight*[10] Pilot out between Capes, passed Cape Henry, Dinner Gen. Phelps at head of table. Letter sent home by soldiers. Scene on deck. Sutlers with tolerances. Gen. Phelps. No staff. Conference with Col. Jones as to quarters of officers and men on ship. *Jackson*[11] Pilot and Capt. Fletcher went on Battis to Fort Sumter before its fall. Pilot entertained me with discussion mosquito, sand flies, green headed flies. More humor in size of mosquito a whole body of sandfly. One sings other small intruders reep upon you. Pilot of *Brooklyn*[12] 30 yrs steady on N.O. packets. Orders about fire. Privateers and waters. Some keen eyed saw rebels on shore of Sacred Soil. Rebel tugs seen from Old point up river.
[7]

Thursday Nov 28th. Passed Cape Hatteras 9 o'clock morn. Run along east part of gulf stream. Clear sky, hot water. Brick house W.S.W. Mild day. One coat discarded. Saw sail to windward off starboard bow. Turtle on top water. Suggestion of Parker and no "mockery."[13] Several sails. Bond on deck. Ladies all out. 11 o'clock opened orders. Night before leaked out that destination of expedition Ship Island. Orders proved report.[14] Took breakfast with Capt. Fletcher. Ate little. Sick again. Tried champagne. No go. Charts studied.[15]
　　Strictly military duties confined to guard mtg. Rw and Pal. The orders opened by Gen. Phelps received from Gen. Butler at Fortress Monroe destination solved. 11 o'clock today. Ship Island six miles long one mile wide 12 miles from Mississippi City. 60 N.O. and Mobile. Great strategical point of importance. Gen. Phelps intimated could not offer brilliant achievement for pen[16] Gov't occupy it as soon as
[8]
xspare available forces from north. Govt having determined to hold Ship and Cat Islands making former rendezvous for fleet and depot for military stores. Camp of instruction for troops and basis of future operations of

offensive character on Gulf Coast. Army will cooperate with fleet in reducing tonnes in Gulf. Gen. Butler called to Washington 10 days ago but times to confer with administration on this subject. He has command of all land forces in Gulf. N.E. Div.[17] recruited for special object—6000 personnel influence secured authority from states of N.E. to recruit men. Mass. 3 Regts. 26th, 28th, and one commanded Col. French. Connt. 9th and 12th Rgts, Me. 12th and NY 1 Reg.[18] "*Constitution*" sailed within 3 days of time Genl. B. promised Adm would start let 3000 troops of his Div. Would have had 3000 but Steamer not having draft, Gallant proved crank, Capt. Fletcher protested M taking Me. Reg.

[9]

confirmed in opinion of impropriety of taking men by exp. off on night between B and P.[19]

Incidents of day — Turtle in gulf stream along edge of which ran. Saw ripple of stream. Visions of Parkins a mockery. Sail ho! Again Bark *Cloud*[20] hauled sails cleared up—fighting trim. Glasses go round. Out sailed her evening. Southern Sky brilliant star light for excdg. Cold North. Sunset. Evening Star. Porpoises. Phosphorescent light. 5 on each side. Comets rebuild. Neptune's wash tub. Longitude — at Meridian — off-distance from land. Contingencies may arise to change the program.

[10]

It is possible that the administration may have been actuated by other and stronger motives than the prosecution of strictly military operations. Signs in the assignment of general officers to the command of the land forces. Men were selected whose views upon the question of confiscating war property belonging to the rebels would render the more present advisors to the cotton planting of the Gulf States than lukewarm servants of the Gov't.

[11]

> *On this page of his journal Bible verses crossed out of journal, Daniel 11:13–16. I have included them because they help to describe his attitude on his southern adventure.*

Daniel 11:13 —: For the king of the north shall return, and shall set forth a multitude greater than the former, and shall certainly come after certain years with a great army and much riches.

14: And in those times there shall many stand up against the king of the south; also the robbers of thy people shall exalt themselves to establish the vision; but they shall fall.

15: So the king of the north shall come, and cast up a mount, and

5. Journal of a Military Expedition from Boston to _____   47

take the most fenced cities; and the arms of the south shall not withstand, neither his chosen people, neither shall there be any strength to withstand.

16: But he that cometh against him shall do according to his own will, and none shall stand before him: and he shall stand in the glorious land, which by his hand shall be consumed.
[12]

Cotton states seat of mischief. Slaves most precious there. Border States slaveholders here accustomed to punish slaves by sending them to cotton plantations and removing evidence of our shame.

Negroes intelligent for their curse should be ready to aid Federalists.

Cold acting on insensitivities of north as much as in design has driven expedition to their port.

Great mischief can be done by entrenching Union troops in Mississippi City[21]:
[13]

Friday Nov 29th. At 8 o'clock Ship off Charlestown.[22] Felt well when woke up, but qualenish as day advance. With difficulty saved breakfast. At 4 o'clock this morning those on deck observed reflection of sky in Western Horizon, indicating great conflagration in direction of Georgetown, SC. Continued fair weather — Conn't band played on quarter deck.

At noon changed course being off. Port Royal and now due South. 22 miles Hilton Head. 27 miles from Tybee Light entrance of Savannah. Wind springing up brought down forces and sails which offered resistance.

Four o'clock made sail off Georgia shore lone trawler waiting for us. Shook out canvas spread all sail and gave chase but she failed to cut us off.

Wind blew strong South mist smelly but good, ship stemmed the waves as smoothly as ever, ferry boat crossed mouth, the Mystic.

Moderate breezes clear and pleasant with
[14]
small sea. Ship sent down fore and port top sail good.
[15]

Ship Island.[23] As a strategical point, Ship Island posses advantages of the greatest importance,

Water at West Point Ship Island. On point where same Island's widens and where Lagoon makes in. At "Litter Bend " Cat Island At Belle Fontaine Pt. Main Shore between Graveline Bay and Biloxi Bay and as a retreat to "North Point, Chandeleur Island. Also at West Point from Island.
[16]

Saturday Nov 30th. One week, first unpleasant weather. Slight rain with considerable wind. Reveille — general timing up in state of Conn under the saloon. Boys fraternized. Nutmeg and Spindles friends and worked together for common cause. Song and laughter. Cleaned off before I left my berth.

"Here's land boy's." Good for sun up. 11 o'clock A.M. Made land on Eastern Coast of Florida at first low sandy beach, then came wooded coast, deciduous growth, inlets, bayous. Palmetto trees. Spruced wooded tops like umbrellas and anchors of vessel onshore, strong breeze first part of day with clear weather, spread fore and aft sails and carried tide came on calm and hot.

Elmore Dane private Co. F 26th fell down a hatch, struck man on hand

[17]

in hold. [illegible][24] of stomach.

Attended by our Bradt 26th.

> As November closed, the expedition was well on its way to Ship Island. Little was happening on land and President Lincoln was questioning why his generals were not on the move. Naval affairs were a different matter. The navy had seized the British ship Trent carrying Confederate Commissioners Mason and Slidell on their way to Europe, angering the British at this unlawful act on the high seas. The Confederate Navy Department called for the building of ironclad gunboats, and conversion of the captured USS Merrimack at the Norfolk Navy Yard began. Elsewhere, Jefferson Davis was elected President of the Confederacy and Major George B. McClellan succeeded Lieutenant General Winfield Scott as General in Chief of the Union armies.

[18]

Sunday, Dec. 1st, 1861. At 4.30 made Light on Grand Key Bahamas. Gun Key Light 24 miles. The ship being designed for southern passenger traffic, better ventilated than northern steamers. Doors and windows thrown open to catch cool breeze. Roomy rout 24 hours light, baffling sea winds, calm and very warm weather. Ship running down East Coast of Florida. 2.50 Friday P.M. made Jupitor Inlet Light House where is a fort.[25] Made land 7.10 morning, At 8.10 made Cape Florida Light and passed Carrysfort LeReef Light[26] at 9½ o'clock. British man of War wrecked many years ago. Light House tender anchor a mile from shore. Boats put off from light on our approach and formed visual. Light House hung not the national banner

and Capt. Fletcher said same. Passed close to light house. Sand keys all along — some decid-
[19]
uous growth wooded hills rose gradually from shore. Wrecks under the land and fisherman. Two mild cases fever onboard. At 12 noon passed Indian Key, fleet under land.

Saw flocks of flying fish. Schools porpoises in wake of vessel. Steamer heeled by men getting out of sun. Took champagne and ice. Thought of dream of vessel's rolling over and only me saved. Opened book to prophetic passage in which a father recorded in his Journal of fiction mention of death of sin. Thought seriously of the matter. Off Sombrero Light at 3¼ Reefs hoisted national ensign. Some Longal men left.

Off Key West at 6½ o'clock. Sand keys most southern point. 8 miles from Key West. First sights since leaving Hampton Roads. Passed Tortugas 12 o'clock Sunday night.
[20]

A life on the ocean mane
The man who wrote it was green
For he had never been to sea
And a ship he never had seen[27]

...

Monday Dec. 2nd
Out of sight of land all day. Not a sail in sight. Gulf as gloomy and unfrequented as in the days of Cortez. Steamer moving N.W. for Chandeleur Island.[28] Beautiful day. Wrote long and dined with Captain Fletcher.

Tuesday Morning Dec 3rd. Slightly quamish, change in weather cold and windy. Nothing new. Got soundings in water 27 feet deep. Land discend one o'clock. Chandeleur Island soon after. Mirage beautiful. Strange objects about point of island — first impressions. Big fleet loomed after steamer. *R.R. Cuyler*[29] came out. Lt. Parker boarded. Reached
[21]
anchorage 4 o'clock. Capt. Smith entrance. Started on *Mass.* to reconnoiter. Damage to *Mass.*[30] by shot from *Florida*.[31] Man passing powder. New rifled guns aboard *Constitution*.

Wednesday 4th. Went ashore on *Lewis*.[32] Met Lt. Buchanon Fontanic and Merrin. Offered cider. Troop landed by noon. Rough prospect. on expedition after Reb. *Montgomery* come up — attacked in forenoon off Grants Pass. Slept on board.
[22]

Thursday 5th. Moved baggage ashore. Wrote and went to cp. Men dug up body of several cannon balls. Dug wells. Cut grass. Gen. Phelps in camp. Shooting hogs. Killed sow litter pigs — brought up by hand. 6th at Relay had kittens and pets. One man pigs in bosom. Inhuman act and will be prevented return. Not spot on island left unexplored. Oyster bed found. Good feed. Cattles got ashore. Steel gun fort in landing from steamer. Spy deserted in boat. Gen. Phelps informed. Sleep on shore first time in Freemans tent. Read 20th chapter Proverbs.

Friday 6th. Took tramp up the island 5 miles. Patterned shells and sent them home. *DeSoto*[33] arrived from Pensacola.
[23]

Saturday Dec 7th (two weeks). *New London*[34] engaged rebel gunboats *Oregon* or *Pamlico* and *Calhoun*.[35] *Constitution* sailed 5 o'clock. Sutler schooner arrived from Key West. Sent report and letters home by Geo. Meval of Harpers Weekly. Had long struggle to decide whether to go back or remain recollected Stockwell's answer. "If you go you will leave to stay till you get instructions to come home "and decided to remain till heard from Maj. Rogers. Ladies all return in *Constitution*. Bands played in fort. Insane Marine. Relaxation and sound sleep.

Sunday Dec 8th. Hot. Calm. *Cuyler* returned from Pensacola. Dined on board. Did not overtake *Connecticut* with mails. I naturally feel better. *New London* went in pursuit of 2 rebel schooners. Under main land.

    9th Conn. Reg. inspected. Met Stair of Artic Exp.[36] Actg. Masters mate *DeSoto*. 26th inspected. Se. Col. Jones off ctg Naval off attend. Dress Parade. *Kinio*,[37] Mass., *DeSoto*. Read 30th Chpt. Ezekiel.
[24]

Monday. Dec 9th. Heavy fog. Flew past like anything sleek. Rainbows. Discharging shell schooner *Rachel Seaman*[38] and *DeSoto*. Feel little under weather. Got pr. Turner's shoes. Went aboard *New London*. Ditto went in pursuing *Pamlico*. Latter turned tail and fled. N.L.[39] pressed and shots exchd. Dined with Dr. Macklin on *"Mass."* Came ashore Capt. Winslow of *Cuyler*. Buchanon drills 5th Batty. M in artillery practice. Fire Columbian and pivot guns. Band of 26th play on ships. *DeSoto* left. Col. Butler getting up stores. Visited off of 26th (one week).

Tuesday December 10th. Queer dream last night. At home all uncles and aunt seated round taken. Went in and expressed wish somebody'd give me a revolver, and I was going that day to Miss. Doley caught me and father and mother came to see me off. Find was going somewhere but I persuaded him to remain at home till I returned.
[25]
    Went on board *Cuyler* and took lunch with Lt. Phillips (a noble hearted man). *New London* came in there prizes. 2 sloops and 1 schooner fisherman for Mr. Maltel. Went on flag of truce to Biloxi and afternoon pursued gunboat *Florida*. Returned to quarters late.

Wednesday Dec. 11th. Hot day but towards night wind rose N.W. clear and cool. Northern opprehendra. Tin D hook. Sky like N.England's. Dined with Col. Butler. *New London* went out after *Oregon*. *Mass.* followed. Schooner off to westward, another rebel steamer. *Florida* and another approached from eastward. Chance for fight. Schooner *Rachel Seaman* gone to Horn Island Pass and to blockade. In danger of being taken by *Florida*. Jeff Davis[40] in danger of *N. London*.
[26]

Thursday Dec.12th. Started 9 o'clock with Freeman and Fontane. Lt. Brady and party of 20 men 4 days rations to head of island to cut wood Steamers. Went up in boats and landed outside. Walked to East Point, passing ruins, and lagoon. Startled by minie ball striking near us and returned.[41] 26th had dress parade near fort. *New London* went out in expedition. Saw schooner *R. Seaman* outside. *New London* not put out.

Friday. Dec 13th. Reconnaissance to Biloxi. Firing on Reb. Steamer "*Grey Cloud*."[42]
[27]

Saturday Dec 14th. (Three Weeks). Store ship "*Pampero*"[43] arrived, supposed to be the "*Kingfisher*" but crowd disp'd Kingfisher arrived. Lost 69 horses in a gale. Sea sick in boarding ship but kept mum.

Sunday Dec 15th. Steamer *Water Witch*[44] arrived for Pensacola. Took 19 sailors and six marines for *Potomac* and sailed for Mobile. Horses landed from *Kingfisher* in shocking condition. Under the weather today. Took medicine and thought seriously of home.

Monday, Dec 16. *Water Witch* returned from Mobile. Discharging cargo of "*Kingfisher*." Took dinner aboard "*R.R.C.*"[45] Board of inquiry on horse commenced.
[28]

Tuesday, Dec. 17th. Arrived *South Carolina*,[46] Cpt. Alden from Passes. Had Secesh capture on board. Two gunboats schooners arrived. Also steamer gun boat *Wissahickon*.[47] (Two weeks)

Wednesday Dec 18. Stupid day. Dined Col. Jones.

Thursday. Dec 19. Started for Pensacola 9½ o'clock A.M. on *Cuyler*. Little tug boat came over to Ship Island to serve Army. Left trap and tent at fort in haste and had just time to catch steamer. Sick in an hour so didn't hold up head. Lt. Parker doud up w/port which expected to send North by *Baltic*.[48] Off Mobile 4 o'clock P.M. Cont'd with Frigate *Potomac*.[49] "*Huntsville*,"[50] steamer ran out to station. "*Supply*"[51] Store ship off Mobile. Saw Fort Morgan in distance and Light House. "Johnny Crapo"[52] Man of war ran down and boarded *Potomac*. Comp's and Capt. Powell Same chap who gave his inspection to U.S. fleet of affair in Miss. River. Arrived off Fort Pickens 8 o'clock. Baltic sailed this afternoon. Missed her by few hours.
[29]

    Friday Dec 20. Had offer to return to Ship Island in "*Niagara*"[53] flag ship. Surf ran high on Santa Rosa. No landing. Boarded *Niagara* evening. Lt. May, Capt. De Kraffs, Purser Berry, and C.C.C. Big ship. Hesitated long about going back in her not having seen "Pickens." Decided to send report back for *Kingfisher* and wait for *Rhode Island*.[54] *Niagara* sailed at midnight. (Four Weeks)

Saturday 21. Forefathers Day. Smooth sea. Stomach right side up. Appetite good. Spirits jubilant. Boat lowered and lands at Santa Rosa with off[55] of *Cuyler*. Island 40 miles dry land locking harbor of Pensacola. Which withins it would never have here. No back country. A dozen semi-nude soldiers leaped into water and dragged boat through surf. No landing at wharf. Sarona pt. (Santa Rosa) Ft. Pickens. Bragg[56] orders to fire on any boats leaving or entering. Boom once forecasts by firing on steamers and c. coming to Navy Yard. So all landing down on beach. Troops supplies

came and c in boats. After reaching land struck across to orig. camp of Pet Lands. Hospitals remained up Island. Enjoy greater
[30]
eminent from danger. 6 and 75th Regts[57] together. Wilson's Surgeon going one of ability and skill. Off regretted Wilson to resign. On lookout met Lieut. off of gd. Night of attack on 2's camp of Rebs. 1st man killed on Spanish Battery. An hour from time Rebs fired 1st shot before reached camp Rebs advc'd as skirmish. Saw place where 1st hurt was brought. "Billy rushed out battery up [illegible]."[58]

Bulletin in fort Pickens picture of Wilson. Strange men seen in camp 2 or 3 nights before attack. Men heard tinking in Navy Yard of Rebs working on Steamer. 4 5 2 killed wounded and taken prisoner. Asks of burned tents. Sentinels on hills checks [illegible]picket guard. Camp now rear fort on inside of island. Met party of 2's. Not very elegant or refined. Light'd at appellation "Pet L's" and all answered "yes." Wanted to go to York but not till enemy driven out of Pensacola. Went to Wilson qtrs. Found Col. in tent smoking. Said took life easy. Bald head bright sharp eye. Black moustache. 2 bottles claret. Never dyes. Nothing artificial about him. Went to Fort Pickens with officers of artilery. Swamp full of
[31]
whole shot and fragments of shell. 2's exhibited bullets lodged in knapsack. None express the dignified could not kill him and looked as if would resist grips of death by time. Slope of glacis of fort. Jarred of shell, buried in earth and exploded left deep holes. Fragments all around of shell and shraps. Before Sally port[59] heavy wall of sand bags protects entrance. Prde[60] dug up to make curtain for officers quarters. Rampart saw battery at Navy Yard. All still deserted. A skeleton of workshop burned still standing. Hulk on stocks. Battery beyond, practicing Friday night to get range on harbor. Chimneys of Washington and Wolsey standing. Yellow flag on hospital. Sandy shore batterys thrown up. At wharf and night in rear of it. Two men fishing Barrancas. Light and sound struck battery at Capt. And ditto further on. Rebs scattered battery in woods. Concentrate fire at night distracts fire of enemy. Barracas injured and respond. McRrae badly wounded. Russell
[32]
L.L. CD of London Times said in a letter, if Rebs had not taken in woods were fools, not heaven and Death's head. Plank road from beach to fort. Enemy encamped in woods. Left barracks when bombardment commenced. Except need to work guns. One woman on Santa Rosa wife of officer of 75th Matron in hospital. Got range for mortars in backside of Pickens and marked on scarp wall lines litter McK. F.B., L.H. Ray, L.H.B. Rg. N.Ydl Rg. Sc. Flag staff hottest place during engagement. Shot went

through cge. Explosion after bombardment 5 men killed several wounded. Same like acdt N. Yd. contrabands and Spaniard come over. 4 contrabands[61] put off retaken and leaving, avg. 1 per day. Vessel off S.R. pt.[62] continuing this morning. Col. Roman(?) went out. Rebs leave 3000 men Oak Island between Pensacola and Santa Rosa. Horses of 75th N.Y. Reg. come out well.
[33]
"To advance or not to advance," that is the question and a matter of grave consideration.

"However skillful the maneuvers of a retreat, it will always weaken the morale of an army, because in losing the chances of success, these last are transferred to the enemy. Besides retreats always cost more men and material than the most bloody engagements; (Bull Run); with difference, that in the battle, the enemy's loss is nearly equal to your own whereas in a retreat, the loss is on your side only."

> *It appears that Hills is describing a raid on rebel fortifications at Pensacola, Forts Barancas and McRae, and possibly the Navy Yard. I have not found any other records to verify his account, unlike the Biloxi raid at the end of the month which is better documented. The 6th New York participated in a battle on Santa Rosa Island in October and around Pensacola in November. It was engaged again at Forts McCrae and Barancas on January 1, 1862. It is not clear if the battle described is the one in January or a different one entirely.*[63]

[34]

Sunday, Dec.22. Rocked in the cradle of the deep and a _____[64] uncomfortable cradle it is. Slept in a hammock cot last night and slept well. But a disgusted stomach rolled out of that same cot this morning. Threw myself on my back on qtr deck and carried studying philosophy of sleigh rides — no I mean the clouds which went floating past. Rain came on and drove me to cover. Old driddhood[65] revived. *Rhode Island* arrived at six and I packed on board. Letters from friends to off of *Cuyer.* Off for Ship Island Sunday night.

Monday. Dec 23. Smooth sea. Cold wind. Firm stomach. Up with *Potomac* 5 o'clock. Hunts isles. 10 o'clock. Off Fort Morgan. Fort Gaines. Run in sight of Sand keys of Ala. and Miss. Reached Ship Island 4 o'clock. Found *Niagara, Preble,*[66] *N. London, W. Witch, Mass, Pampero, Supply,* 3 Schooner gunboats, *Wissahickon, Kingfisher* in fort.
[35]

5. Journal of a Military Expedition from Boston to _____   55

Tuesday. Dec 24th. (Three weeks). Cold last night and hot today. Took horse back ride. Gen. Phelps went on board *Niagara* rec'd 11 guns Naval depot to be established on Ship Island. Fort Mass[67] to be turned over to 4th Mass. Battery. Flag officer McKean came ashore salute 13 guns by battery. Inspected fort and reviewed troops with Gen. Phelps. Personal difficulty with Butler.

Wednesday. Dec 25th Christmas, No boxes and no Santa Claus. But serenade, Sack Race and c. Flag staff off 26th and 9th aboard *Niagara*. Fort evacuated.

Thursday Dec 26th. Moving Day. Fort evacuated. Norther in night bands ashore. *Connecticut* stores up and c.

Friday 27th. Dined Col. Jones. Fire off Biloxi.

Saturday 28th. (5 weeks). Dined aboard *Preble*. *New London* fired heading H. Island Pass.[68]
[36]

Sunday 29th. Went to *Pampero*. "*N. L.*"[69] came in with cotton prize "*Gypsy*,"[70] owned by Marcy, N.O. came from Portsmouth. Letter from Samuel Marcy and mother and c.

Monday 30th. "*Rhode Island*, in morning *DeSoto*, "*Mulan*,"[71] "*Huntsville*," arrived. A stormy day.

Tuesday 31st. (Four Weeks) Expedition to Biloxi. *Rhode Island* at night, "*Preble*," and "*Fearnaught*"[72] sailed. Grand inspection reviews and muster. Quarters. Gen. P.[73] meeting 1st time.

> *Ship Island was a Union encampment by the end of December, but forces still needed to be collected for the move up the Mississippi River. Elsewhere, the Mason and Slidell incident that had angered the British ended with their release; they were allowed to continue on to England and France. The Biloxi expedition provided a great deal of excitement for Hills. A letter Hills acquired describing the action of the U.S. Steamer Henry Lewis and its capture of the "Captain Speider" has been transcribed below. Union ships capturing rebel vessels with cargo could be eligible for a share of the prize when sold, so detailed records were routinely kept.*

[*Biloxi Battle Letter*]

The date given is an error. The date should be January 2, 1862.

U.S. Steamer Henry Lewis
Off Ship Island
January 2nd 1861

Sir:

I have the honor to report that on the 31st of December 1861 I got underway by order of Commander Smith, he having previously come on board with the Marine Guard of the Massachusetts and a guns crew of sailors, also the Marine Guard of the Niagara under command of Lieut. Geo. Butler, and in company with the Water Witch and New London stood across the sound to the town of Beloxi. On arriving outside the bar, I came to anchor in six feet of water, when Commander Smith accompanied by Acting Master Ryder went inside, under a flag of truce, to communicate with the authorities, and demand a surrender of the place and free navigation of the waters, informing them that should we open fire on the battery which was near the Light House, there would be considerable destruction of property and life which he wished to avoid.

His demands were acceded to where he returned to this ship. I there got underway and crossed the bar and anchored in six feet of water, close to the battery, where I sent two boats on shore under the command of Act. Master Ryder and Mid. Woodward to bring off the guns, belonging to the battery. The guns were brought off as expeditiously as possible and without trouble. There was one nine pounder weighing 1300 lbs. and one six pounder weighing about 800 lbs. They are both of iron and of old make.

In the meantime I had sent Act. Master Freeman with a boat's crew of trueline men to capture a schooner which was beating up behind Deer Island. After a pull of about an hour and a half he succeeded in boarding her. He brought her down past the town of Beloxi without molestation when I ordered him to proceed to Ship Island, I then got underway and joined the Water Witch and New London when we returned to this place. The Water Witch and New London were not able to cross the bar on account of their draught of water.

On my arrival here I found the schooner we had captured to be the "Captain Speiden"[74] of New Orleans, Francisco Martinez Master and sole owner, and to be loaded with hard pine lumber and of 34 63/95 tons burden. All the papers found on board are in the possession of Acting Master Johnson of the New London. No manifest of the cargo was found but the Master of her states that there is at least 30,000 feet of lumber on board.

The crew consists of Manuel Castro and Joseph Pedro Martinez. I forgot to state that Act. Master Wiggins was on board as pilot and took the ship

5. Journal of a Military Expedition from Boston to _____   57

over the bar in fine style. I herewith enclose a list of the officers and crew of this ship entitled to prize money.

                      I am respectfully
                      Yr. Obdt. Servant
                      Thos. McKean Buchanan
                      Lieut. U. S. Navy

To.
Flag Officer W. W. McKean
Commd'g Gulf Blockading Squadron

Wednesday Jan 1st 1862. "Happy New Year" to all. Flag of truce to N.O. postponed. "Ready" to go. All day getting ready. Closed up letters and sent aboard *R*.[75] Navy consider it their plunder and "*Water Witch*" goes at 10 o'clock tomorrow. Slept on board *Lewis* and wrote account of Biloxi. [37]

Thursday Jan 2nd/62. On board *W. W.* early. "Very fishy morning dis morning," and lasted till 3 o'clock. to late for "flag," and called on Lt. Oliver in evening.

Friday 3rd. Up at 5½ A.M. Off to W.W. to breakfast. Fog — fog — fog. Till noon. Dine on *Mass. Merdicelita*[76] arrived. Went to flag ship — got Cap.

Saturday 4th. (Six Weeks). Fog! for a wonder. Up at 6 o'clock. The biggest jollian day of my life letters from home and file of the Journal all at once. *Kingfisher* towed down to mouth of harbor. As the moon waxed the bay rose earlier and the wind increased.
[38]

Sunday Jany 5th. Clear and bright. Off to "*Water Witch*" or Frenchman off to NO. in his own boat. Afternoon ride with Robinhart of Battery to East Head. Evening gun booming. Two new gunboats arrived and Schooner and *New London* also *Sagamon* and *Winona*.[77] *Kingfisher* went to sea evening.

Monday Jany 6th. Wrote all day. At sundown went on board "*Mass*" for Expedition. Rathole fleet. *New London, Sagamon*,[78] *Winona and Wis*— gunboats. 1st death 26th Reg. John Graudrau. Co. H. (Five weeks)

Tuesday 7th. Off Horn Island Pass.[79] All but *Mass*. went into Sound. Run up to 15 mile of Grant's Pass.[80] Rebel schooner and 2 Reb gunboats. Shoal water. Water in gun. Lt. Cmdg. ordered to *New London*. Steamed off of Rebel Bois. *Kingfisher* sailed for passes.

Wednesday 8th. Off Rebel Bois Pass[81] still 4 o'clock P.M. Some rough! Should think. Left for Ship Island on yacht *Zouave*[82] Cpt. James Packer. Arrived safe at tent 8 o'clock eveng.
[39]

Thursday. Jany 9th. Fog. Thunder.Rain. Anxious about "*Water Witch*" going to Key West. Got letters aboard in hurry after it had rained *some*. Letter dated today.

Friday 10th. Went down to flagship. *Water Witch* still here and likely to be. Refugee arrived Ship Island.

Saturday 11th (seven weeks) *Water Witch* sailed. Steamer arrived. "*Zouave*" sailed. Sent letters to Journal. Jane the Contraband. Married at 11, had 1st child at 12 and one every year till 15 yr old, had three bastards. Sister had 36 children. Her own sold away from her and her husbands ditto. Stewardess on Steamer *Luis*.[83] Now washerwoman for Reg. Had one child by white man. Health broke down by early maternity. Her mistress wanted her to marry, and she thinking it was what the girls played keeping
[40]
house, thought would be fun. Last mistress wouldn't let her marry but sent a white man to her. Miss Adron her mistress.

Gray, Hospital Steward informs me that weather (damp) and diet (rations of fat pork and hard bread seven days out of ten, no potatoes arrived) laying foundation for pulmonary diseases and scurvy.

Soldiers steal molasses, but defend selves from accusation by averring that 6 sailors steal from 10 of soldiers Conn 9th. Stole shoes off each others foot on "C." Lt. Oliver in to see me tonight. Predicted that in 3 mos. he be back to Mass. And that Butler never sets foot Ship Island. Discussed Expedition which was chastised as humbug — got up to make money out of gov't. War danc'd as preconcerted affair which will last till leaders on both sides had filled pockets.
[41]

Sunday 12th. Dined with Capt Warren 26th. "Whistler" served at table. White napkins. Corn. Peas. Mackerel. Soldiers firing at target. Gen. Phelps said "Do your best boys. This is all the shooting you'll have to do. You'll go home in the spring when the birds fly north." Conn't soldiers pulling guard. Genl. said "If you pull that guard off you'll have to pay for it. You'll find the trigger lower down." Steamer *R.R. Cuyler* arrived.

Hopkins says *Kingfisher* chartered for $6,000 per month. Reed post Sutler, brother in law of Butler. Pref given to his stores and no potatoes sent to the troops, who are getting pork rations 7 days out of 10. Poor quality of hardware stuck onto the fort. *All shot for rifled cannon ⅛ inch too large.* One day Gen P. catechized a soldier who had been arrested for refusing to obey an order — "For what did you enlist! Said the Gen'l. "For a soldier! Was the reply. Oh! I thought you enlisted to command. You might make a good commander, but I don't think you are.

The case of the sick horse. Case of Lieut. Sola. Case of larceny of chickens on board on *Constitution*. "Nickle Wrangler."

Officer of Conn't 9th lost hat returned.

Monday. Jany 13th. "*Mass*" returned from expedition. *New London* arrived. Attempted to board *Mass*, got wet and gave it up. Hog attacked by dog in fort. "Jack" set on by roguish soldiers, who applauded his courage and said "Good boy Jack." Go it Porker, root hog or die. Oh! Wife — you'n the joy of my life." And look for a letter by the *Constitution*. *Cuyler* brought news confirming surrender M and S and that "*Constitution*" sailed Jany 3rd news came via Pensacola paper. Soldiers declare peace declared. *Mass* from Horn Island Pass brought mailbag and tomorrow troops to be inspected and sent home on "*New London*." Took tea Reed sutler. Wiggins came gave report exp. Five contraband escaped from Bob Saffo — Bay — met 26th Reg. just off parade.
[42]

Tuesday Jany 14th. Weighed 144¼ pounds after dinner. Last night Capt. Fairbanks of ship *Geo. Greener*,[84] forcibly compelled to leave ship by Master Mate of U.S. Schooner "*Kittatinny*"[85] strange proceeding. Battery fired at target. "*Milan*"[86] sailed for Havana. (six weeks.)

Wednesday Jany 15th. Ship "*Black Prince*"[87] arrived. Gale 3 days out Boston destroyed 147 homes (awful.) Lt. Palmer M.D. came out. "*New London*" went on reconnaissance.

Thursday Jany 16th. "*Lewis*" Steamer. To be turned over to Army. Gen. Phelps[88] says troops will have a good drill and very little fighting to do. Phantom Ship. "Dress up then Paddy Green." Be Gorry says Paddy I'm am well dressed as yourself Capt. Garvy having the sword and sash." "*Milston*"[89] arrived. Flag of truce after noon.

Friday Jany 17th. "Clam chowder *Mass.* Porter, C.N. Berkin and Pickman in a *funny* way. Writes to Mrs. D. Con. W.C. Prescott Battery boat crew loose raft and like to loose themselves.
[43]

Saturday Jany 18th. Had interview with Dr. Wells. Good as oats to see him. Ship *Bullion*[90] towed down. Sent letter to Journal and Sallie. Board "*Portsmouth*"[91] evening. (Eight Weeks from Home)

Sunday Jany 19th. Fine day sir. Spiritual influence. Rank odor of excrement. While passing to determine its origin, get good ideas suggested by spirits who raised a stench to attract my nostril. Lt. R. didn't smell it. I went out of tent but couldn't find cause of it. Sure I am improving in style through some unseen agency. At 11 o'clock A.M. hear heavy guns Fort Pike. Hollins came out *Pamlico* and *Oregon. N.L.* and Hills went out to attack them. Rebs ran as usual.

Monday Jany 20th. Reviewed 4th Batty. *Portsmouth* sailed. Met Dave Horn, Ed. Gorham, and took tea Capt. Jones. Great fires opposite shore.
[44]

Tuesday Jany 21st. (Seven weeks) Went down to Str. *R.R. Cuyler.* Yesterday 20th *Cuyler* captured Schooner. 4 men shot: Slept on sofa.

Wednesday 22nd. Put letters on "*Supply.*" Norther. Seven times raking shore.

Thursday 23rd. Cold and dreary. On board ship BM Pce.[92]

Friday 24th. Supply sailed last night. Sent letters of 14th and 18th and Col. G. [illegible] date 24th by *J.W. Hall*[93] of Providence going to Key West and Havana.

Saturday Jany 25th. (Nine weeks). Ride to East Head. Bk *J.W. Hall*[94] sailed morning. Pkman and self sang songs on beach.

Sunday Jany 26th. *Water Witch* returned. Ride into ports up East Head.

Monday. Jany 27th. "*Connt*" arrived.
[45]

Tuesday Jany 28th (Eighth week). Rebel flag of truce Str. *Crescent*[95] Mobile. British consular dispatches.

Wednesday 29th. "*Santiago de Cuba*"[96] arrived. News from Passes. Secty Cameron succeeded by Staunton of Penn.

5. Journal of a Military Expedition from Boston to _____   61

Thursday 30th. "*Water Witch*" went to Pensacola. *Niagara* sailed for Passes and Galveston. "*Mass*" returned to port.

Friday 31st. Monthly Inspection. Slept on Steamer *Santiago de Cuba* last night. Had queer dream about Louisa Gorham.[97] 2nd Mass. Ship "guard" sailed for So. West Pass. *Niagara* had steam up 380 days.

Friday 31st. Discussed policy of leaving Ship Island. Col Jones, Capt. Butler, Commander Smith and others advised trip to Key West. Capt. Ruglesbe offered me passage. Went aboard
[46]
after borrowing $20 of Capt. Howe of Ship *Black Prince* leaving him packages for home. Told Reinhart, Manning, and Annable was going and went.

Saturday Feb. 1st. (Ten weeks from home). Sailed from Ship Island in Str. *Santiago de Cuba*. Left pr. Shoes (Parser) straw hat, bar soap, and c in tent. Kind of home some for 2 mos. Ship Island had dif't look when left it from that presented at first approach. "Count this day lost who's low declaring son sees from thy hand" and c. So I felt for 2 days.

Sunday Feb 2nd at Sea. Inspection go on. Auction Dead man shoes.

Monday Feb 3rd at Sea. Hard struggle. Reached Key West at dusk. Dark outline of shore and darker still of fort and vessels arose before me. Exct of everything port dissipated sea sickness and felt bully. Went ashore met Mrs. Cashship (white woman). Big thing with ice water.
[47]

Tuesday Feb 4th. "*Oriental*"[98] arrived on shore. 47th Penn. Reg landed and marched through "Conchtown"— niggers, cocoanuts and secession. Three classes of Society in K.W. "Kingfish, Groupers, and Conches." Sunday prayer for Pres. of US. Secesh close prayer books. 2 Comde Porter's expdy schooner arrived.

Wednesday Feb 5th. Fort Taylor. U.S. Bks *Mg* or *Hill*.[99] Lt. Gibbs of Boston, ride Key West. Music Sorie evening. Russell House. To bed at Russell House.

Thursday Feb 6th. Dinner on Oriental. US gunboat Kanawha[100] Lt. J.C. Febigner comdg, arrived. On 5th got file of Journals. 150 miles E of Portugese Bay.

Friday Feb 7th. "Oriental" sailed morning for N.Y. Sent Gibbon's party to dix and five packages Ship Island 8 other letters to Journal also. No. 1 letter from Key West.
[48]

Saturday Feb 8th. Kanawha sailed dispatch. "*Mass*" passed. (Eleven weeks from home)

Sunday Feb 9th. Fire this morning Sch. *Emma*.[101] Attempt to destroy gov't property. Arrived last night Schooners *Matthew Vasser Jr., Chas. H.H. Savage,* and *C.P. Miller.* Capt. A.R. Laugthome, Brig *Sea Foam*, Mortar flotilla.[102]

Monday 10th. Connct. Arrived. *Constitution* passed. Sent letter to Journal via Havana. "*Roanoke*"[103] met C.W. French, John Blake, Merrill, Capt. Blood and others.

Tuesday Feb 11th. Pensacola[104] arrived K.West off Keys. Richardson, Watson, Locke, Torbell, and glad to see friends, salutes and c.

Hartford[105] Flag Officer Farragut arrived. Big day.
[49]

Wednesday Feb 12th. Met Lt. Thornton, Lt. Heisler, and Flag Lt. Osborne of *Hartford*. Chf. Eng. Hilbert of *Pensacola*. *Connecticut* sailed 4 o'clock. *Hartford* coaling. Called on Mr. Ferguson eveng. Arrived Sch. *Oliver Brach*. Mortar Schooner's *Adolph Hughes*, Capt. F___, *Geo. Nahaw* Capt. Collins. G.A. *Ward* seen.[106]

Thursday Feb 13th. Arrived Sch. *Isabella* late. *W.R. King*[107] captured 1st by *W. Montgomery*.[108]

Friday 14th. Bk "*Tenseta*"[109] arrived. "*Santiago de Cuba*" sailed Ship Island. Sent letter to Sallie by bk *J.W. Hall*.

Saturday 15th. Hartford sailed daylight. Wrote out pens strong. In Cupola Russell House. 47th and 90 Regts.[110] Paraded. *Rhode Island* arrived. Rec'd one Sallie's journal. *Saxon*[111] arrived and got letters. Good ones from home and paper for Zenas and officer, and Reg pld Rye unknown friend. Oh! I'm so happy, so happy am I. Not from the effects of the whiskey though. (12 weeks). Bk Hall sailed. *Owasco*[112] gunboat Porter arrived.
[50]

5. Journal of a Military Expedition from Boston to _____   63

Our dinner table. Capt. Marks. Soldier drinking water. John Venerable drinking and Matilda.

Sunday Feb 16th. "*Reaney*"[113] arrived from Ship Island and Fort Pickens. Seized by gov't at Phil. Pas and So. Fitting up gun boat. Brought levies $20,000 expd. and sent out Str [*illegible*][114] to Gen Brown to be and as dispatch. Bay Ship Island. Laid 2 mos and now back here. Not worth the gov't expense to come.

Saxon trying to spend all my cash. 20 arty to work guns and 2 officers [illegible] six men [illegible] had works and fight ship. Govt got to feed and pay the men unless.

Bright 75 to and 150 by better hours. This then extended at $120.

Bartlett's Reg. learn halt and blend.

Saxton sent to sea shameful condition. [illegible] compelled to take not true.

After keeping boat 2 mos. might have made loaded too deep. [illegible] on upper deck.
[51]

Spring head of air pump and injection pipe. Too big a load fits a [illegible] so too big a load [illegible] a ship. Potatoes 10th Jany 150 bushels there freezing and lay till 5th Feb right made trip now rotten bushel full. No circulation 90 and 95 enough to cook. Flour baked. Why not start off.

Monday 17th. *Blank day.*

Tuesday 18th. *Saxon* sailed. *Rhode Island* sailed daylight. Fisher a nonpaid master mate and talking about taking oath. Oh and its just as airy to take the oath as 'tis to sing a song.

Sail brig *S.H.* and *Engl.*[115] Sat smoking. Wish to god blew out faster. What devil that for. Leave the seas open. Let's all go to put a dent hole in murdering but give chance to plunder. Why god do you spurn Society by working $20 month, 'tis that so. No man.
[52]

Wednesday 19th. Bummer[116] _____ arrived. Case of _____ "*Geo. Snow*"[117] of Deer Isle. [llegible] of underwriters. Experiments with 8 inch howitzer Fort Taylor. Gave C and E. Have draft for $140 on *C.O.Rogers*.[118] Pd $20 board Russell House.

Thursday Feb 20th. Most sick today. Took pills and Sedlitz powder. Steamer. *Phila*[119] arrived with Gen Brannan and staff.

Friday 21st. Brig Gen Brannan staff arrived by *Phila.* L Steamship. *Richmond*[120] ashore Sombrero night. 8 ft. [illegible] 19 at 3 o'clock. *Phil* and *Owasco* sent. Tucker came down. Serenade. Cheer. P. de. Albany.

Saturday 22nd. Nash birthday. Address Brigade parade. Races at Barracks and C. Richard arrived safe. (13 weeks).

Sunday 23. Three months from home. Refugees arrived. Brig (*Horace*) *Beals* arrived. Alden gave dinner to officers. Went with Gibbs and Maj. Fchgler to nigger meeting. To Fort Taylor and back for journals.
[53]

Monday Feby 24th. *Pensacola* sailed of 47th. Evening with Furgason's. Found the odor of oleander on voyage home. Hot and salty. Close and sticky. Mosquitoes and sand.

Tuesday 25th. False run about "*Columbia.*"[121] Left Key West 10 o'clock P.M. in *Sophronia.*[122] D. Havana sick nigh unto death. Arrived at 4 o'clock Wednesday afternoon.
[54]

Trip from Key West to Havana and back.26th. Arrived Wednesday afternoon 26th, passed Morro on one side and Ponto fort on other. City low and surrounded by fortifications. On hills comdg town and harbor. Tug like Ray Towed in Sph [illegible], ferry boat, brass gun in Moro. Waited ½ hour for boardg off. Gave up passport. I went in boat [illegible] over to *Columbia.* "Mather" the Purser. Ashore. File of boats. Spanish and French men of war in port. English S.S. sailed. Lanaid on Spanish I___ Columbus. Rain. Southern Cross. Cabago Head Quarters of U. men. Garden of Gov. Gen'l of Cuba. Palace. Rolden. White and red uniformed police. Statues. Teles on roofs. Bells. (d_ _m). Dominica Dos Jincock taken. Bands played. Too much brassllant. Union Hotel! Supper. Steep price. Circus. Spanish beauties. Americanos. Lottery ticket under "Posso" when all elite of Habonida out. Therton T____ [illegible].

[Drawing of stick figure with wheelbarrow at bottom of page]

Hills clearly enjoyed Cuba, and although there are no journal entries found for 1864 he returned to Havana that January as editor of the Era.

[55]

5. Journal of a Military Expedition from Boston to _____

Pass for a trip to Havana in 1864.

First night in Havana. Went 9 miles to a circus. My first and last circus. Spanish beauties in Lawrence calico and valencel lace. Volantes and negros gowns. Slouch hat. Some lining. Silver buckles. Volantes of rich plated and lined velvet. Statue in parlor on front of house. W.C. in kitchen. Close to furnace. Hotel de Union dining room open air. Northern females at circus. Fancy woman at Louvst Bravo and Hanlan performance. Stall for drinks outside. Passo lighted gas. Streets watchman black cloaks, a halbeard or spears cry out "all's well" every ½ hour. To bed. Cell in hotel one square window. Tile floor. Cot corrugated India rubber mattress. Mean after. No sleep. Every bone in body sore next morning. Guns, bells and c. [56]

Havana Thursday Feb 27th. Rose disgusted. Walked to Gov. Genl's gardens. Begged flower of garden. Went to Cabarga's. Met Caps. Berry and Dennison. Went to breakfast at Mr. Fultous. Coolie waiters. Madrid. Tops of masts over brown vessels entering port. Long narrow breakfast room. Garlic in everything (smell odor now) and actually did off Morro going out of Havana. After breakfast started for H.R.R. to see Gonzales. Passed vegetable market open air. States all round. Negro women selling fruit and veg. Beautiful jargon of "voices." Found R.R. Station and Philadelphians. Took cruise to find G. Came back met him in office. Arranged ride 2 o'clock. Back to city and called on Am. Consul. Shufeldt and Savage. Lady in office. She left. Shfld and self had talk. Knows of temper secesh down in mouth. Stock of S.C. falling. Yancey had hair cut and left H.

Called on Mrs. Polhemus at Hotel Cubana. Saw Helme ex consul, and judge Huntington and son from West. Saw Frank of N.Y. Sardines ship at Louvre no Le Grand Hotel. About supper 22nd Feb. Rode to R.R. Station to say oldest go to courts. G.

[57]

In suburbs at 4 o'clock. G. Savage and self started from Caboyes and went out on Cerra Road. Beautiful. Beautiful. Beautiful. This ride was a big thing seen with brig Syes. Back to Havana. and circus last night. Down town with two friends. To bed on canvas sacking. Nervous fear *Nonpareil*[123] bears me. No sleep out at daylight silent struts. To Carboyes. Met friend Dr's G. Ckts. Board *Nonpareil*. Back to Sch. Pilot Cyrus of Orange. Scene on wharf. Negros naked to waist onloading ship. By ring head to gray fleet of boats. Importunate boatmen. Unft New York Hackmen.

Friday — [No entry]

> *While Hills was exploring the Gulf and Cuba much was happening on the war front in February. Union forces were aggressively moving to close Confederate ports, and captured Roanoke Island on the North Carolina coast to hamper traffic in the Albemarle and Pamlico Sounds. In Tennessee a Union combined land and river force forced the surrender of Fort Henry on the Tennessee River and Fort Donelson on the Cumberland River. This opened central Tennessee to invasion and by the end of the month Nashville became the first Confederate capital to fall.*

[58]

Saturday March 1st. Left Havana. Arrived K.W. 3 o'clock. Mail. Letters C.O.R., Sallie, and Ship Island. *Santiago de Cuba.* (14 weeks)

Sunday March 2nd. Disabled "bummer" arrived. Last one here.

Monday March 3rd. Str. *Cuyler* arrived. Norther.

Tuesday 4th. *Oriental* sailed. *Harriet Lane*[124] returned from Havana.

[59]

Wednesday 5th. *So. Carolina* and *Magnolia*[125] arrived.

Thursday 6th. *Phil.* Sailed daylight. Went to concert and jail. Beauregard prisoner.

Friday 7th. Coldest day K.W. this winter. The [temperature][126] down to 60°. Dull stupid day.

Saturday 8th. "*Mallory*" passed. "*Bainbridge*" went to sea. (15 weeks)

Sunday 9th. *Water Witch* arrived.

Monday 10th. *Niagara* arrived. *Rhode Island* or *Westfield*.[128]

Tuesday 11th. "*Clifton*"[129] and "*Cuyuga*" arrived.
[60]

Wednesday 12th. "*Rhode Island*" sailed. Tappan and Dr. Lane left for home. Had blues desperately. Gunboat *Chambers*[130] arrived. Paid Russel $24. Rode to South Beach. Got in Chaparral.

Thursday 13th. Left for Tortugas at 10 o'clock with Genl Brannon staff on Schooner *Reaney*. Arrived six o'clock evng. Met Lt. Col. Mrs. Abcott. Quartered Col. A.S.

Friday 14th. Inspection of N.H. 7th and Fort Jeff.[131] Supt at cook night for Key West most painful night in experience of writer.

Saturday 15th. Arrived K.W. at 9 o'clock. (six weeks) morning and went to bed sick. *Dr. Bates my friend.*

Sunday 16th. Met Mr. Price. Addressing Miss Jameson, Chelsea.

Monday 17th. Nix countdown.

Tuesday 18th. *Constitution* came and went to Havana. "*Oneida*"[132] arrived. *Nightingale*[133] here [Acting Master][134] Dave Horn.
[61]

Wednesday March 19th. *Cuyle*r sailed. *Kingfisher* arrived. Breakfast at Fergurson. Good bye to ladies thought I was oph by Kalhcaids but too much motion. "A burnt child dreads the fire."

Thursday March 20th. *Water Witch* returned with her prize "*Mrs. Mallory.*"[135] Collision with "*Mohawk*"[136] in harbor. Ship *So. Carolina* from N.T. to Honduras for mahogany arrived. News of naval fight at Old Point

received. Natural excitement. Old Ben McCullogh died. Peace to his ashes. Salute of 4–8 inch casemate guns Fort Taylor[137] in honor. Looking for *Connecticut* all day. Anxious to get back to Ship Island before the advance of New Orleans. In a hammock. Music on *Niagara*. Poor Hayse disappointed not going home. *Katahdin*[138] sailed.
[62]

Friday March 21st. Went on board *Kingfisher*.

Saturday 22nd. Busy closing up letter. *Constitution* sailed for Monroe at 6 o'clock. Met Brooks of Band of 26th Reg., Lt. _____ and Major Watson. "*Connecticut*" arrived. Read letter from Stockwell dated 6th inst.

[*Hills' report in the* **Boston Journal:**]

A SUB-MARINE TELEGRAPH

The Connecticut brought out from New York six cylindrical cases containing about thirty miles of submarine telegraph cable, which was directed to Commander Porter, and landed at Ship Island. The necessary instruments accompanied the cable, and two skillful operators, Messrs. Sweet and Grace of the American Telegraph Company, came out in charge of the cable. The precise locality where the telegraph will be laid is not generally known, but the fact of its having been left at Ship Island instead of its being delivered to Commander Porter at this point leads me to suppose that it is to be used to communicate between Ship Island and the main land.

Sunday 23. Day passed without incident. Strong gale from westward. Decidedly winterish. Pse Sch. *Cora*[139] arrived. Boarded *Connecticut* and secured passage Ship Island. Dined guard "*Kingfisher*." 10 gal.

Monday 24th. Closed letter and gave to Clapp to go by *Magnolia*. Wrote Stockwell.

Tuesday. Had gay times saying goodbye to Key West. Daring Bgley.

[*Hills' report in the* **Boston Journal:**]

CAPTURE OF COTTON SCHOONERS BY THE OWASCO

During the passage of the Owasco from Ship Island to Pass l'Outre, in company with the mortar flotilla, she fell in with a captured two

schooners laden with cotton, which had succeeded in escaping from New Orleans out of Chandaleur Sound and Isle au Briton passage. One of them, the President, had 100 bales, and the other, the Eugenie,[140] 275 bales of fine cotton.
[63]

Wednesday March 26th. I went on board "*Connecticut*" at 5 o'clock after a merry night at Russell House, in company with Dr. Bealer and Oltmanus of Coast Survey. Str. Sailed at 8 o'clock. Out of Main Channel and down Gulf. Rounded Rebecca Shoal and leaving Tortugas on the port bow headed for north. Anchored off Tampa.

Thursday March 27th. Entered Tampa Bay at 8 o'clock' Passed Egmont Key on starboard hand and caught glimpse of union family of refugees. Whitehouse trunks and boxes from Key West sent them by "*Connecticut.*" Growth of Palmetto on Key useful for piles on wharves wood which worms will not eat. Wharves at Charleston built before Revolution and Cabbage Tree fruit very nutritious. Leaves like coconut. Shape like pineapple and eaten like cabbage. No wonder people on isle. People come and bld but on shore. From back door [illegible] short [illegible] with which get whiskey and coffee and one day's hiking get enough to live on well. Need only thin clothing to live like lords. Light House
[64]
on Egmont Key destroyed by rebels. Tampa Bay is 90 miles up coast of Fl. From Fort Poinset on Cape Sable and 40 miles above Charlotte Harbor. It Is 15 miles wide and 25 miles long and consists of Tampa Bay proper and Hillsboro Key. There is a very straight fine entrance at Egmont Key. Anchorage for 12 miles, above which it gradually shoals and at Tampa Head of Bay carry 9 feet. Bay abounds in green turtles, red fish, groupers, barracudas, and deer, wild turkeys. Climate fine. Resources of Florida not developed. Enterprising Yankee could make fortune in 2 clearings. Spanish Bay one and a kind of cactus grows wild 100s of acres. Make best manila root. Machine wanted to manufacture it. Arrowroot called Cooney by Indians kind of yarn is a mine of wealth. Meat like chestnut. Powder equal to Bermuda arrowroot. Can be manufactured at 100 per cent for 10 cents per pound.

Bk *Ethan Allen*[141] and *W.B. Eaton*[142] in
[65]
Tampa Bay. Met Fornby of East Boston, John Turner Hale of Barnstable. List of officers. 4 Key Westins deserted from Rebel Army. Left Tampa at 10 and anchored at 6 P. M. off Cedar Keys. Saw Bail (cotton gun).[143] At

10 o'clock hailed by a schooner (tender to Str. *"Tahoma"*[144]) Gave the mail and c. and she lain by all night.

Friday March 28th. Supplain *Tahoma* will provision Lieut. ____ informs me.

Cedar Keys is a group of 4 or 5 large islands and numberless smaller ones. Few spots where can rain anything. They are grown over stumped and shifty Palmetto and Mangrove. Del House Key in South on and 50 feet high above LH on highest elevation. May Key and North Key uncultivated and uninhabited. Depot Key 20 or 30 ft. and 3 or 4 workhouses. 2 families. May Key largest of all and terminus of Fla R.R. to Key by Marsh

[66]

Island tressel work. Were large exports belonging to R.R. which he burned. Islands used during Seminole War Sel and Word and present work on old hospital and off quarters from point of buildings of islands. Judge Steel (Augustus) enforced island in land office. Order armed occupation Law of Florida. and got title several groups, 7 or 8. Bought all buildings sold at public auction after termination of war $120 and consequently owns whole settlement with exception of some. Good businessman at heart but has to howl with the wolves. Owns all property here. Did good deal of business. All cotton from Swannee, Vacasasa, and Whisloocochea Rivers sold here. 7–8,000 bales. Larger exports wood and timber for Devare river in floats and sent to Texas and Mexico. Water and fish and oysters and climate healthy. But works of harbor landlocked. 9 ft.

Fort No. 4 over in the sand work and on mainland almost May Key where R.R. crosses beaches and may be occupied by rebels.

[*Hills' report in the* **Boston Journal:**]

CEDAR KEYS

> Is a group of four or five large islands and a number of smaller ones, which were occupied by the United States army during the Seminole war, at the close of which the government buildings were purchased by Judge Steele, who entered the island under the occupation law of Florida, and consequently became their owner. He is believed to be a Union man at heart, but is obliged to howl with the secession wolves around him. All the cotton from the plantations on the Suwanee River, amounting annually, in time of peace, to between seven and eight thousand bales, is shipped from this port. The U.S. gunboat Tahoma, Lieut. Commanding Howell, was at anchor off Sea Horse Key. From Lieut. Howell, I learned that since the expedition from the steamer Hatteras against the place the rebels have maintained a picket guard of fifty men on May Key, the largest of the group and the terminus of the railroad from Fernandina; and also on hundred men on Black Point, at the entrance to Suwanee bay. There is a fortification called Fort No. 4, which

was held by the United States forces during the Indian war, and which, from its position on the main land, commands the approach on the railroad from Way Key, where our forces destroyed the warehouses and depots. Three men belonging in Key West, who were captured by the rebels while fishing off Cedar Keys, and impressed into the Confederate army, recently made their escape while doing picket duty, and are now on board the Tahoma. They confirm all previous reports in reference to the distress among the people and the hopelessness of the rebel cause.

[67]

Reached St. Marks at 4 o'clock and raised the brig *Bainbridge*,[145] hlkdg. Steamer anchored and brig beat out to communicate. Approached Bay at head of where the St. Marks River empties. 5 miles above mouth of river divides and Walk River.[146] On point where the river divides is village of St. Marks. Prosperous and (No.) 2 cotton port in Florida. 10,000 bales exported per year. It is connected by R.R. with Tallahassee Ht and for my [illegible] only R.R. in Florida. The country below St. Marks grows Cyprus and cedar and above it pine commerce whence this immense portion exported from Apalachicola. An old fort at _____ was surrendered by the Spanish in 1815 to General, then Capt. Twiggs. The fort was subsequently demolished and used to build sea wall around Light House on St. Marks Point, which wall is now a rebel batty. 7 to 8 feet water can be carried to St. Marks and off mouth river, is safe anchorage called Spanish Hole where 11 feet can be carried.

[68]

"*Bainbridge*" hon CO ofs. Seen nothing but boats. 19 this morning. Boat seen steering direct for ship. Boat sent flag and armed. Fired at her and put for shore. Afternoon shift disarmed leeward and came out two contrabands. Shirt flying for flag of truce. Said looking for friends belonged to Bratham living plantation up _____ River. Said rebels had plan to trap Union forces by getting them into interior surrounded. They keep sharp lookout and demonstrations made to show strong force, such as signal lights and guns. Pickets out on coast. When Connecticut arrived guns fired at Fort L. House. Tallahassee 26 miles distance. One dky shot in back and org B traced shot. Rebels have a steamer 2 engines. 1 rifled gun and 2–32 pounders. Burnt boat of helped negroes to vessel. Upped Bdge and left at 8 o'clock for Dog Island.

[69]

Steamer left St. Marks 7½ o'clock Friday evening and anchored off Dog Island. Sight at 11 o'clock P.M.

[*Hills' report in the* **Boston Journal:**]

ST. MARKS

The Connecticut arrived off St. Marks on the evening of the 28th, and supplied the brig Bainbridge, Commander Brasher, blockading that port. The brig had been ten days off St. Marks, but had seen no vessels attempting to run the blockade. On the morning of 19th a boat was seen standing out directly for the Bainbridge. A shot from the rifled gun of the latter caused secesh to put about and return to port. The maneuver was a mystery at the time, and was explained in the afternoon by the appearance of a skiff containing two negroes, pulling up from the leeward where they had been driven by the boat seen in the morning, which attempted to recapture them. The contrabands displayed a flag of truce, using a shirt as a substitute for bunting. They came alongside the brig, and when asked why they came, said they were looking for friends. They were taken on board and cared for. They were held in bondage by a man named Bratham, who has a plantation a short distance from St. Marks. From these men Capt. Brasher learned that the rebels intend to entrap the Union forces whenever they shall land on the coast by enticing them into the interior and surrounding them.

My own impression is that the armed rebels of Florida are few and far between. They kept up a show of strength on the western coast, but from all I can learn I am of the opinion that the State is as good as reclaimed from the hands of the traitors. The same story — distress among the masses; desperation of the leaders and a general withdrawal of every available soldier from the State for the defense of Mobile and New Orleans. The people around Fernandina told Commodore Du Pont that they had never seceded from the Union; that it was the work of strangers from Georgia, and that they were glad to welcome the old flag again. The same is doubtless true respecting the people of the other sections of the State, who are only awaiting the approach of the Union forces to declare their loyalty to the United States.

St. Marks is the second cotton port in Florida, ten thousands bales having been exported annually before the rebellion. There is an old fort at the junction of the Walkulla and St. Marks rivers, which was surrendered to General, the Captain Twiggs. The fort was subsequently demolished, and the material used to construct a sea wall around the light house on St. Marks Point, where the rebels now have a battery. The enemy keep a sharp lookout, and demonstrations in the shape of bonfires as signal lights to convey the impression that they are strongly fortified. When the Connecticut arrived off the harbor, a signal gun was fired from the battery. The contrabands, one of whom was shot in the back in making his escape, report that the rebels have a steamer at St. Marks armed with one rifle gun and two 32-pounders.

Saturday March 29th. Got underway and went in to supply *Sagamore* and Bk "*J.C. Kuhn.*"[147] Lt. Comdg. Broler and Acting Master Comdg. Lee. No news. Dog Island laid within six miles of main entrance of Apalachicola Bay. Plain sight of both steamers from Dog Island. Dog Island six miles long, partly overgrown pine. Sand hills. St. Georges 22 miles long. Whole sand flat few hundreds of pine trees. ¾ to a mile wide and is distinct per

dark line of pine forest of main land. 8 miles back of island sailed along shore and in plain sight of St. George Island to M(ain) entrance which is formed 8 St V and St G. islands.[148] St V. peculiar formation divided in parallel ridges of pine and marshes. 8 miles wide 10 miles long. Dell
[70]
North of St. Vincent lies city of Apalachicola 10 miles distant. Apalachicola lies in softest and driest sand desert imaginable while on opposite side of river open marsh. On St. V. rebel troops formerly encamped.

12 o'clock came to anchor at 5 miles due south of Main or West Entrance and found "*Mercedita*" at anchor inside Dr. Georges Island. *Mercedita* got under way and came out for supper and mail.

St. Georges Island is now broken into three pieces.

Officers of *Mercedita* reported that on 12th inst. They relieved the *Marion*[149] and next day an expedition landed and found the embrasures in sand batteries for 5 guns all of which had been removed. Found remains of encampment for 1,000 men.
[71]
Distances from Key West. To Tampa 200. Tampa to Cedar Keys 95 miles. C.K. to St. Marks 75. St. M. to St. Georges East 35 miles. St. G. East to St. G. West 40. St. G. West to St. Andrews 50. St. A. to East End Santa Rosa Island 55 miles. St. Rosa East to Fort Pickens 35 miles. Pickens to Mobile 45 and Mobile to (Ship Island) 55 miles.

Next day the str. Sounded out the channel and went in and a shored one mile up. 2½ miles inside of harbor. 2 contrabands came of formerly deck hands on steamer Young. Which with small schooners and other light draft vessels have been moved up Apalachicola River. Apalachicola abandoned of Rebel troops. See *roster Book*.[150]
[72]
After leaving main entrance of Apalachicola Cape St. Blas and run for St. Andrews where "*Permium*"[151] supposed to be anchored 11 o'clock and lay till six next morning.

[*Hills' report in the* Boston Journal:]
APALACHICOLA
Off the west end of Dog Island, and guarding the main entrance to Apalachicola Bay or St. George's Sound, we found the gunboat Sagamore, and the U.S. barque J.C. Kuhn. The Connecticut kept on her course to the western entrance to Apalachicola. We ran in plain sight of St. George's Island, 22 miles long, and beyond this had a fine view of the dark prime forests of the main land of Florida. The U.S. steamer Mercidita, Lieut. Commanding Stellwagon, was at anchor inside of the west end of St.

George's Island. From her officers I ascertained that on the 13th ult., an expedition from the steamer landed on St. Vincent Island, on the west side of the entrance, and burned the remains of a rebel fortification, where until quite recently there were five sand batteries, the guns of which had been removed when our party landed. There were indications that a force of at least 1000 men had been encamped on the island. Two contrabands came down the Mercidita, and reported that all the rebel soldiers had left Apalachicola for some place where the Confederates are collecting all their available forces. The enemy according to the story of the negroes are making extraordinary exertions to raise one hundred thousand men for the defense of New Orleans and Mobile. All the steamers and vessels in the harbor of Apalachicola have been removed up the river and secreted, to prevent them from falling into the hands of the Unionist. A detachment of troops, said to number 640 men, had been sent up the Apalachicola river to a place called Ricos, for the purpose of fortifying the river.

Sunday March 30th. Saw hills of St. Andrews Hurricane Island. Saddle Hills on island 85 feet high. River in sight of coast to 10 miles west of East End Santa Rosa supplied schooner *Maria A. Wood*.[152] Expedition on Topis vs. Rebels steamer reached Pickens at half past 3 o'clock P.M., no blockading ships there, and after leaving fort mail started for Mobile. Officers of fort said heavy firing heard on Saturday night. Carried batteries below McRae and went all round Navy Yard. Can they afford to burn gunpowder for nothing. Not more 800 troops at Pensacola. All seem to be concentrating at Mobile and New Orleans. Sutler of *Pensacola* and boat builder deserted and took off large amount of money. Built three boats. 2 of which were destroyed by rebels.

Arrived off Mobile at 7½ o'clock P.M. Sunday night. *Vincennes*,[153] *Preble* and *Kanawha* blockading, latter gone in chase of a gunboat for Mobile trying to get out. Rebels attempted to destroy light house on Sand Key which serves as beacon for Union ships running for Mobile. Comdr Febiger of *Kanawha* reports all ships but *Colorado* over bar at Passes. Rec. Febiger fact wood cut away — 140 heavy guns. *Kanawha* and *Wissahickon* 3 miles of fort rifled range. Russell, Allen Smith, find St. P. fired shell 20 yards of this and stack 4000 and 200 days wood held back for mos. to obstruct progress of fleet and keep as long under fire.

Departs plan of elliptical sailing. 1½ hour under fire forts 1000 yds. apart. Some vessels disabled. Smoke, both forts firing.

[*Hills' report in the* Boston Journal:]
REBEL ATTEMPT TO DESTORY THE LIGHT HOUSE OFF MOBILE

The Connecticut arrived off Mobile on Sunday evening, and remained at anchor until 5 o'clock the next morning, in the meantime supplying the sloops-of-war Vincennes, Preble, and gunboat Kanawha, the two latter blockading that port. The latter was absent from the station at the moment of our arrival, having gone in chase of a rebel steamer which attempted to get out of Mobile Bay. The rebels, after having removed the lenses from the light houses on Sand Island, at the entrance to the harbor of Mobile, attempted to destroy the structure itself a few nights before we arrived. By placing a quantity of gunpowder at the base of the tower, they succeeded in blowing out a section of the work, and, if persistent, they have doubtless ere this leveled the structure. The light house was very high, and served as a beacon for our vessels running from the eastward to steer by. The rebels have lighted false fires of late to mislead the Federal vessels, and their object in destroying the light house was unquestionably to remove the only sure guide in approaching Mobile. On the last trip of the Connecticut they nearly succeeded in running her ashore on the shoals off this point.

[74]

Monday March 31st. Steamer *Connecticut* got under way at 5 o'clock A.M. and run for Ship Island at 9 o'clock P.M., up with Island and anchored in fog — cotton city. Tents all over western end of island. Reached Island at 11. Saw Gen. Butler. Camp of Conn. 9th, 26th Mass. And others all confusion. Western regiments embarking on steamer *Mississippi*.[154] Vessel disabled. Got to be sunk in St(illegible). When got almost forts let go dam. Object insuperable. Mad not to think of it. But suppose from line and river 700 yds. of fort and debris. Current taken on bow and drifts down. When she drifts down out of range of guns and if she has turn. Never present in raking position because standing across and current caters down, and another _____ fire and come down right banks.

Place boys which in driest smoke know where to turn.

[75]

Left for Passes at 4 o'clock.

[*Hills' report in the* Boston Journal:]
   AFFAIRS AT SHIP ISLAND

   The Connecticut run from Mobile to Ship Island early on the morning of the 31st, bringing your reporter to that point after an absence of exactly two months. A dense fog enveloped sea and land, and delayed our entrance to the harbor several hours. When the murky barrier was removed, the long low ridge of sand hills, grown into a "cotton city," and peopled by thousands of sturdy soldiers of New England and the West, appeared before us. Two months of time and General Butler have wrought a remarkable change in the condition of affairs at Ship Island. During the former, the army in the Department of the Gulf has been swelled to _____[155] thousand men, while the latter, by his presence, has infused new life, confidence and ardor into the dispirited and impatient ranks of the first comers.

Landing upon the island indications of a "forward movement" were seen on every side. Troops were embarking on the steamship Mississippi, the quarter deck of which was radiant with the brass field pieces of light artillery, while the ships Black Prince, Undaunted, Wild Gazelle and others lay in the harbor ready to receive troops; and steamers, the Winona, J.P. Jackson and others, were waiting to take the transports in tow. Proceeding to Fort Massachusetts, the place resembled New York on the 1st of May rather than a permanent garrison. Everybody was on the move, and no one could afford time to answer the simplest interrogatory. Entering the quarters of Maj. Gen. Butler, near the fort, I met the Commander-in-Chief of the Department of the Gulf, who manifested the same quiet composure and masterly determination in his responsible military position that I have seen him display in his forensic efforts.

Hastily visiting the camps of the 26th Massachusetts, 9th Connecticut and several other regiments, I found all confusion and activity. The camps of some six thousand troops had been broken up for several days, and the men were momentarily expecting orders to embark. The troops had provided themselves with four days' rations, beside which they were to take nothing with them but their blankets and knapsacks. Their destination was kept secret, although the impression prevailed with the men that they were coming to this point. A large number of scaling ladders for storming forts, and shovels for throwing up intrenchments were embarked, and little doubt existed but the troops would soon meet the enemy face to face. The health of the troops was generally good, although several cases of small pox were reported.

>   *Hills thought about returning home but decided to see the campaign through, and he was glad that he did. Elsewhere during March the Army of the Potomac moved its base of operations from just outside of Washington D.C. to Fortress Monroe to threaten the Confederate capital at Richmond. Major General McClellan was relieved of his duties as General in Chief and took direct command of the Army of the Potomac. Also near Fortress Monroe the ironclad CSS Virginia attacked the Union fleet with success, only to fight to a draw the Union Monitor a day later. On the Mississippi River Union forces took Island No. 10 near New Madrid, Missouri. Rebel defenses on the river would now be tested from the north and the south, and power of ironclads would again be tested.*

Tuesday April 1st. Arrived at South West Pass in fog so thick could cut it. Saw *Colorado* outside bar. *Pensacola* on it. "*Iroqouis.*"[156] (Bampton). *Verona.*[157] *Kittatinny.* Inside Mississippi. (Bortleman, Wiggins). Smith Cmdr. Guns in tops. Spars down.

Connecticut aground.

[*Hills' report in the* **Boston Journal:**]
REBEL TROOPS RUN THE BLOCKADE OF MISSISSIPPI SOUND

A day or two before the arrival of the Connecticut at Ship Island two steamers, said to have been loaded with Confederate troops, passed through Mississippi Sound from Mobile, and went toward New Orleans. An attempt to intercept them failed, for want of light draft steamers. These troops were unquestionably intended to reinforce the Confederate army in New Orleans. Had the Government sent out two steam gunboats of six feet draft to blockade Mississippi Sound, the enemy, who is understood to be pouring troops into New Orleans by every available avenue, would be cut off from at least one channel of communication. As I have before remarked, the rebels appear to be fully alive to the danger which threatens New Orleans, and they are making every exertion to repel an attack.

Wednesday April 2nd. *Connecticut* got off and lay all day in fog. More dense than ever.

Thursday April 3rd. *Connecticut* and one Hills disgusted. Went up to Delta (Head of Passes). Hot food and *Brooklyn* at Delta. Corbett telegraph operator. Met Ransom (*Kineo*).[158] His plan of attack. Eliptical sailing not practical owing to strong current.

[*Hills' report in the* **Boston Journal:**]
ARRIVAL ON THE MISSISSIPPI

The Connecticut made but a brief stop at Ship Island, and as every movement at that point seemed to be directed to a co–operation with the navy in the grand advance against New Orleans by the Mississippi, I promptly decided to retain my seat at the ward-room table of the steamer, and come at once to the scene of active operations. Previous to leaving the Connecticut, however, I desire to say that the steamer is a credit to the navy; her officers skillful, high-minded and courteous, and the service in which she is engaged one which redounds to the honor of the government.

[76]

Friday April 4th. Skirmish between *Iroquois*, *Kineo*, and rebel gunboat. 10.30 rebel steamer drew fire forts in sight for con't within 2½ to 3 miles of B & K before turned. K. & I. gave chase and fired at her. Rebel steamer sending first shot which I. and K. returned out of sight. *Iroquois* fired 2 shots. *Connecticut* got under way and came down to Pilot Town. Hill of *Richmond* came aboard and Waud and self discussed with leisure. Had interview with Farragut. Got permission to occupy cottage at Pilot Town. Lt. M. Felton in charge. Saw picture of wife of Fred Hill. Thought of my Sally.

Forgot to say that at Head of passes met Bampton. Good boy. Received letter from Sallie. Promised to show it to me. Happy meeting. Surreal. Libations on soon of old friendship. Did not see letter though!

[*Hills' report in the* **Boston Journal:**]
"Press Cottage," Pilot Town, La., April 8, 1862

It is with no little pride and contentment that your reporter, after ten days' confinement on shipboard, finds himself the joint occupant, with one of Frank Leslie's accomplished artists, of the most charming cottage in the deserted village of Pilot Town, on the Southwest Pass of the Mississippi, which, before the rebellion, was the headquarters of the Louisiana Pilots' Association.

Saturday April 5th. [159] Pickel out stores. Paid $10 for same Waud paid mess bill on *Connecticut,* and after saying goodbye to all on board steamer (wood, hull, and *forced*) went ashore and took possession of cottage of L.F. Higgins. See plan of same. Pilot Station. Pen where put broken pilots to keep them from falling out.

[*Hills' report in the* **Boston Journal:**]
A Union Foothold in Louisiana

Pilot Town was taken possession of about three weeks since by the naval commander of the Western Gulf Squadron, for the express purpose of occupying the place as a hospital for the sick and wounded in the expedition against New Orleans, and as a naval depot for the fleet. A single family, besides a few oystermen, who supply the men-of-war with bivalves of enormous dimensions, remain in possession of their homesteads, while the majority of the dwelling have been deserted, their owners leaving behind splendid mahogany furniture, side-boards of exquisite carving, tables with marble labs, billiard tables, and tester bedsteads, with lofty canopy and luxurious beds. A bayou from the Southwest Pass, through the which the rebels have been in the habit of running the blockade, passes through the village, and on either side is a row of buildings — dwelling houses, boat sheds, &c. To cross the street, one must do as in Venice — take a boat and paddle over. The houses are built upon piles; the sidewalks and passages from one to another are plank and logs, and if you are not nervous at the sight of lizards, fiddler crabs, and other tropical insects, you may walk the narrow path without sinking in mud beyond your depth. I regret to say that the sailors from certain ships in the squadron have indulged their destructive propensities in the demolition of furniture and other articles to that extent which led to a rigid enforcement of martial law throughout the town.

Dr. P.S. Wales, Surgeon of the Colorado, has been detailed to take charge of the hospital, and is actively employed, under the direction of Dr. Foltz, the Fleet Surgeon, in fitting up several large buildings formerly occupied as public houses during the watering season, as a hospital.

Sunday April 6th. Intended to go to work on letters. "Up all hammocks"[160] at 5 o'clock. Capt. Blanchard of "*Amelia*"[161] off in the fog to see mortar practice. Sold—retrieved to P. T. and what with Waud and Muser to get boat given us by Capt. Guest. Hard job. Smoked a cigar. Burnt my finger and made myself sick.

[*Hills' report in the* **Boston Journal:**]
   A RECONNAISSANCE IN FORCE

   On the 5th inst. Commodore Farragut, accompanied by Fleet Captain Bell and several other officers of the squadron, made a reconnaissance up the river. Six steamers, viz: the Iroquois, Sciota, Katahdin, Kineo, Kennebec, Wissahiccon, proceeded up within sight of Fort St. Philip, one of which passed between her masts, directly over the smoke stack. Nothing further was discovered beyond what was seen on a previous reconnaissance.
   A strict guard is now maintained on the river for several miles above the point where out(r) fleet is anchored, to prevent the enemy from examining our force. Three steamers are sent up every night, these being relieved upon alternate nights by three others.
[77]

Monday April 7th. Took good bath with cackle of marsh hens. *Pensacola* came up to Pilot Town. Steamer *Saxon* arrived with Gen. Butler and brought me letters from Sarah. Fred, father, Charley, Itochereli, Olive, Irene, Abby Hale, Amie English, and c.—big batch. Feel better. Waud has bunch flowers on his table.

Tuesday April 8th. Good bath. Freedom from restraint. No neighbors to see one in disheveled. Marsh hen cackled. Step light when there was prospect of treading on hazard and c.

Wednesday April 9th. Met our Folter that told me about flag of truce. Time for me to go to Passes. "By the mark three."

Thursday April 10th. Left Pilot Town and went to Head of Passes on *Mississippi*. Met Wells, noon with Bartleman.
[78]

Friday April 11th. The *Connecticut* has sailed and with her goes my last chance for reaching Ship Island, before the attack on New Orleans. Today I have had a mental struggle as to the proper course for me to pursue. I ought to follow Gen Butler, and I ought to remain on the *Mississippi* and see the bombardment. I am convinced after looking at the case in all its bearings that the fleet leave have got to do the work, before Butler can accomplish anything. I may err in this, and therefore note down for future reference the points which have lead me to remain at this point. For the first time since leaving home, I feel the importance of recording my private feelings in view of the dangers which threaten me. If I were an officer in the Army or Navy and had nothing to do after the battle

[79]

I should select the place most likely to afford me an opportunity to do my duty to my country. But as I have to record he acts of other rather than myself, I feel it my duty to select a position which will ensure my personal safety. There is no place in the squadron where I should be exempt from danger, hence in remaining here to witness the battle, I consider that I shall escape the imputation of cowardice. It is my present purpose to stick by the ship *Mississippi* and witness the bombardment. And when the barge ships move up to engage the forts I hope to go on board the "*Horace Beals*."[162] Today I went on board the steamer *Mohican*,[163] and met my old friends, Gurdes and Oltmarius. On my return I found Bampton on board and with Bartleman had a happy meeting. Bampton has received a letter from Sally.

[*Hills' report in the* **Boston Journal:**]
SAILORS DROWNED FROM THE MORTAR VESSELS

While the mortar flotilla was at anchor off Pilot Town, a sailor attached to the schooner Norfolk Packet, while at work on the outside the vessel, accidentally fell overboard and was not seen to rise. Every effort was made to recover his body, but without success, the swift running current carrying the unfortunate man down the river. I have not been able to ascertain the name of the man, but learn that he belonged in East Boston. A few days after the above accident, a boat containing Capt. Charles G. Jack and a crew from the schooner Maria J. Carleton, was upset alongside the schooner T. A. Ward, and the coxswain of the boat, an Englishman named Francis Bird, was drowned. Capt. Jack narrowly escaped a similar fate.

[80]

Saturday April 12th

Visited the *Richmond*, and had lunch with Fred Hill. Hoyt[164] making tracing of map of river and forts. Next went to Cabels the notorious rebel spy who lives on bank of river at Head of Passes. Received with a yawn and "bad weather this morning, didn't go out fishing." Took seat on stoop by shanty. Wife, two daughters, one dry nurse to negro baby which Cabel raising. Cats, dogs, pigs and poultry living in greatest degree of domesticity. Cabel agent and telegraph operator for Good Intent Tow Boat Company.

5. Journal of a Military Expedition from Boston to _____   81

Received $115 per month and salary up to now lost. Lost one negro by flood, and two by rebellion later at work in forts. Cost $700 and $150. Woman cost $1150 and had two children since bought her. Cabel part of Attantie Ditto.
[81]

    Visited flagship and dined with Ward room mess. Had talk with Flag Off Farragut, who told me looked Butler every moment. Later could do nothing til forts are taken. Fears of riflemen in reeds on bank of river picking off our officers. When fleet move will be all together.

[*Hills' report in the* Boston Journal:]
    RECONNAISSANCE UP THE RIVER — IMPORTANT DISCOVERY

On the 28th ult. a reconnaissance was made up the Mississippi, for the purpose of ascertaining the position of the reported obstructions across the river, and of drawing the fire of the enemy's batteries, by the gunboats Kennebec, Lieut. Commanding Russell, and the Wissahickon, Lieut. Commanding Albert Smith. Fleet Captain H.H. Bell being on board the former vessel, proceeded within two miles of Fort Jackson. No batteries were discovered below the fort, but as soon as the steamers approached within range of Fort St. Philip which is situated o the left bank of the river, the rebels opened fire upon the Kennebec from tow rifled cannon, and threw some thirty shell, which exploded above and all around the steamer. Lieut. Russell, who will be remembered for his bravery in connection with the Judith affair at Pensacola, maneuvered the Kennebec so skillfully that, although she was twenty minutes under fire, not a single shot took effect. The fire was not returned by our steamers it being useless to contend with such a superior force. The shell have been 100-pounders, of which caliber there is supposed to be four rifled cannon mounted on the fort. Fort Jackson, which did not open fire, is reported to mount ninety-five guns bearing upon the channel through which our ships will have to pass, and Fort St. Philip, eighty-five guns, all of which command the approach up the river, which at this point is only seven hundred yards wide.

    A deserter from the rebel army reports that they have powerful batteries at English Turn, a short distance below New Orleans, each one of which commands a reach in the river. A diagram of the position which these batteries occupy has been shown me, which represents the first as raking the river a distance of one mile and a half. Above this is another which commands the first turn, running easterly a distance of half a mile. The third battery at the third turn which the river makes at this point raking the river two miles, and the fourth battery at the upper bend of all is reported to be one and three quarters miles from the last mentioned work. I am not prepared to vouch for the truthfulness of these statements, which will be verified or contradicted as the fleet advances up the river. Should these fortifications exist, and the rebels fight with half their boasted determination, our ships will meet with a warm reception.

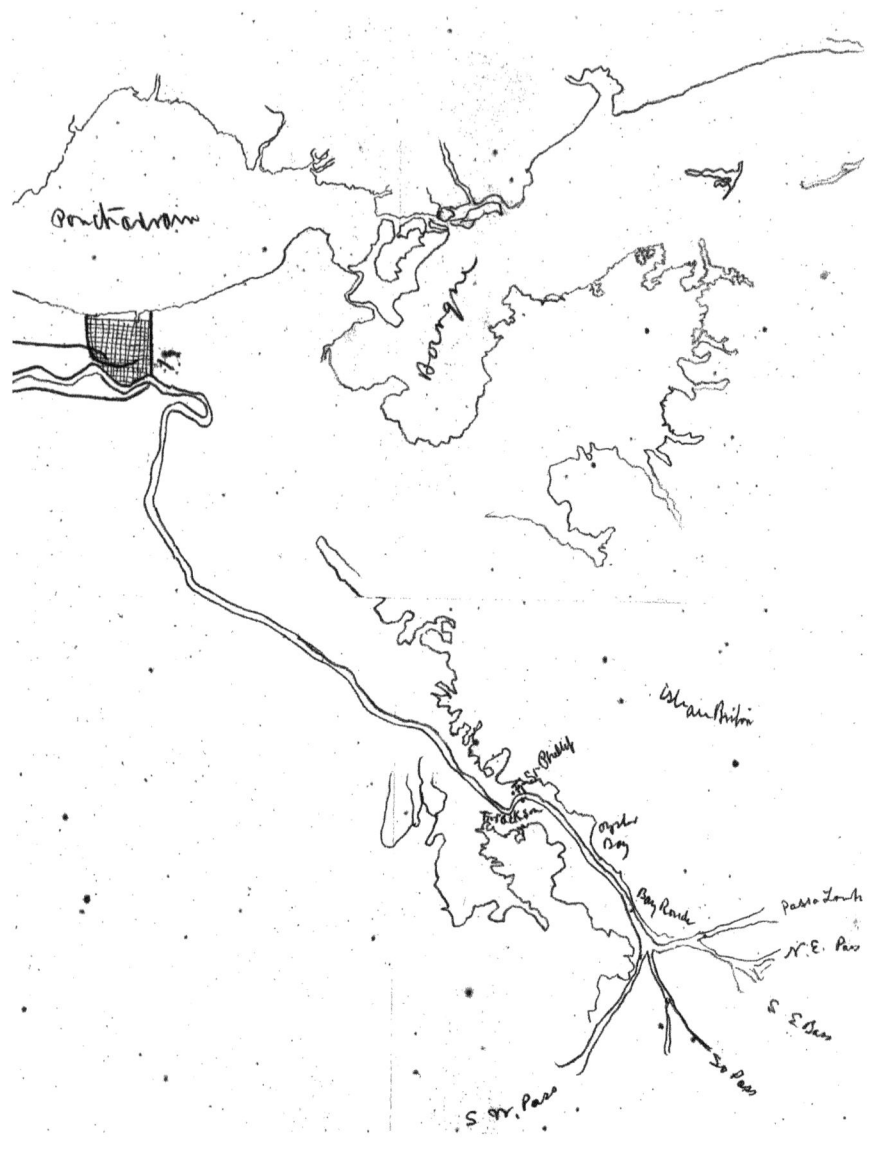

Sketch of the Mississippi River from New Orleans to the Gulf of Mexico, presumably by "Hoyt."

5. Journal of a Military Expedition from Boston to _____ 83

By this reconnaissance our officers have at length obtained something reliable in regard to the much talked of obstructions which the rebels have placed across the river. At a point about three hundred yards below Fort Jackson, the officers discovered eight schooners, some of them as large as five hundred tons, anchored fore and aft with the current. These schooners are loaded with cotton to prevent them from sinking in case they are stuck by our shot. A heavy chain cable is stretched across the river over the decks of the schooners, which are securely linked together, and another chain is reported to be secured to the hulls under water. The main channel of the river through which our ships will be obliged to pass, runs close under the guns of Fort Jackson, and here the rebels have a light a chain, one end of which is secured to a schooner and the other to the shore. This is dropped when any of the rebel steamers pass down and up, and is drawn taught by means of a steam engine on the bank. On one side of the river the rebels have constructed a mud battery with which to protect the chain from any attempt which may be made to cut it.

It has been observed that the quantity of drift logs which usually come down the Mississippi at this season is much smaller this year than ever before. In fact I have not seen any pieces of drift wood larger than a man's body, which fact is accounted for on the supposition that the rebels are holding back all the logs they can obtain, for the purpose of constructing a barrier against the Union fleet. The readers of the Journal will recollect that

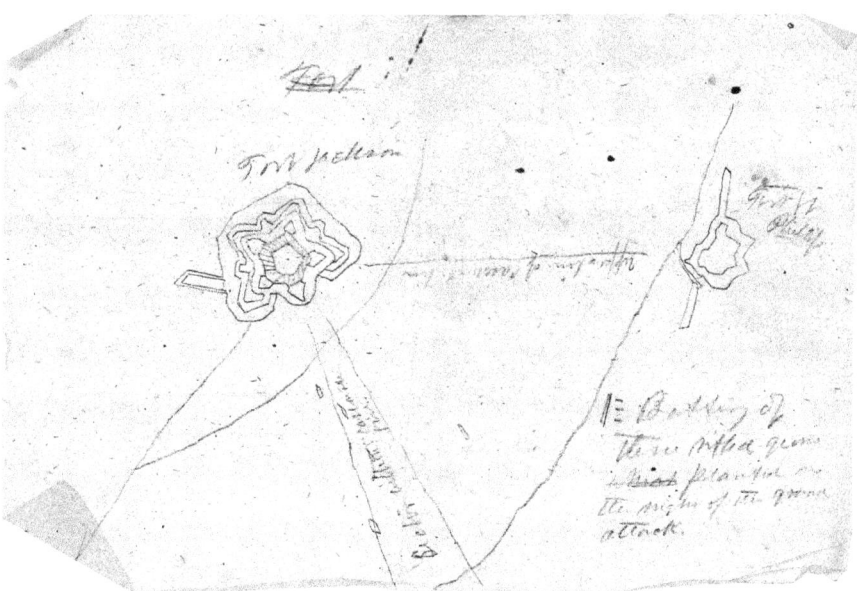

Sketch of Fort Jackson and Fort St. Philip showing water battery and section of Jackson without casemate.

in a former letter I referred to an immense raft of logs, which a rebel prisoner informed me was moored across the river; which being true, will account for the scarcity of drift logs. I should not be surprised if, at a convenient moment, the rebels let loose this immense raft, which, borne by the swift current, may sweep down upon our fleet and create dangers for which we are not prepared.

[82]

Sunday April 13th. Anniversary of Fall of Sumter. Divine service on *Mississippi* (Steamer of that name.) Comdr. Smith observes day. Chaplain better than hand cuffs. Service impressive and solemn, boom of cannon up river mingles with the voices of singers. Crew on one side of deck, officers and marines on other. Canopy arriving. Visited Capt. *Preble* gunboat *Katahdin*. Dined and talked.

Report that Steamer *Westfield* fired into rebel gunboat and fort over‐reaching range of both with 100 pdr. Gun. Flag went upon *Harriet Lane*. "*Montgomery*" arrived.

Schooners *Orvetta* and *Arletta*[165] went up river.

[*Hills' report in the* Boston Journal:]
Trouble Among the "Bummers"— The Captains of Three Mortar Vessels Suspended and Sent Home

A difficulty has arisen between Commander Porter of the mortar flotilla and the Action Masters commanding the first division of bomb schooners, growing out of an order issued by Commander Porter to which the officers took exception. A correspondence ensued, which has resulted in the suspension of Capt. Thomas E. Smith of the Orvetta, John A. Darling of the Sophronia, George N. Hood of the Para, Amos Langthorn of the C.P. Williams, Washington Godfrey of the Oliver H. Lee, and William P. Rogers of the William Bacon. Captains Hood and Darling will proceed North on the Connecticut, with orders to report to the Secretary of the Navy. The other officers have been reinstated after coming to a mutual understanding with Commander Porter. Another Acting Master, Hollis B. Jenks of the Adolph Huger, has been sent home for misdemeanor.

It has been ascertained for a certainty that there are four chains stretched across the river on the decks of the schooners; one large and three smaller ones.

[83]

Monday April 14th. Went on board schooner *Dan Smith*.[166] Waud sketching mortars. Visited Cpt. Breese on *Horace Beals* and hurriedly took up quarters on this vessel. *Hatteras* arrived from Ship Island with mail. Officer reports 20,000 troops there, 24 ships and several steamers. *Southern Repub‐*

lic[167] lost rudder. *Idiho* and *Bowsprit*.[168] Butler waiting for movement there. *Mississippi* went up river and schooners.

All hands up anchor and get under way. Have taut your topsail halyards. Port four helm, she's over run her anchorlis. And a ¼ 5 close to shore. And then deep six. By mark 7 — no bottom by forts, man the starboard gun. Rebel pickets train sharp on bow.
[84]

Monday night going up Miss. on *Horace Beals*. Run on East bank, in water six fathoms, narrow strip of marsh, river one side and ocean other. Guns loaded and run out bained sharp on the bow, to give rebel riflemen in the reeds foretaste of what they may expect before week is past. Capt. Breeses seated on the quarter deck cool and collected. Anchored some time during night off the Salt Works, a dilapidated establishment where a N.O. company formerly manufactured salt.

[*Hills' report in the* **Boston Journal:**]
PREPARATIONS FOR THE ATTACK ON NEW ORLEANS

Before landing at this point I had a fine opportunity to observe the condition of the great naval fleet on the river, and the preparations which have been made for the bombardment of the rebel defenses between here and New Orleans. The reports which reached Key West in reference to the efforts made to get the large ships over the bar and the commencement of hostilities were scarcely truthful. It is not true, as has been stated, that the masts were taken out of the Colorado in order to get her over the bar. The vessel was lightened by discharging her armament, coals, and provisions but after all it was found that the depth of the water on the bar was not equal to the launching draft of the ship, the Flag Officer has reluctantly given up all hopes of engaging her with the forts. This is to be regretted inasmuch as the noble frigate would have proved a formidable auxiliary to the expedition. The vessel lies outside the bar, and will be used as a hospital and store ship during the siege. Capt. Bailey, her commander, will take command of the division of gun boats during the attack, and her officers and men, unwilling to remain idle spectators of the bombardment, will join various vessels in the squadron. Her armament, being superior to that of the frigate Mississippi has been placed on board the latter ship, which now mounts sixteen broadside guns. I have been agreeably surprised to find the Mississippi in command of Commander Melancthon Smith, formerly of the steamer Massachusetts. Those who are acquainted with the career of this gallant officer will require no word of mine to convince them of his fitness to manage so powerful a ship as the Mississippi in the coming attack. The vessel is now in fighting trim, and with the Pensacola, which after ten days hard labor is at last safely over the bar, lies in the stream off Pilot Town.

[85]

Tuesday April 15th. Breakfast with Capt. _____ of _____[169] and then went on board *Sachem*. Wrote all day. In the afternoon the British steamer "*Barracuda*" — 9 guns 3rd class sloop of war, side wheels, came steaming in with English Ensign at peak. Deck full of men. Officers in white pants. Two hours later the *Richmond* steamed past in him, only the *Richmond* went up first. Her decks were full of men. Her guns were out and she looked the personation of all that is formidable, and Englishman anchored below flotilla. Raft blown up by Kroul.

Attach in Surveyor. Difference of ¾ mile in shots. Greater noise in air. ½ mile stern of *Owasco*. Bullovich supply of steamers of mortar fleet. Shot *coon* one live. Took survey of ship and out stern bar rite of Cpt. L. took [illegible] to fort full of men.
[86]

Wednesday 16th. *Mississippi, Richmond, Iroquois, Oneida*, 2 or 3 gunboats, *Owasco*, ahead of bum in W bank of river. Can burnt 19 sec. fuses at moment it touches. Will be ½ mile nearer at South. 1st one *Orvetta*. Capt. Frank Blanchard. 2nd over. *John Griffith*'s Cpt. brown. *Harriet Lane* Capt. Porter, *Owasco*, Guest. I went up on *Owasco* and was for 2nd time under fire. See report of affairs.

[***Hills' report in the*** **Boston Journal:**]
The Mortar Flotilla

Arrived without accident at Pass a l'Outre on the 16th ult., and after being towed up to the Head of the Passes, the vessels all came down to Pilot Town, where they have remained till today, when, the wind being favorable and the time approaching for opening the bombardment, they got under way in fine style, and sailed up river. Although several weeks have elapsed since the flotilla arrived here, the time has not been wasted. On the other hand the men have been constantly drilled at the mortars and heavy thirty-twos in maneuvering which they have become remarkably expert. The vessels are already for action, having struck their topmasts, and lashed their fore rigging to the mast, in order to obtain a clear range for the bombs. Commander Porter has labored unceasingly to perfect his part of the expedition, besides devoting his days and nights to the furtherance of the whole. Much of the success attending the passage of the large vessels over the bar is due to this acquaintance with the channel and the currents, and his personal labors as pilot. His careworn features evince the toil and mental anxiety which the expedition has already cost him. Still he is well and eager for the fray.

Some excellent practice has been had with the mortars since the fleet entered the river. The mortar of the T.A. Ward, flag ship of the second division, Lieut. Commanding Queen, was fired the other day, with charges ranging from two pounds five to two pounds seven ounces, and threw thirteen-inch shells eight hundred and twenty six yards. Lieut. Queen also fired his long 32's at the extreme range, and struck a target six feet square four out of six times. Commander Porter is delighted with these experiments and confident of his ability to dislodge the rebels from their batteries up the river.

Thursday 17th. Rest of mortar fleet towed up to west bank of river and anchored.
[87]

Friday April 18th. Bombardment of Fort Jackson commenced at 9 o'clock, for which I have been waiting nearly five months. Went on board *Hartford* and got in mizzen tops. At 10 and 15 *Hartford* got underway and steamed up to line of fire from Jackson. She [illegible] from that time forward at head of squadron in position which exposed her to fire of rebels. Left her in boat which came from *Mississippi* to attack fire rafts and met Waud and Winser in fore top of *Mississippi*. Went from the *Miss.* gig and came down to *Horace Beals*. Got dinner and went on board *Portsmouth*, took baked apple and tod with Dells, MD., and went to "*Saxon*" which arrived afternoon. *Wissahickon* passed up squadron announcing that Norfolk and the *Merrimac* were taken. Officers of Butler's staff, Col. Jones, Strong and others went to flagship. Goodrich showed me letter from Fred Fulcher up to *Harriet Lane*.

[*Hills' report in the* **Boston Journal:**]
    A VISIT FROM GEN. BUTLER TO THE FLAG OFFICER

At a late hour yesterday afternoon I discovered a small steamer in the river which I at once recognized as the Saxon, and in going on board found, to my great surprise and pleasure, a voluminous package of letters and papers from friends whose kind remembrance does much to mitigate the privations of your exiled correspondent. Upon inquiry I learned that the Saxon came down from Ship Island to bring Maj. Gen. Butler who, accompanied by several officers of his staff, was on a visit to Flag Officer Farragut. The Flag Officer was on board a gun boat off Pilot Town, where Gen. Butler joined him and had a consultation in regard to the method of attacking the forts. I understand that Gen. Butler proposes to land a large body of troops at a point several miles above Fort St. Philip, there to await the result of the naval attack. If the fleet fail to dislodge the rebels from the forts then, I understand, it is the intention of Gen. Butler to advance his troops and attempt to carry the works by storm. Of one thing, however, I am satisfied, that if the immense naval force which will be arrayed against the rebel works fails to route the enemy it will be useless for Gen. Butler, with his comparatively small force, to attempt it. The General returned to Ship Island the same evening. I understand that the troops which embarked on the steam ship Mississippi on the day the Connecticut was at Ship Island, were subsequently landed and returned to camp, the movement being premature.

[88]

Saturday 19. Night before schooners on East side Miss. River were forced to retire from position and took up point rear of others. Re-commenced bombardment at six o'clock morning. While on board *Richmond* today shell whistled off bow and crew seen to come down quickly. Was on board schooner.

Capt. Savage when firing mortar shells struck all around. One passed over my head as I stood in companion way of cabin. Had an errand on ship lower down river.

[89]

Easter Sunday 20. Rained this morning and continued to do so until noon. Went up river with Waud and Winser in *our* boat, couldn't fetch for up, all under fire and heavy current running. Fell back and went on board *T.A. Ward*, saw half of shell. Queen objected to having his stores destroyed. Molasses and butter mingled up. Left and went on board *Oneida* which was also exposed to fire. Dropped down to *Richmond* when same peculiar experience awaited press gang. This time we went to *Portsmouth*, and after look aloft, set Waud and Winser on *Sachem*[170] and went back to *Portsmouth* to dinner with Hall and Wells. Went to *Sachem* and timed in 10 o'clock Big Bombdt to help cut chain. *Pensacola*[171] and *Itasca*[172] went up. *Kineo* would but didn't get mast out. (See notebook for cutting chain for 2½ o'clock fire raft.)

[90]

Monday 21st. Went to *Kineo* and with Ransom to *Hartford*. Wells and Hall to *Brooklyn*. Wells and *Mississippi*, and *Sachem*. Halter to *Harriet Lane* and then to *Pensacola*, *Iroquois* where met Bampton and read Sallie's letter to him. Berch to *Pensacola*, and with Halter to *Sachem*. Bodfish on *Medora*[173] sailed for New York, sent 4 lines to C.O.K. to *Portsmouth* tops. 4th day of bombardment. At night dropped down to *Itasca* and got her record.

Tuesday. Man Winn on *Oneida* lost leg and arm on same side, been through Peruvian, Mexican and Crimean wars, and was in California.

[91]

On board *Horace Beals*, Tuesday night, the grand attack. The hour has come. I went aloft gazed upon the scene on the river.

Below me lay the fleet swinging with the current their anchors hove short ready to weigh at a moment's notice from the Flag Ship. A deathly stillness reigned throughout the squadron broken only at irregular interval by the deep boom of the mortars. One could scarcely bring self to realize that the hour has come for which thousands had waited anxiously to see. In the distance the enemy is enveloped in darkness and silence. His guns have not been heard since four o'clock. What can be the cause of his silence. Has he evacuated the fort, or is he lying secure behind his casemates
[92]
awaiting the spring of the tiger that well beard him in his den. Every shell from our mortars explodes within the fort, which must now be piled high with iron, and shattered by the ponderous shell. On board the *Hartford* are heard sound of the artisans. Now the mortars open smartly, and as the hour of midnight approaches there are indications of the fleet getting underway. The signal officers have been gone several hours and are waiting on the opposite shore for the advance of the armada. While they move on does the absence of Lt. Lea delay the movement. Stillness everywhere except among the mortars where men who have stood
[93]
to the wide mouth dogs of war and pound their sulphurous fire and iron hail upon the heads of the rebels five days and nights, are still true to their breast, and though ready to fall with fatigue they still continue to hurl their missiles at the enemy. Single lights shine out from each of the ships in squadron, but along the line of mortar vessels, there are glomming lights and casks of gunpowder, which tell of powder boys hurrying to and fro with their leather boxes, and shell carries dragging wrath along with their globular bundles. Men are tugging away at the mortar and the lookout aloft, cries port or starboard to the helmsman, as he orders him to shift the helm to give do
[94]
proper direction to the mortar. God help the brave men that go this night upon a desperate errand into the very jaws of the enemy and into the presence of the Death Angel. A country's praise avails you, go and reap the reward of your valor.

The time has now come for the squadron. The big ships which have serving idly in the stream from weeks to play their part in the tragedy. The bummers are growling at your inactivity. Why will you not show yourselves men and not sleep while your brothers are awake and doing. Mothers, wives, sisters thousands of miles away, pray that a kind Providence may watch over and guard your loved ones
[95]

as they move into the blind path, and pass through the fiery ordeal. Oh God, if dear lost love thy children, bring them safely to behold the dawn of another day. Turn the hearts of the enemy and cause them to pull down the bloody flag which has flaunted its recreant folds in our faces so long.

Frail it is the dust before us. It is only once in the life of a man that he looks on a scene like this. Hearts are beating anxiously for us and, here I sit composedly in the midst of one of the most determined and terrific battles, which the world has ever seen. Writing my calm reflections undisturbed, I have though to see a battle and I have had my fill. This is war.
[96]

Up all hammocks. The fires have been raked open, and the hissing stream is screaming as it escapes from the surcharged boiler. The *Hartford* noble ship, pride of New England mechanics, is under way and steams ahead of the fleet. Several gun boats follow and move to the front. The *Mississippi* with Butler and the _____[174] moved up and have first arrived 12 o'clock at night below the fleet.

The mortars having got hot from constant firing now sting out and as there is no sign of a forward movement till near morning when the garrison are in profound slumber for all of us friend and foe sleep now in the midst of bombardment. The
[97]
Ward 100 yards ahead of me is firing and yet I shall have a good nap. Turned in — shell from mortars went hissing through the air shaking the ship and jarring my head upon my pillow. A report as if from Jackson, quickened my pulse, and I held my breath expecting to hear a shell whistle over my head or knock my brains out. Just as I had got ready to fall asleep then fire bells rang out alarm and going on deck saw lights of infernal rebel raft approaching. Don't mean to let us have any rest. A large wicker raft approaches lighting up fleet and spreading appalling darkness over sky. Serpentine pall of smoke floating in advance of the raft boats tackle it and tow it away to rendezvous.
[98]

Went to bed and slept without fear or trembling save from the jar of the mortars. Morning dawned. Disappointment in fleet. Men wrought up to pitch of battle. Excuses. Reasons for not proceeding. Machinery of *Sciota*[175] disabled. Six carpenters away from *Mississippi*. Mortars fired by Division once ten minutes.

Reports from aloft say fort being repaired and new guns mounting, or evacuating. Steamers seen and men on ramparts while our shell falling all around them.
[99]

5. Journal of a Military Expedition from Boston to _____   91

This page lists titles of articles pondered by Agaius to report the events of the campaign. Actual article titles were somewhat different.

The Great Naval and Military Expedition Against New Orleans
Reduction of the Sebastopol of the Mississippi
Reduction of Forts Jackson and St. Phillip
The Rebel Fortifications Bombarded Six Days and Nights
Brilliant Success of the Mortar Flotilla
The Union Squadron Assailed on the Fifth Day with Fire Ships and Rafts
The Confederate Navy Driven up the River
The Chain Across the Mississippi Removed and the Hulk Set Adrift
Grand Night of Attack by the Squadron

[100]
    Equal in magnificence to at every shot fired rose clouds of white smoke which drifted off to eastward, one after another till sky overcast.
    As the clouds lifted we saw flash of fire, jets of blaze and a zone of light from a raft which rebels set on fire, and still the black ponderous mass rolled away. Thunder and lightning or the roar of a volcano are same in comparison to awful sublimity of scenes. The eastern sky meanwhile was lit up by the roseate tints of morning, which appeared in beautiful omsolis and startling contrast to the scene before us.

[*Hills' report in the* **Boston Journal:**]
    IRON CLAD SHIPS IN THE EXPEDITION

> The neglect of the government to provide iron clad steamers to contend against the ram Manassas and similar gunboats which the rebels are reported to have on the river, has been partially supplied by the ingenuity and skill of the officers of the Richmond, with whom the plan to which I refer originated. In order to protect the boilers and machinery from the fire of the enemy, the sides of the ship have been covered with chain cables, hung perpendicularly and securely bolted to the hull. An additional preventive to this mail being shot away consists of a shield of heavy hawse running fore and aft outside of the chain the whole forming an armor, which though not perhaps invulnerable, will at least break the force of shot and shell hurled against it. This excellent plan has been followed by the Hartford and Brooklyn, and I presume it will be adopted by the Pensacola and other ships. Captain Alden has hit upon a novel expedient for disguising the Richmond, or rather for rendering her a less prominent target for the rebels. By mixing oil with the gray alluvial deposit of the Mississippi, a composition if produced with which the hull and smoke stack of the Richmond have been painted. The color this imparted to the ship renders it difficult to distinguish her from the water in the river when seen at the distance of rifle range. This disguise has

been imitated by Lieut. Commanding Guest of the Owasco, which being a much smaller vessel, will prove a very indifferent mark for the rebel artillerists. My artistic companion suggests that this expedient of producing phantom ships in our navy would be much more successful if they were painted an atmospheric color, and as an illustration on a small scale, I might instance the smoke stack of the Iroquois, which cannot be distinguished at a distance of a mile.

I went on board the gunboat Owasco a few days since, and found her officers and men busily employed in protecting the boilers and engines from the shot and shell to which they will be exposed. A solid bulk head of logs, obtained at Pilot Town, has been built on each side of the machinery the which it seems impossible of the machinery through which it seems impossible for a shell to penetrate. Similar precautions are being taken by other ships in the fleet and extra pains are taken to protect the most valuable parts.

I have been surprised to find with what pride the sailors regard the guns which they are soon to bring to bear upon the rebels. While every other part of the ship is plain and unvarnished, the greater care is taken with the "Treason Crushers" which are kept scrupulously clean inside, and outwardly brilliantly polished. The crew of the Owasca have christened their 11-inch pivot gun the "Growler;" their 20 pounder Parrott bears the appropriate mane of "Teazer," while the two brass howitzers are called respectively "Scorpion" and "Viper." The same affection, if I may so term the passion, exists among the "bummers," who have painted on the face of their gaping mortars, such as "Pet," "Spitfire," "Uncle Abe's Physician," and similar appellations.

Nearly all the vessels which will participate in the attack are now at the head of Passes, and as soon as the Pensacola, and Mississippi receive their armament from the lighters, and have taken in coal, they will join the squadron, and "on to New Orleans" will then be the word. "No retreat" is the order of Flag Officer Farragut, who is determined to send his entire fleet before abandoning the attempt to drive the traitors from their last great stronghold. Commodore Farragut may be seen daily, with his blue pennant, on at least half a dozen different vessels. Now his barge is flying with the swift current down the river to the bar; the next moment he is on board the Colorado, then his pennant is run up on the Richmond, and so on wherever he chances to be. He is well nigh omnipresent in the fleet, making every vessel his flag-ship for the nonce, while he is closeted with the various commanders, consulting plans and arranging the details of the expedition, everything relating to which is distinguished by activity, zeal and courage.

This ends the first of A.G. Hills' journals describing his observations throughout the Gulf of Mexico and during the New Orleans Campaign of 1862. There is a gap of five days between the first two journals, although the events of these five days are covered in his reports. The following journal was given to Hills to use at the Head of Passes off Pilot Town on April 27th by A. McPhee of New Orleans.

5. Journal of a Military Expedition from Boston to ____   93

Sunday, April 27th, 1862. The Lookout at Pilot Town. Gardens fenced in like turkey krauls instead of parsnips beds, birds chirping, marsh hens cackling. The hospital, poor fellows, heros of siege of Jackson and St. Phillip. Fleet in Pass, *Portsmouth, Norfolk Packet*,[176] and mortar flotilla, *Fearnot, Bliar, Hallett*,[177] gunboat *Itasca*, painted and prim and ready for fight again. At bar, *Colorado*, not in fight, and Englishman who says "we shall all have to turn farmers now. What is the good of wooden sailing ships when you have vessels as *Monitor* and steam vessels that pass forts."

Monday morning, April 28th. Orders from Porter to flotilla to hold selves in readiness to recommence bombardment. Yesterday Porter sent flag of truce to Jackson and demanded surrender of fort. Received polite note from commander stating that he has no official notice that N.O. was in possession of U.S. forces and that until he did so he could not think of surrendering. French steamer *Milan* received permission from Porter to pass up and went to New Orleans. The rebels still hold out, smoke of their fire rafts curls up and their tarry scars drift down upon their inoffensive mission. We hear that Gen. Butler landed his troops yesterday morning, and though anxious to be with him cannot perform impossibilities. Our gig is not a steamer. Though we have got up considerable muscle we not equal to the task of rowing round to Quentin's Bayou. Explosion seen up river at 11 o'clock. Our gunboats sweat it. Report of heard at Pilot Town. *Owasco* approaches. *Portsmouth* cheers. Mortar fleet commotion would pass at a "All hands cheer ship." *Owasco* of ensign signs up. What is so desponding changed to joy. All fleet cheer. Buzz of joy. *Itasca* hoists secesh flag under stars and stripes. The fleet is decorated with flags. Pilot Town taking up cheer and poor wounded sailor writhing in pain joins in general acclaim. Current never ran so strong. Cannot bear the delay. Secession has received its death blow with "one foot in the grave and the other on the priest." The forts have surrendered to Commander Porter. Jackson, "Open her wide and give her all the steam you can."

News of attack on Ship Island by Mobile steamers *Morgan*,[178] *Gaines*,[179] *Florida*. *Morgan* and *Gaines* 8 32 pounders, draught 6 foot, and 2 pivot, 4 rifled. Fla. 8 32 pounders and one rifled 64.[180] Going up Mississippi on steamer "*J.P. Jackson*," which is impatient to reach forts, drops schooners and steams up all knows while I write. Pass "Jump" and eager to see all and hear all. I ascend her near deck and look at scene now robbed of all dread, no fear of rebels lurking in reeds and cane brakes. At anchorage in Oyster Bay under Sable Island. Ships *Great Republic, Matanzas*,[181] and *Lewis* alongside *Mississippi* disembarking troops. We take no heed of thatched cabins on banks of river. Secesh cattle whose fellows have furnished many a dish of "sirloin rare" and "well done" stand meekly in water on the shore. No fleet now below forts. We are after the *Owasco*, but steam chase is a long one, and we gain on her slowly off the point which our gunboats approached so cautiously. The *South America*[182] is at anchor. The scene has under gone a wonderful change since the night before the grand attack. Guns no longer trained sharp on bow. Shore is lined with logs and charred wrecks of fire rafts which have affrighted none but those who dispatched them on their harmless mission. Now we are over the spot where the rebels rained their iron hail upon the Union gunboats; before this we cross the river to the west shore where the bummers were stationed. No boom disturbs our ears. "*Miami*,"[183] " *Sachem*" and two schooners rear of St. Phillip.

Cranes stretch up slender necks and gaze at us as we pass. Now we pass wreck of *M.J.C.*[184] struck by rebel shot and blown up by Commander Porter to prevent falling into hands of enemy. We have been under fire here. As sun sunk in west I left sumptuous [illegible, crossed out] later of Lt. Commander Woodworth, open forts, see battery where black smoke vomited forth upon pour gunboats. Another fort which troubled us more than any other wicked raft full of wood on west shore, wreck of raft and *Westfield* off landing. *Clifton* and St. Phillip signal of rebel soldiers with bags back in white shirts winding on ramparts. A motley crew. Hospital building riddled, one corner knocked in.

Looking back got view of such of river which rifled cannon of Jackson hurled missiles. In river three hulks. How could our ship have passed this Jackson fire. *Mississippi* and *Harriet Lane* just ahead of us. They fought long and well but did not pile the ground with Yankee slain. One hulk is from *H. Toone*.[185]

Jackson ordered back from fire with our gig pulled up past raft, feeling wood and barrels of tar to sand bag landing.

Capt. Porter, Renshaw, Smith, and Col. Jones came along side full dress and landed at fort. Our painter made fast any secesh Sgt. and will pick our way across short board lumber of bldgs. Destroyed by our shell out to the mote across which we were ferried much.

Talk about Mobile. Way is to open Grant's Pass.[186]

As *Mississippi* going up tried to turn and struck limbs. Crowd called out three cheers for Jeff Davis. Ladies waved handkerchiefs and parts of dragoons rode down and drawing revolvers fired into crowd. Band played Yankee Doodle. Three cheers more. Levee crowded with women and child.

Marsh surrounds forts and into this our shells struck and put up columns of mud and water. Only two small bldgs. left outside fort.

Harriet Lane's record 28th. Came to anchor off Jackson 9:45–10 A.M.

5. Journal of a Military Expedition from Boston to _____   95

Two steamers towed ram to other side of river and set it on fire at 10:52. At commanding officer came on board 4 rebel officers. Ram exploded 10:56. Marines of *Westfield* reached fort 1:20. Rebel flag lowered both forts 2:48. Stars and Stripes hoisted 3:15. If anything calculated to affright the souls of adversaries — mortars. Plan of rebels to send all fire rafts together but miss [illegible] and Mitchell attributes defeat to this.

Appearance of Rebel soldiers at word given to go to *Burton* rushed to hospital and soon stopped, leaving bedding bundles, knapsacks, bullets, bags like from embarking from emigrant ship. Wear felt hats, plantation clothes, gray-black shirts, carpet vests of gray, white jackets and black. Regulars distinguished from volunteers by uniform gray and caps.

[*Hills' report in the* **Boston Journal:**]

The Captain of the French Steamer Milan goes to New Orleans — The Rebels Burn one of their steamers — Visit of Confederate Officers to the Gunboat Union.[187]

U.S. SHIP MISSISSIPPI, April 10.

On the 8th inst. an affair occurred up the river, which has created an unpleasant sensation in the squadron. Capt. Cloue of the French Steamer Milan, desiring to visit New Orleans on business connected with the removal of the disaffected French residents there, Flag Officer Farragut dispatched the gunboat Winona, Lieutenant Com. Nichols, to convey the Captain under a flag of truce up the river.

The Winona proceeded within five or six miles of the forts, and Capt. Cloue landed on the right bank, whence he walked up to Fort St. Philip, intending to communicate with the city from that point. Upon his arrival at the fort, the Frenchman was treated with great indignity by the rebels, who refused him permission to proceed or even communicate with New Orleans, assigning as a reason that he was accompanied by Federal gunboats who took advantage of the flag of truce to examine their works. He was held in custody twenty-four hours, and was sent back down the river on the following day.

The most singular part of the affair remains. The sloop-of-war Iroquois was up the river on picket duty, and upon the approach of the Winona, Capt. DeCamp of the former vessel went onboard and, as the report goes, took charge of the vessel, and ordering a full head of steam run her up towards the forts with the flag of truce still flying. The rebels open fire upon her from Fort St. Philip, firing first a blank and then a rifled shot at the steamer to bring her to.

In the course of the run up the river the Winona encountered a small rebel steamer, filled with people and having in tow a raft of logs, which the enemy were securing to add to their raft above the forts. At the approach of the Winona the rebels were seized with a panic, and running their steamer under the bank, set her on fire and fled without even stopping her engines.

The steamer was destroyed, notwithstanding an attempt was made by our men to extinguish the fire.

Two rebel gunboats, the Tennessee and Defiance, the former commanded by a traitor named Wilkinson, formerly an officer in the United States Navy, who, together with another officer and a man attired as a civilian, to whom his companions showed great deference, went on board the Winona, and were received with great cordiality by Capt. DeCamp, who invited them into the cabin where the party spent several hours in confidential and animated conversation. The rebel guests informed their host that they knew all about the movements of our fleet, the number of vessels, by whom commanded, and, what is more strange, that they were divided into three division, a fact which has not been generally known among our own officers until within a few days. The most serious charge brought against Capt. DeCamp is, that he showed his rebel guests about the Winona, and they obtained a complete knowledge of her armament, steaming qualities, and everything, in fact, they desired to know. Other reports are afloat with regard to the proceeding of Capt. DeCamp, which coming to the ears of Flag Officer Farragut, he has ordered a court of inquiry to investigate the matter. Capt. DeCamp is a brave and skillful officer, and his course in thus entertaining rebels, and giving them important information, has caused much comment.

Tuesday April 29. Stopped last night on *Harriet Lane* and nearly devoured by mosquitoes. Back to Jackson in gig. Coffee, toddy, pipe. Secesh flag and ammunition found by officers of Jackson. Launch raft one of many Secesh navy helped on shore fort Jackson. Man fell off stern of *N.A.*[188] morning and two boats put off but current carried down. White party seeking trophies of war into extent of danger.

Fort Jackson. Inscription on gun. "We fought but fought in vain. But B[189] will come with us again. Hot shot for you damned Yankees. Dirt and filth. On Wednesday man deserted and laid two days behind bayou. Captured and taken to Philip and to (be) shot.

From Jackson up, rafts on right bank. Alligators basking in torrid heat. *Burton*[190] discharging soldiers. Jack pirates. Red River boat. Bull Run confederate flag. Burton smoke stack riddled, shot through section chimney.

Now go to Landis. St. Phillip post command of Lt. Lea, *H.L.*[191] 2.20 in pm take *Burton, Landis,*[192] *Defiance.*[193] Sailor and artillery on La. Bayou to in dead battery La. Blown up. Mortar fleet post guard Co. K 30th Mass.

Upper battery 17 guns 2 destroyed 4 disabled. Piles of shells unbroken. Lt. Dixon CO of upper battery sent board La. Battery. Volunteer fired 20 shot: Ft. Jackson shot first. 2 guns dismounted, out by exp. Flying battery. Co. F Lt. La. Artillery Capt. Squires. Four or five bombs fell in crop and many over and short. One the east parapet and carried away brick and sand and gored cattle, Two magazines lost bench to.

Surprised to find old friend Maj. H.O. Whittlemore commanding St. P. expedition, embarked Ship Island 15th April and H. of P. 17th, bombardment 18th. 28th read northern forts surrounded and surrendering N.O.

> The remainder of the entry for April 29 consists of Hills' descriptions of the garrison details for the forts, especially regarding the detachments of the 30th Massachusetts Regiment. These he describes in great detail (when legible) observing that his notebook would have been very helpful to rebel spies in the area. He also mentions the work of the Owasco removing hulks of burned out vessels to improve river access and allow for better navigation of the fleet. Of interest is Hills' being able to interview rebel prisoners without any apparent interference or restrictions from Union officers. One rebel he interviewed said he expected a land attack on New Orleans via Alabama more than the possibility of a land and river attack directly up the Mississippi. The rebels appeared to be stunned by the relative ease of the Union success but were still confident that they could do better "next time." At 5 o'clock in the evening Hills started up river to New Orleans, noting the abundant waterfowl, as well as "negroes, orange groves, and oleanders." Ship bands played "Dixie" and "Yankee Doodle," and the J.P. Jackson continued up river all night.

Wednesday Morning, April 30th. We have steamed all night going up Mississippi in steamer *J.P. Jackson*, officer Woodworth. Plain bldgs., long lines of magnolia trees. Opposite bank gang of field hands at work on sugar plantation. Overseer on horseback. A church and Campa Santo of N.O. Sacred earth. White sepulchers of past generations.

Passage of fleet 8 miles in passing English Turn. Each ship fires two broadsides. Ship bells and scuttles in disarray. Beautiful fields of rice level as billiard table and plush as new carpet. As in midnight of life we are in death. So on man of war end as of peace, end as of peace and prosperity mold sides. However bitter may be felling no northern booms can but rejoice in south which opens a new era.

Sycamore trees [illegible] every morning, bend beneath [illegible]. Cottonwood, ash, willow boughs dipping branches in river. Extensive sugar plantation wealthy planter has built a prosperity sovereign in small scale. Boiling hour and extensive negro quarters. The morning panorama of Mississippi. Right and left bank of river has a sliding of 25' side. One rich planter, other more plantation field hands cease their plodding labor and for moment gaze at us as we pass. A year has passed since ships towed up river. *E. Wilder* is first ship towed up since enforcement of blockade. Banks of river lined with waste cotton burned by fire of traitors. Domestics and negro children come out and warm welcome with this party. After five months of exile from all amenities of civilization your correspondent can appreciate beauties of sunny south. First troops facing groups in front of charming villa. Hesitated whether friend or foe, or let Stars and Stripes and bhkps. out. Negros danced with joy. Another did jump. Soldiers returned greetings of those released from terrors of rebellion. New growth of sugar like peas. *Oneida* and *Pinola*,[194] Plantation Bell tolls 12 A.M., we pass extensive sugar house and all quiet cane plantation. Plant only their cane to [illegible] two long rows of negro quarters. Took of Yankees and cane to feed their slaves. English Turn. We've had a at [illegible] of bend (fresh smart herds of cattle) shouting, and reuniting. Small boy disappears after gazing eagerly and c., and doubt taken place. Like divoling veins. A lot of negoes arriving whom old man more or less [illegible] slow appalling time.

> *Hills goes on to further describe the excitement he witnessed along the banks of the Mississippi River as he neared New Orleans. There were slaves of all ages excited at the approach of the Union fleet with hats and bandanas waving. Hills was very emotional witnessing these scenes, and remarked that the staffs that had carried the Confederate flag were "not strong enough to carry the stars and stripes." The enemy had retreated from New Orleans. To him it was a turning point of the war and he thanked God for the outcome as did slaves "in groups of twenty on bended knees, hardship lifted, Bless Lord you come at last, black faces radiant with joy."*

Planters stood looking sullen and dejected. Not much Secesh on river below New Orleans if below Delta, which 22nd contains unjust appeal for aid to garrisons Jackson and St. Phillip, charging them not sending fresh regiments to forts.

Not a planter has manifested the least interest in the affairs of the forts. Men in forts mainly from the city. They have cheerfully immersed selves in wet, vermin infested, ill ventilated and unwholesome place.

Field hands men and women are at work. Cane looks tall; war not interfered with agriculture. Planting goes on as usual. The *"Landis"* approaches bearing American flag. *Harriet Lane* passes Commander Porter bound New Orleans off to Mobile. Pt. La Harota[195] and now English Turn. Have been told by quid moves Delta over times that at English Turn but like pilots of Mississippi. Woodhull *Ct*[196] steamer makes slow progress vs. current. Steering east of great artery of Union, fields of cane. Patch work Magnolia[197] passes zephyrs wafted fragrance.

5. Journal of a Military Expedition from Boston to _____

Negro quarters at English Turn type of La Plats up river Pavilion. All ought to be confiscated if libel sch. The estates of men who plotted rebellion ought to be divided among conquerors. Very fact that navy past up and down river not harboring spied is evidence out to suppress rebels. Fort Lin[198] faces city pen. Negro quarters below of modern state.

N.O. still in distance. Oh for a Joshua to command sun to stand still.

Every planter on property and preparation, [illegible] feudal system which has engendered rebellion. Now pass most mag b [illegible]. Scene pales on the senses and lost in maze of novelty and splendor.

Stern of press gig grows heavy and fear of swamping. Majestic trees on right bank of river. Steam from sugar houses not much evidence "six bells gone" and we round the last turn in river below N. O. Look in vain for formidable batteries commanding every bend in English Turn. How the rebels have attempted to scare us. I lay aloft on furling and seeing city, smiling with peace, folded hands returning from daily toil. Soldiers lay aloft too and contemplated scene of future operations. It is a little ahead of N.E. verdure, and as seeing of men on Washington St. with their white hats looks like forcing season.

Hulk of ship northern neck. Bells of city strike 11 as we drop anchor. The last 10 miles has been slow progress and dark the lights on levee on *H.L.*[199] ahead.

Here am I, A.G.H. off N.O. of Slaughterhouse Point.[200]

[*Hills' report in the* **Boston Journal:**]
SHOCKING ACCIDENT ON BOARD THE PENSACOLA

It is my painful duty to record the particulars of a melancholy accident which occurred on the 30th ult. On board the sloop-of-war Pensacola. While efforts were making to get the vessel over the bar a large hawse, drawn beyond its tension, parted, the inboard end sweeping the deck, which was filled with men. A large number of sailors and several officers were knocked down; one man, Frederick Beth, captain of the after guard, was instantly killed; another seaman named Conner was rendered insensible and died on the following day, and five other men were more or less injured. Among the latter was Acting Master J. D. Robertson, of New York, who sustained a compound fracture of one leg. It was at first feared that amputation would be unavoidable, but the surgeons are now confident of saving the limb, and the officer is in a fair way of recovery.

> *At the end of April the surrender of New Orleans was imminent, which would be a major blow to the Confederacy. It had seemed to fall far too easily, and Confederate inquiries would soon look to point the blame. Troops that had been available to defend the city earlier in*

the spring had been withdrawn to reinforce Confederate General Albert Sidney Johnston's Army of Mississippi to the north at Corinth, Mississippi. On April 6–7 at the Battle of Shiloh just north of Corinth along the Tennessee River, both sides experienced the extreme casualties of typical Civil War battles to come. The battle was a strategic defeat for the Confederacy, resulting in a Tennessee now largely occupied by Union troops. Certainly, no troops were available to reinforce the defenses of New Orleans. Union forces were also finally advancing in Virginia on the Peninsula. All in all this April was one of the worst months in the history of the Confederacy.

U.S. Steamer Jackson May 1st. May morning, called 4½ o'clock. Boat up Algiers side to *H. L.*, passed French steamer *Milan* back to Jackson. Cast off *W. Farley*.[201] Secesh scattered along levee. Confederate soldiers on guard. 3 march down to relieve guard. City Hall held by enemy. U.S. Hospital 200000 apptd. over of Jeffs pet jobs. Cook, H and Co Old Hospital rear. River 2 inches of levee. One of their fears 3 batteries on stocks at Algiers.

One steamer cut down at Bellville iron works.[202] Aught [illegible] N.O.O. and G.W.R.R. Great city before is hold of half our ships, great moral power exerted by two war ships. Dome of St. Charles. Have long talked of taking breakfast there but not safe. "Last Chance" Hotel, Mint, but few mint drops. Spirit easily ctd. Gunner of Jackson ordered to put charge of cement on top of 32lb starboard bow. Breastwork in front of Mint. Liberty House "creole excp." Boston House English flag on Picayune Pier. Levee crowded people. Statue of Jackson in Jackson Square. Redoubt thrown up. No guns on C.H.[203] Nearest approach to cannon is water pipes. Gunboats 1 & 7, *Brooklyn* and *Hartford*.

Str. *Sallie Robinson*[204] only docks sunk. 2 English ships. *Richmond* cheers ship *H. L.*[205] passing. Cotton smoking which vandals set on fire. *Richmond* ahead. *Pensacola* #8, *Hartford*, *Brooklyn*. Boat from *Brooklyn* puts off levee at Algiers. Blacks and creoles look sullen, not a sign of Unionism, and why 35,000 confederate troops up and d[206] in rear. Sides vibrate sensations at gazing upon hostile city where enemy are seen, to all appear our enemy looking upon with hatred. Flags French, German, English, Secesh. No S and S[207] on shore but river looks cheerful. Pen and coal for our ships. Bosworth and Co. ice depot if behave selves, may take one in julep then.

We should like to drop in at St. C. Theatre for gaieties or varieties, tis not convenient.

9 o'clock, S and S on C.H. Pic[208] Pier in front filled people. Can hardly believe eyes that old flag again floats. This is hour when stores open but shutters taken down. Not 20 open doors along levee as if stricken with

5. Journal of a Military Expedition from Boston to _____   101

plague. Beholder is lost in amazement. Do not care to go on shore set fires break out in dozen places professions did not tempt me to go and obtain loss and insurance.

Only sign of industry is ½ dozen black smoke curling up and drifting northward, and ferryboats plying and now and then a sail boat. This is home of Slidell, of Soule, of Roula. Few women, one black with umbrella, who mourns the loss of some loved one killed in unholy war or he may have died of yellow fever, sisters of mercy on pious works. Where out happy darkies. We fair would visit callboard, dread of sailors. Slave pens. Wonder if trading brisk in niggers about this time.

No jubilant sounds. Tis a tame understated, including no band to play hail airs. Now crowd increases to greet soldiers from forts, women with throbbing hearts, whose dear ones lie moulding in dark deep sleep of death in ramparts of forts. Now and then the sharp report of a musket.

Ferryboats come in at A[209] where we lie, full of passengers. There is type of slave driver. Southern faces and end times origin betrayed secesh soldiers. Look with a must upon heavy walking beam of Jackson, none like it, so different from lofty palatial steamers on river.

Fight. Shells bursting so ran away.

[At this point in the May 1st entry Hills inserted casualty results of the Union fleet as he knew them.]

Before attack 18th to 24th, 2 killed, 19 wounded.

Hartford	3	10	
Brooklyn	9	26	
Pensacola	4	33	
Richmond	2	4	
Mississippi	2	6	
Iroquois	6	22	
Oneida	none during battle		
Cayuga	–	6	
Sciota	–	2	
Katahdin	none		
Wis.[210]	–	2	
Varuna	3	9	sunk
Winona	3	5	
Niagara	4		

Mortar Fleet 1 killed, 1 during 24th, k 1–10

Pen[211] led way all up to New Orleans. *Varuna* 1st ship passed forts at Chalmette. *Penco* attacked battery, ½ mile under fire, 1 of 4 guns and 1 of 8, each side of river upper part English Turn on any levee. Fgt.[212] Ordered

Morris to send full marine guard, commanding Lt. Stillwell and Paymaster Davis to secure all specie and dies in Mint and howitzer s & d over it, which did. Found machinery all good order and vault locked. Davis reported to Morris send guard of marines and thence to Flag Ship. Flag hoisted. Farragut ordered her marines all posted to pull down fire main up howitzer. Thanksgiving and prayer held 11 o'clock, and while raising on flag denizens fired killing one man, prisoner dead been previously taken out, and men so excited by insults to flag reached to guns.

Assailed officers with indecent insult and threw tobacco in their face. Major said if ordered city would die by brute force. Prisoners from forts on arriving were treated with brutality, kicked about streets. Meeting on board steamer which came up under flag of truce and sunk at levee next morning.

10 ships. 2 confed batteries,[213] one near finished. *Hartford* 32 shot. *Brooklyn* suffered most when *Hartford* vanishes and took fire. B. Kennon on *Gov. Moore*[214] steamer came up on *Hartford* and had 15 out of 90, fearful harvest.

At Carrollton 15 miles 2 batteries. P.M. up and out and deepest set fire and abandoned. At Quarantine[215] 3 o'clock P.M. Camp Lovell. Frasers Hill hoisted first flag at one of the forts. Col., Major, Lt., Captains, and _____. *Miss* ram pca 20 guns in ram filled combustibles and set fire and one iron cased battery out of 6 batteries.

12000 bales cotton burned and tobacco. Peace of city provided by European guard, French man of state. Man named Summers, two years recorder N.O. on *Richmond* was compelled to leave lines up at Ring Woods. Compelled to come down affected self on ships when Bailey went shore and offered courtesies (and) a mob nearly killed him. Sight nephew on *Richmond*. Son in confederate army.

Union feeling in city plenty but none shown till city finally occupied.

> *A barely legible section at this entry describes a warning to the fleet sent by a woman living in New Orleans, of the value of commodities stored in the Custom House at $50,000, and of the steam ship Tennessee*[216] *and the tow boats* St. Charles,[217] Diana,[218] *and* Sallie Robinson *captured on the Mississippi. Praise was also given to the officers and crew of the USS* Katahdin *for their bravery and cool determination in support of the USS* Preble.

Chalmette Reg., Col. Skimansky of Portland, Me[219] drowned out on other side where was six hundred men not molested. K[220] took 150 suits of clothing belonging to the regiment. K stk. 3 times.

5. Journal of a Military Expedition from Boston to _____   103

The next page lists the numbers of guns for both Fort Jackson and St. Phillip. An attempt to break out each type by number is not complete. The totals — 78 for Fort Jackson and 44 for Fort St. Phillip — differ slightly from those in other accounts.

Landing troops N.O. 5 o'clock Thursday evening. Crowd with the 21st Indiana, company from platoons across pier and forces back armed crowd. Crowd cheers in hatred, much damming as any other crowd would so band strikes up and the Stars and Stripes are carried ashore.

Owasco's foremast goes by board in contact with *Brooklyn* Yankee. Enemy case hidden secesh Otis,[221] and then *Jackson* going to assistance. This then to *Owasco*. As we approach *Owasco*, excise boats capsized men overboard. Otis weak of misuse. Wipes out excise counts taken some over. We look upon these things coolly now. Sensibilities have been seen full.

What King says sugar house full of sharp shooters. *Richmond* and *Mississippi* fired and in 7 guns on sight Hon Pt. *Hartford, Cayuga*,[222] and *Pensacola* engaged on other side, 9 guns.

Havoc of camp H.[223] when arrived, cotton and tobacco. Went up same order. American flag only dock on Algiers starting Union stk. down.

1 yrs' men on Mississippi.

Friday, May 2. Down river last night brought up Pass a Loutre, collided steamer *Matanzas* bound up Gen'l Butler's troops carried away out ahead and anchor of *Owasco* and take off rail of *Matanzas* ___ to toprail.

Friday go off to Pilot Town, Saturday or ditto, Sunday 5th (4th) ditto.

All guns out of van of *Mississippi*. All rigging and one man found, Capt. Green.

Mississippi Record. King on spk. noon, our M. at wheel. Curving ship, holding at mark, all thought engaged, where out of cannot fire, drifts, grounded ashore and meeting between fire at both forts, working both broadsides. During this time fire sharp both sides. It was grand and terrific. Had 17 shot struck. Shot from forts fired high. *Miss.* fired St. P. broadside, shot of all guns on solid 42 pound shot through both decks, took away chart and implements, down several through bulkhead into engine room. Butler narrowly escaped first shot.

The remainder of the May 2nd journal entry is largely illegible. The few words I can transcribe describe a continuation of the fight of the USS Mississippi *as it passed Forts Jackson and St. Phillip and later saw action against the CSS* Manassas, *suffering some damage but able to unleash several broadsides despite the rush to pass the forts. The fight against the ram Manassas is also described. It is likely that Hills was copying this account in a hurry, accounting for the poor handwriting. A brief description of the* Iroquois *in the battle as she suffered six dead and many wounded is also given.*

Monday Morning, May 5. 3rd Div. Mortars sail to Ship Island. Chain for Redman.

Tuesday May 6th. End of *Jackson's* trip. Negroes mending lines, arrive of mules. On our right Magnolia Estate, broad avenue lined of Linden trees.

Hills describes the estate as a palatial mansion. Some in his party hope that the mansion will be confiscated. Others may have had notions of liberating the site of valuables. The entry is a difficult read, with words such as "confiscate" and "marble" in the same paragraph. Hills goes on to describe a section of the city as "The Battery," having sustained some damage (he refers to "shot holes in the roof"). Some damage was attributed to vandals, not just the Union fleet. On board he also saw the position of the Parapet Line of breastworks upriver of New Orleans. The lines extended as far as he could see from the river. He also noted the abandoned works of Fort Leon with guns dismounted and carriages burned by the retreating rebels. At every site he noted that for the present at least it was business as usual along the river plantations, with slaves working in the fields under the watch of overseers on horseback with their dogs.

Iroquois N.O. and Op boat *H.L.* took *Landis, Burton,* and (*Defiance*). Capt. Mitchell in command. Navy assault St. Wilkinson board *Colorado*. Accident on *Rhode Island.* Men drowned. *Sea Pennell, Whit.*[224] *R.I.* at Algiers, crowd of laborers flocked to shore to get work. Accident on *Hartford*. 24 men injured by capstan.

Richmond took *Tennessee* and found excited crowd on board that should not take her. Laid trolley on her and found water near up to the fire room. Great loss. Had names only demoralized men armed ships rifles. Started fires, got underway and pumped out and brought down to *Richmond*. Terry in charge and Hoyt chief engineer, to Island for troops and Ship Island one of most Connecticut[225] vessels. Every evidence in ship that her steering below Ch[illegible]. Had French flag when taken.

Union sentiment, incidents on increase. Rapidly informed by gulls on shore that there are many Union people here. As soon as have any union man arrived on to ships and manifest union feeling showing slyly white Hk[226] at enemy. Last night elegant, caught 2 young ladies elegantly dressed with negro driver. After people left pier lad turned to leave, showed hhhf.[227]

5. Journal of a Military Expedition from Boston to _____   105

Officers on shore. Page 15.[228] Much Union sentiment manifests self in solo voice, hurrah for Union. Only insults is at cannon. Store keeper received all silver change. Conclusion we have come to is that erupting stocks and silver change will accomplish anything. Ships passed 30 yards of forts.

Our terms of surrender were all fortifications of city, Forts Lio,[229] Pike, Wood, and battery at Proctorville. Portion 8th N.H. Pike.

All appears to city cut off. Yet levee road along bank of river which is almost impassable from height of river.

8th N.H. Butler went to meet where pieces all loaded canister and 2 pcs. General Butler placed foot of C. Hill seceding for any Engineering on hill Sunday night.

Leave. City in possession of Butler and staff.

Rumor at Ship Island General Shipley acting Brig. Gen. in command of all forces at S.I. Sent troops 3rd May by *Calhoun*[230] and bark *Lincoln*.[231]

N.O. May 7th. Leave for Home for Steamer *Rhode Island*. Port with Wells. Prefer with whom slept last night at St. Charles. As we sat on balcony smoking miserable cigars part of stock of centroland[232] tobacco found Custom House and gobbled up by Quartermaster Hormal. Crowd assembles opposite side and pressed. Some with gladness stopped unfestive in street up by gas lights which here lights all over city, and some scowling at "invaders." This is extent of disaffected probation. Federal cannon return their stare and form back in return. In cool of evening a lady sit in trestled verandah bare headed rocking to and fro with what reflective best judge by petulant cast of her charming features, and shade of ax by which overcast face of her legitimate lord. Sound of music, Union band playing national airs. Passing up canal through crowd like all rabble in towns and cities, follow some grinding teeth. In mastering imprecations on Lincoln's minions, others so full of patriotic feeling as soon would kiss hem of garments of brawny sons of New England. Peculiar sound wreaks on ear as watchman from beat to beat drops his staff with a ring on the side walk. In Havana island through one night the cry in Spanish all's well, the cowled and blacked mark like watchman, and from the ships have heard as tossing in disturbed berth. Fighting mosquitoes their grum shouts, forecastle, fore capstan [illegible].

Ships at N.O. *Pensacola, Katahdin, Portsmouth, E.W. Farley, So. America, Mississippi, Tennessee*. Col. Jones at 2. Mails from Forts, *Varuna* and Morgan. Pilot Town, 80 ironclad, 5 died at hospital.[233] *Matanzas* towed "*City of New York*,"[234] over bar with 8th N.H. Received prisoners. Officers confederate navy so-called, Nis and Thy[235] refused to sign, and next signed as prisoners of war.

Cross the line between muddy and blue water. Steamer *Whiteman*[236] by *N.L.* Provost Marshall Allen, 8th, 48 men named although Rx found man with blood and made up a confession. Telegraph describes 7th no battle at Corinth. Enemy still hesitates.

Called meetings of city. Forbid drafting for Confederate army and truce of lines.

Reinhart charge of artillery Ship Island. Ship *Eliza Siler*[237] got ground Horn Island and stove hole in bottom. Tried to beach bar but drifted off and sunk between Mississippi and Biloxi.

Rebel officer weighing his words in letter sent to friends. Mortar fleet 7th to Mobile. 8th, Sondid and forts occupied. 7 or 8 hours *Westfield* found got off. Afternoon 3 rebel gun boats landed troops Fort Morgan and rested, back Friday rebel navy schooner ran past fleet at Dauphin Island and back to fort. Mortars back on Thursday and decided could not make attack. Heard how abandoned expedition to fort. Wood and *Richmond* on 4th occupied. Forts abandoned and guns spiked, *Richmond* with files and Wood cut nails.

Major Hallbrook 7th N.H. 250 men Fort *Richmond*. Lt. Col. Lull to take possession of Fort Wood, convoyed *New London* and *Calhoun*. Fort Pike have brick casemated circular fort to pass good condition. Officer quarters burned but barracks good. Shell road only effect to ford covered by.[238]

Below is a transcription of Hill's ticket home dated May 3, 1862, signed by both D. Porter and D. Farragut authorizing him to board the Rhode Island en route to New York:

U.S. Str. Harriet Lane
May 3rd 1862

Dear Sir,
The bearer Mr. A.G.
Hills, correspondent of the Boston Journal desires to obtain a passage to New York on the Rhode Island. By granting him such a privilege you will oblige.

Yours truly
D.D. Porter

D^r. Sir

You can take Mr. Hill if you think proper, as I have no objection.

Respectfully,
D.G. Farragut
F.O.

5. Journal of a Military Expedition from Boston to _____   107

Friday 9th. 11 o'clock fired of guard 200 single shot. Signal lighted McRae and everything on fire, McRae, Navy Yard, Hospital, Lamp oil factory Pensacola (could have captured garrison if had a gun boat or steamer of troops). Beautiful sight. Warrington and Woolsey[239] not suffered much.

Sunday 11th. Off Pensacola. Entrance Pensacola Harbor Water Battery. Scan which have seen before. No one seen on McRae. Glowing flag sight to see. Old flag flying where rebel ensign so lately flaunting in insolent fold. Hole where magazine blew up. Flag breezing, drooping over gap. Light Horse Battery. Pickens opposite it, stern grey walls which defies a rebel hill. Now pass channel where Bragg refused to allow even a boat to pass before. St. and Sp. over McRae, Barrancas. Union soldier on ramparts and under shade of trees. Deep in detection in scarp as *Rhode Island* passed *Harriet Lane*. Band of Str. Star Banner. Cheer ship, lay aloft. Lt. Lea Staid by to fire 3 here by. Cheer Dixie. Thrilled. Horses embarking.

Flag on McRae hoisted by Lt. Leroy L. James of 2nd Artillery, Browers. Capt. Dear? Navy Yard.

Harriet Lane after *Jackson* went to Pensacola, Porter way off Mobile case the Secesh adv [illegible]. Pilot circled to ready and rear up to town. Capt. Wood[240] got up to *Jackson. Pensacola* met *Niagara* and set for Morgan to cir. Officers C and Porter waited to know what condition of cities P. and Aipia[241] got no inf[242] regard to c troops and A at night landed 1200 men. What fighting thru til airs that gun boats entering Mobile and fear retreat being cut off left. In firing, guns may be buried in sand. Left flags flying Gaines.[243] No flags flying where mortar fleet. All wanted war for squadron to have been off Mobile and would have gone in.[244]

Appearance of Navy Yard and buildings standing. Smoke still rises from ruins. Several pile drivers remain. Scene of desolation and ruin. Provis buildings store houses on fire, flames still raging. Wharves still burning, all burned. Wharves, Prov. Store, parts shop, officer quarters, iron and brick buildings, main quarters. Burned buildings all government. Dwellings outside yard occupied by employees of government.

Rhode Island left N.O. May 8, Pilot Town 9th, Ship Island 10, Mobile ditto, Pensacola 11, arrived Key West 14th, left Port Royal 18th, Fortress Monroe 20th.

The arrival of the Rhode Island at Fortress Monroe was reported in the New Hampshire Sentinel *of May 29, 1862:*

Among the passengers from New Orleans are Col. Deming of the 12th Connecticut, bearer of despatches from Gen. Butler, Captain Albert

N. Smith late of the gunboat Wissahickon, and A.G. Hills correspondent of the Boston Journal: also between forty and fifty prisoners, naval officers captured on the Mississippi, below New Orleans. Among them are several formerly of our navy, including J.K. Mitchell, commanding the confederate naval forces on the Mississippi, W. Wilkinson, second in command on board the *Louisiana*, Beverly Kennon of the *Gov. Moore*, destroyed, and A.F. Warley, commanding the ram *Manassas*. On the passage the passengers were obliged to take their turn doing guard duty over the prisoners."[245]

> *As Hills left New Orleans for New York, Farragut was sending the fleet up the Mississippi to probe rebel defenses. Baton Rouge and Natchez surrendered but were not occupied. The ironclads that were supposed to prevent the Union Navy from gaining control of the river had not worked well as a deterrent, and most were being destroyed by their own crews so they wouldn't fall in enemy hands. The same was true for the CSS* Virginia *in Norfolk, also in May. The Confederate Army in Corinth, Mississippi, was in retreat. No rebel army was in any condition to consider retaking New Orleans. In the east, "Stonewall" Jackson was battling General Nathaniel Banks in the Shenandoah Valley. Banks would replace Butler by the end of the year.*

6

Sketches Showing the Action on the River

Included in Hills' journals are seven sketches that show the progression of the river battle above Forts Jackson and St. Phillip. The first of the sketches shows the position of the rebel fleet at 3:45 A.M. on April 24. Confederate gunboats are shown on both banks of the river above the forts. The number of guns per vessel is given on the bottom half of the right side of the page. Beverley Kennon's name, as commander of the *Governor Moore*, is prominent at the top of page. Hills wrote of atrocities committed by Kennon. Those reports were not accurate and may have been harmful to that officer's parole efforts after the battle.

The second sketch shows the scene of battle at about 3:45 A.M. as described by Hills: "*Resolute, Reliance*, and *Louisiana* destroyed by orders of Commodore Mitchell after passage of the fleet. *Manassas* scuttled by Lt. Warley,[1] by cutting her pipes. *McRae*[2] sank at New Orleans. '*Jackson*'[3] Lt. F. B. Renshaw C.S.N. ran away with his vessel and destroyed his ship when out of harm's way."

The time of the action for the fourth sketch was not given, so it must be assumed that it follows close behind the action of the third.

The descriptions of the fire for the fifth sketch are not entirely clear, but it is evident that the firing distances between the *Governor Moore* (CSA) and the *Varuna* (USA) closed from 30 yards to 30 feet.

The sixth sketch shows the *Governor Moore* ramming for the *Cayuga*. *Moore* set fire to bar after receiving repeated hits from the *Varuna*. C. O. (*Cayuga, Oneida*) *Pinola, Pensacola, Mississippi, Iroquois*.

The seventh sketch shows the punishment of multiple Union warships upon the *Governor Moore* at the end of the engagement. According to this

The first of Hills' river battle sketches.

Opposite: Hills' second river battle sketch.

6. Sketches Showing the Action on the River

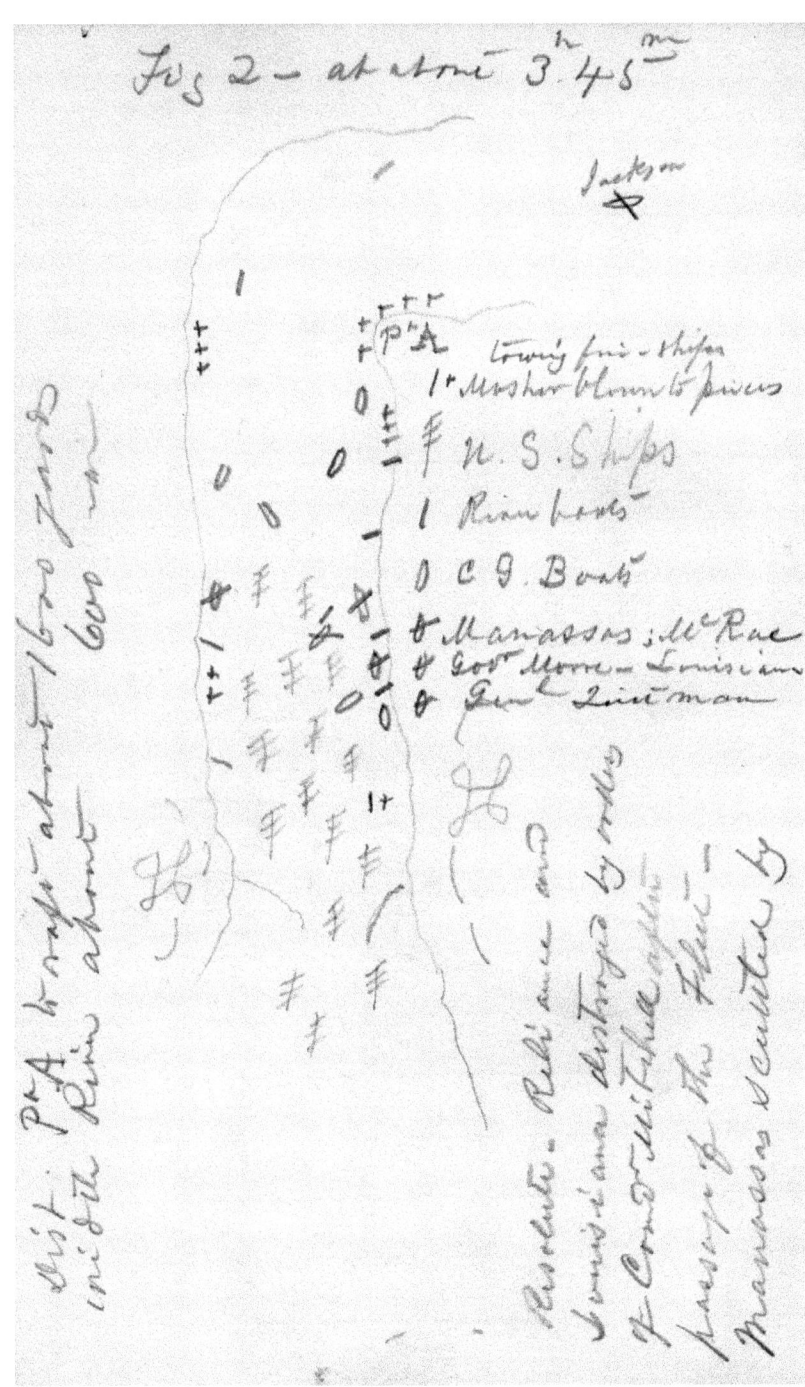

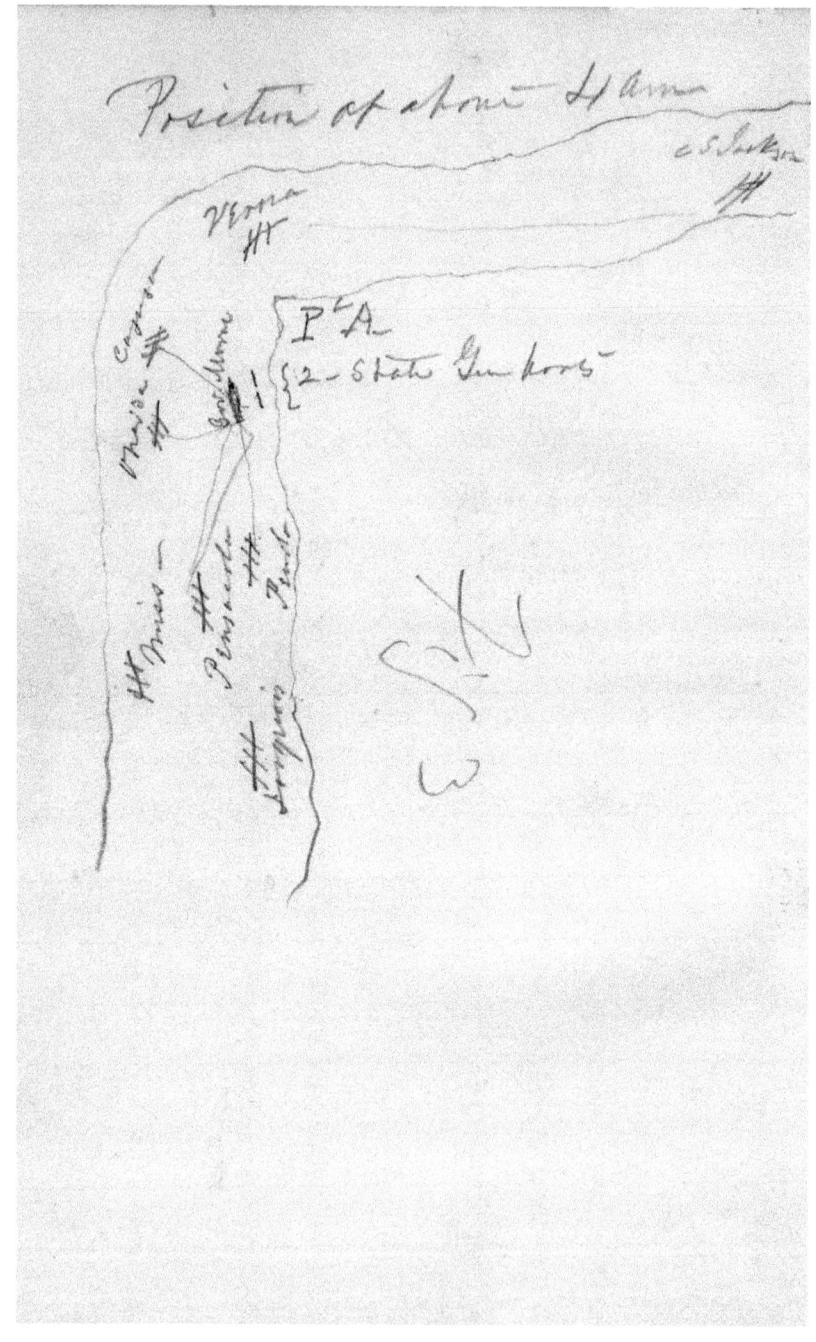

Hills' third river battle sketch.

6. Sketches Showing the Action on the River

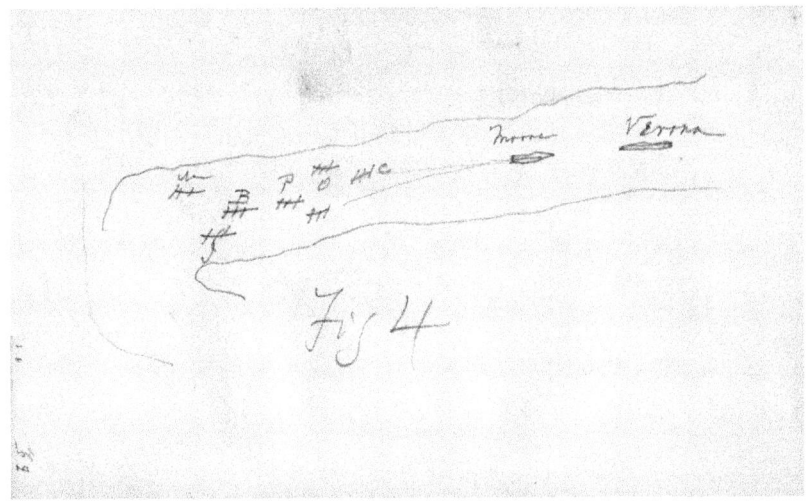

Hills' fourth river battle sketch.

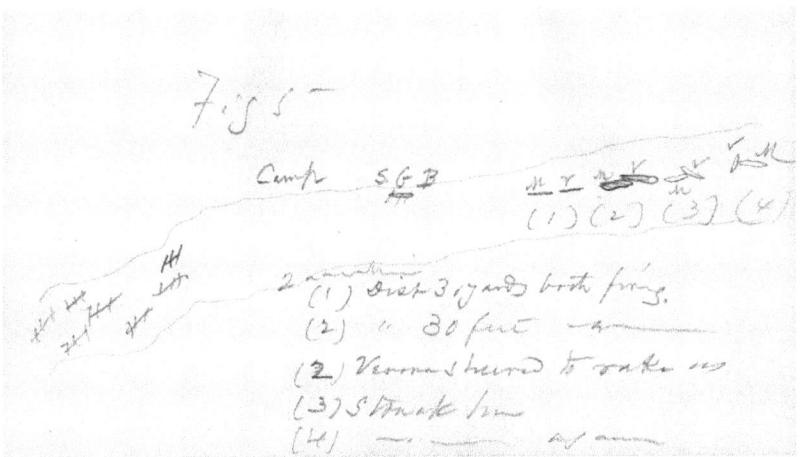

Hills' fifth battle sketch.

sketch the Confederate gunboat *Jackson* withdrew from the battle and moved toward New Orleans. The site of the sinking of the *Varuna* is also shown.

> "*Breckinridge*[4] destroyed by her captain up the river two miles above Quarantine and on opposite side of river. *Governor Moore* was set fire to by her commander. The other vessels were destroyed, I know not how, only whom. These four vessels were destroyed between Quarantine and Forts."

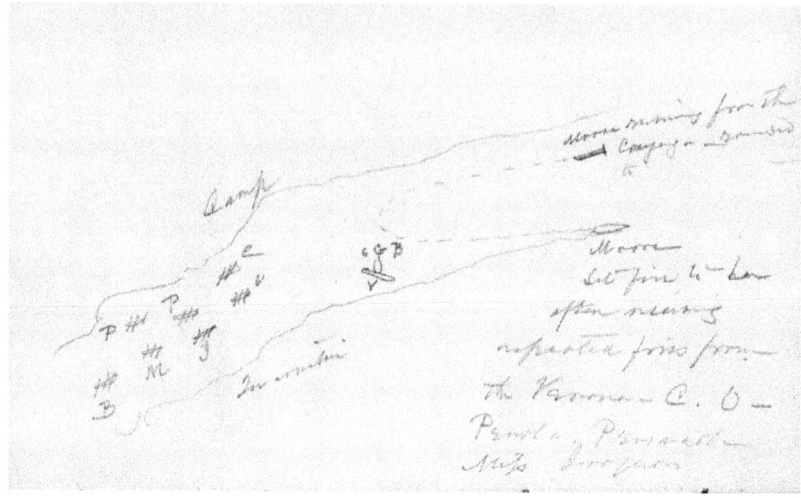

Hills' sixth battle sketch.

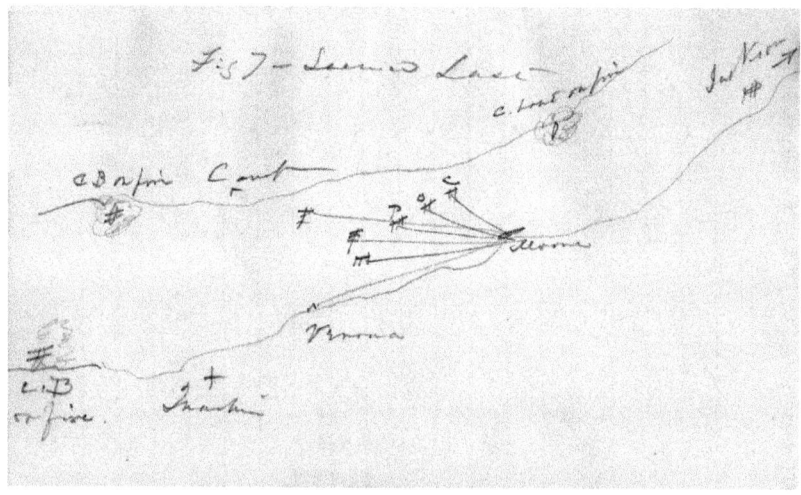

Hills' seventh battle sketch.

Hills compiled totals and mentioned some of the Confederate commanding officers and numbers of crew members of vessels as follows:

All total:
Louisiana, 200 men, J.K. Mitchell, McIntosh, Wilkinson
McRae, 130, T.B. Huger
Jackson, 75, F.B. Renshaw

6. Sketches Showing the Action on the River

Governor Moore, 93, Beverley Kennon
General Quitman,[5] 90, Grant
Warrior,[6] 75, Stevenson
Resolute,[7] 75
Breckinridge, 75
Lovell,[8] 75
Stonewall Jackson, 75
Manassas, 30, Lt. Warley
Total 910 men

Hills added an additional 150 men for a revised total of 1060 men.

Nearly all of whom were soldiers. The forts had about 1000 men.
Little *Mosher*,[9] not larger than any oyster Prongy was destroyed with all hands when taking a fire raft alongside *Hartford*. "*Star*"[10] River steamer (telegraph station), *Diana*, loaded with loafers, gentlemen, etc. from N.O. who came to see the fight. *Burton* and Landis, river boats, tenders to Louisiana as her engines were not ready for use.
Belle Algerine[11] — River boat — *Diana*, escaped.
Louisiana lost 1 killed, 2 wounded (Capt. McIntosh wounded seriously)
Manassas, none
McRae, 8 killed, 30 wounded (Capt. Huger wounded)
Quitman, don't know
Governor Moore, about 50 killed, 14 wounded (64)
Lost in river vessels unknown, Cpt. French
Resolute (Hooper) mortally wounded, died

The next two lines were written after the sketches but describe his return to Boston.

See Major about J.N. Smith. Spotts. Money spent. Clothes worn out and lost.
C.L. Hathaway Chief Marshall. 2½ o'clock near Flagan bldg., Water St. Father here.[12]

This ends Hills' second journal of the New Orleans Campaign of 1862.

7

Memoranda of Letters Sent to the *Boston Journal*

A.G. Hills wasted little time in reporting back to the Boston Journal the history he was witnessing. These letters formed the reports printed in the Journal under the signature of "Agaius." In the preceding journal A.G. noted when letters were sent, but it appears the more newsworthy ones began in February of 1862 as follows:

February 7th. Steamship "*Oriental*" sailed from Key West for New York. Sent "No. 1" from this place and four packages Ship Island letters.

February 10th. Schooner *Nonpareil* left for Havana. Sent letter No. 2 to go thence by steamer *Roanoke* to New York. Letter dated 10th.

February 12th. Sent letter No. 3 by Post Office clerk of Steamer *Connecticut* going to New York from this place. "News from the Gulf" dated 12th.

February 14th. Sent Letter No. 4 of this date care Acting Master Cook by bark *J.W. Hall* to New York.

February 28th. At Havana. Sent Nos. 5 and 6 and 7 by Purser of *Columbia* to New York.

March 4th. *Oriental* sailed for Port Royal to New York. Sent No 8 by Major Hill. 20 pages and the story of Refugees.

March 5th. "*Philadelphia*" sailed for New York. Sent No 9 by Purser.

No 10 sent March 12 by "*Rhode Island*," care of Lt. Semmes. Porter fleet and news by *R.I.*

No. 11 sent of Capt. Wilson of *Nonpariel* to Porter "*Columbia*," from Havana 20m pages dated March 14 at Tortugas and 17th at K. W.

No.12 dated March 22nd sent by Wesson on steamer *Constitution* sailed same date for Old Point.

No. 13 dated 24th March, gave J.C. Clapp, U.S. Marshal. "*Magnolia*" sailed for New York. Wrote Stockwell in answer to his of letter and also father.

No. 14 by *Connecticut* from Head of Passes dated April 10th.

8

New Orleans Under Occupation

The New Orleans to which A.G. Hills returned at the end of 1862 was of course different. Its formerly rebellious spirit was gone replace by a spirit of suspicion and dread due to the Union occupation. Although there were some reasons for encouragement among southern troops on the battlefields of Virginia, there was little to be happy about in the western theatre. Less of the Mississippi River was open to the Confederacy. Union armies had taken much of Tennessee. Ship Island was now a prison for captured rebel soldiers. Blockade runners were finding fewer ports of safety along the coast. The occupation was almost seven months old, and the spirit of rebellion displayed in May was no longer tolerated. According to the *Soldier's Newsletter* "The soldiers of this command are subject, upon the part of some low-minded persons, to insult. This must stop. Repetition will lead to arrest and imprisonment." Butler would have none of this. Under the iron rule of Major General Butler (who was relieved in December 1862) and now of Major General Nathaniel Banks, personal liberties were severely restricted. While Hills was absent General Butler had made life difficult for anyone loyal to the Southern Confederacy. Almost immediately following the surrender there was suspicion. From the *New Orleans Delta* in early May came this report:

> STRANGE FACES—*We noticed a number of strange faces on our streets yesterday in citizens' dress. This appeared to us somewhat strange, as all public modes of ingress to the city are cut off. The police should keep a sharp look out for the possessors of those new faces, as they might not be all right on the goose question, and here for no good. It would be well for our citizens to be on their guard in more ways than one.*

William Mumford, a New Orleans resident who had cut down the newly raised Stars and Stripes from the U.S. Mint, had been executed as a traitor in June 1862. General Order Number 27 forbade the observance of a day of fasting and prayer because it was proclaimed by Confederate President Jefferson Davis. Women who insulted Union officers had been labeled "women of the town" through the infamous General Order Number 28. Residents who knew anyone keeping arms without a permit were encouraged to produce names for a bounty. Poverty in New Orleans had affected a large number of the population even before the occupation, and General Butler demanded that locals in better fiscal condition alleviate the suffering. Companies and individuals were levied fees to feed poor residents of the city more than once. Later there were assessments for those who had aided the Confederacy in the initial defense of New Orleans. Loyalty oaths were required for those sixteen or older who entered the lines; those who refused to swear the oaths would be considered spies. Foreigners were required to be registered through the Provost Marshal's Office. Persons refusing to sign a loyalty oath were forbidden to transfer property, and an inventory of their personal property was also required for not signing an oath.[1] Butler overstepped his bounds as a military leader and was also accused of helping friends and family gain financially from the occupation. It was no surprise that Butler's tour of duty was coming to an end as Hills made his return to New Orleans. The change of Gulf commanders had grabbed Hills' attention, as is evident in the following article from an unknown newspaper[2] that had been cut out and tucked between the pages of journal:

GENERAL BUTLER AND THE PRESIDENT — COMPLICATIONS IN NEW ORLEANS

The curious coincidence in point of time of Major General Butler's order practically applying the writ of proemumie to a whole population in Louisiana, and of the President's proclamation, putting the execution of the act of confiscation under the control of the Attorney-General, has already, I perceive, attracted public attention. I have reason to believe that the proclamation has been hurried forward to Butler by extraordinary express, and that much anxiety is felt here lest it should not reach him and arrest his arbitrary and high handed course in time to prevent a serious collision between our own authorities and certain foreign powers. The affairs of France in particular at New Orleans are known to be in the hands of resolute men, backed by a strong naval force, and it is not considered improbable that angry discussions between the French representative and General Butler might arise upon the construction of his order, the effect of which would be to complicate in a very undesirable manner the already delicate condition of our foreign relations.

On the battle front, enemy activity was a considerable distance upriver, with Union forces descending against Vicksburg from the north and ascending from the south against Port Hudson just upriver from Baton Rouge.

Port Hudson and Vicksburg, with their formidable fortifications on bluffs overlooking the Mississippi River, were the last two major obstacles preventing the Federals from taking complete control of the river and splitting the Confederacy in two. Baton Rouge had surrendered to the Union Navy in May of 1862, and was soon occupied by some of Butler's regiments that had been cooped up on transports much of the time after leaving Ship Island in April. A Confederate attack in August had been beaten back, but soon after Union forces were pulled out and sent back to New Orleans. On December 17 Union naval and land forces returned, and after a few shots fired by the USS *Essex*[3] the mayor of Baton Rouge offered to surrender again. These land forces would prepare for eventual assaults on Port Hudson.

Expeditions also originated from New Orleans to attack Galveston both success and disaster. Galveston had been occupied by Union forces on December 24, but a stunningly successful rebel counterattack on January 1 (news of which reached Hills on January 4) resulted in the city's recapture and a defeat of the Union flotilla there. Some of the ships mentioned in Hills' earlier journal entries were no longer afloat or soon would not be because of this battle (*Harriet Lane* and *Westfield*) and other battles (USS *Mississippi* in March 1863 at Port Hudson). Some were lost to the sea itself (USS *Bainbridge* in August 1863 off Cape Hatteras).

With the Emancipation Proclamation taking effect on January 1, 1863, many of the Negroes lining the banks of the Mississippi or working on plantations when Hills first steamed upriver would soon be serving in the Union Army, first as soldiers of the Louisiana Native Guards and later the Corps d'Afrique. Ranks were filled in these regiments despite the exemption from the proclamation of southern states currently in federal control, as is evident in this transcribed letter from Hills' records explaining the conditions in which servants could be retrieved by a master:

> Thibodeaux January 21st 1863
>
> Mr. J.T. Lidet has permission to take his servants by forces whenever he may find them except in the camps of the U.S. Army or in the employ of the U.S. or an officer thereof and compel them to return to their obediences to him and their quick application to their business. In case any of his servants are found in the camp of the U.S. Army not in the employ of any officer and chooses to return home with their master, they will not be hindered. The master is enjoined to treat his servants Kindly and Justly as a Judicious man would treat his servants.
>
> O.W. Lull
> Provost Judge of Lafourche[4]

The jubilation of the Emancipation was even muted by General Banks. At least one plan for a demonstration — in which effigies of a slave family in chains were to have those chains removed in celebration when the Proclamation became effective — was suppressed.[5]

Despite months of Union occupation the streets were not entirely safe, and A.G. was issued permits to carry weapons for self defense. He and his reporter friends traveled in groups but by other accounts had an agreeable stay. When not reporting the news the journalists engaged in considerable loafing and drinking, and though there was some boredom to endure Hills and his group were content not to be in Virginia.[6] Sometime during one of the New Orleans stays his wife Sarah (Sallie) accompanied him for at least a little while, but he stopped his journal entries before her arrival. There is no doubt that her presence curbed his activities with his fellow reporters.

New Orleans was experiencing an occupation force that would soon descend on many other southern cities. A.G. was part of the occupation force as an editor for a pro–Union newspaper, a lieutenant in a colored infantry regiment, and an official registrar loyal to the Union. Through the *Era* Hills attempted to build positive regard for the Union presence to the citizens of New Orleans, but there was no doubting where the blame for the war was laid:

> SATURDAY EVENING, FEBRUARY 21, 1863
> There is a strong Union sentiment in New Orleans, which is every day developing itself and which finds constant encouragement in the security of life and property, under an impartial administration of law. It is impossible for people to live together long in close relations, and hate each other very sincerely; and it is equally impossible for people not to respect a Government which affords them perpetual protection from violence, and secures to them the enjoyment of every privilege compatible with a state of war. It matters not whether we hail from Louisiana, Massachusetts, or New York — we are all members of the same political family, and our interests are common. So long as we remembered this fact, and acted upon this principle, our country was blessed with freedom and prosperity such as could not be found elsewhere among the nations of the earth. It was only when this principle was forgotten, and the Union assailed by open and armed revolt, that commerce languished and sorrow came upon the land.
> ... It is our wish to be fully identified with the cause of the Union; and we are grateful to the citizens of New Orleans for the kindly spirit in which they have received The Era. We wish to make it a paper for the people, and the flattering patronage we have received encourages us to hope in our success. Our circulation has already increased beyond our expectations, and we shall labor diligently to deserve a much greater.

There was a lot of war yet to be fought, and with the exception of Port Hudson — where Hills found the effects of combat a bit overwhelming — there wasn't much happening near New Orleans. Perhaps for this reason Hills shuffled between New Orleans and home. Leaving for home at the end of June 1863, he missed the surrender of Port Hudson in July, just after the fall of Vicksburg.

As 1863 drew to a close the war was becoming more distant from New Orleans. The Mississippi River was firmly controlled by Union forces. Any concerns about Confederates massing to retake New Orleans had faded away. Union forces were driving deep into southern territory, at least in the west. Confederates were trying to defend the Red River instead of the Mississippi. Tennessee was firmly in Union hands, with the capture of Atlanta within range. The war in Virginia was a brighter spot for the Confederacy, but strategically it was on the defensive. Losses on all fronts were not sustainable. There were still a few coastal holdouts such as Mobile and Wilmington, and expeditions against these would certainly be routine for a reporter like Hills to cover. Hills' days in New Orleans were coming to an end. His venture with A.C. Hills running *The Era* hit a snag in March 1864 after the two had a disagreement, and the financial fallout would take nearly two decades to settle, by which time both had died.

I have found no concrete evidence that Hills covered the expedition that captured Fort Morgan and Mobile, but it does appear that Hills' next reporting assignment was the assault on Fort Fisher that finally closed the port of Wilmington. Who he was reporting for is not known. He was not with the *Boston Journal* again until about 1870, after he returned from Europe. But Hills remained in war zones until the South had capitulated, and he was well known enough to have his reports picked up by other papers.

9

A.G. Hills' Third Journal and His Return to New Orleans

This next and final journal was begun when A.G. Hills joined General Nathaniel Banks' expedition that eventually captured Baton Rouge and Port Hudson, first relieving General Butler of his command. It is not complete, is largely illegible, and ends abruptly. It began with another expedition to points unknown, although other correspondents in his group thought the destination was somewhere off the coast of Texas. Accompanying him this time were Gunn of the New York Tribune, *Hayes of the* Boston Traveller, *F. Schell of* Leslie's, *A.C. Hills once from the* Evening Post, *and Hamilton from the* New York Times. *Hills started his voyage from Boston once again and joined some of the others while in New York City.*

The route taken to the Gulf was of course familiar to him, as was his constant battle with seasickness. After reaching Ship Island once again the North Star battled the current of the Mississippi instead of continuing west, and back to New Orleans Hills went, passing the orange trees and sugar cane fields along the way. He was able to point out to his companions the still-present remnants of the failed fire rafts from the previous April. While the correspondents noted the warm welcome they received from groups of Negroes along the river, vestiges of the defiant populace were evident in the fist-shaking of an overseer with his slaves on the river bank — a reminder that he was returning to land that might be occupied by friendly forces but in an unfriendly place.[1] *The last dated* entry is December 14, the day the North Star went over the bar and up the river.

Journal of A.G. Hills, Special Correspondent of *Boston Journal* Attached to Gen. Banks' Expedition

New York Nov. 20th. Arrived here this morning from Boston to assume the duties devolving as above. Called upon Gen. Banks at Headquarters 759 Broadway. After having seen him at breakfast Astor House,[2] where met Mrs. B. who hoped to have Gen. at home with her at Thanksgiving. No doubt *some folks* would like to see me same time in Chelsea. Hope they may be so fortunate.

Met Col. Howe Mass. State Agent, who has received 4500 troops today mostly for Banks Expedition. 50th Mass. Regt. arrived this morning. Took up quarters temporarily first in Park Barracks and next in Franklin Street for night. Officers feed at Astor House when I stop. Saw memorandum books of Col. ____[3] containing names of transports.

[2]

Met Carl, NY Herald and his wife, also Sawyer same paper. Parted with Major Rogles and M.L.W. Clapp.

Received of C.O.R. $60—had when left Boston $10—Total of $70. Went to Serenade to Gen. McClellan at 5th Ave. Hotel. General has all the elements of obstinacy force of character and caution. He is in the hands of the Democracy, was introduced by the President of a Democratic club, and will in my opinion be the next candidate for President in opposition to the Republicans.

Returned to Hotel 12 o'clock. Retired.

Nyk. Nov 21. Anniversary of departure from Boston on Butler's Expedition.

While at breakfast 52nd Mass. Regt. marched up Broadway in rain storm. Met Col. Howe, went to quarters in Franklin Street.

When Gen. Banks commenced organizing his expedition, Col. Howe Asst. QM was detailed by Sec. of War to assist him and has since proved an invaluable asset.

Was introduced today to members of Banks

[3]

Staff. Went to Howe's house after which in company with him went to see McClellan[4] and Scott. Shook hand with "Little Mac," who received us all cordially, and was closeted half an hour with.

Sent dispatches to Journal which no paper, not even in New York had today.

9. A.G. Hills' Third Journal and His Return to New Orleans

United States of America,

STATE OF LOUISIANA,

REGISTER'S OFFICE----CITY OF NEW ORLEANS.

OATH.

Albert G. Hills, do solemnly swear, in the presence of Almighty God, that I will henceforth faithfully support, protect, and defend the Constitution of the United States and the union of the States thereunder, and that I will, in like manner, abide by and faithfully support all acts of Congress passed during the existing rebellion with reference to slaves so long and so far as not repealed or modified or held void by Congress or by decree of the Supreme Court, and that I will, in like manner, abide and faithfully support all proclamations of the President made during the existing rebellion, having reference to slaves, so long and so far as not modified or declared void by the Supreme Court. So help me God.

A. G. Hills

I do hereby Certify, that on this 29 day of Jany 1864 appeared before me Albert G. Hills who subscribed the foregoing oath.

Signed: *W.R. Fineshmayder*
Register

Hills' loyalty oath from January 29, 1864.

Learned today that Gen. B. and 41st Regt. going on *North Star*.[5] Saw Major Gen. Auger assigning troops to various transports.

Nyk Nov 22nd. Weather clear and cold. 42nd Mass. Regt. arrived, 50th and 52nd Mass. Regts. Went to Camp N.P. Banks.

Sent second letter to Journal. Met George Hemony, Tom Lee and Lt. Mcanty U.S.N. Went to Mallacks evening.

Nyk Nov 23rd. Met Sallie this morning. Went with Col. John H Olerry, Amos Lamond and Sgt. Conlan to Camps. At Camp N.P. Banks Union Course.

Nyk Nov 24th. Troops arrived. Embarking 169th Nyk. *Northern Lights.*[6] Sent letter to Journal.

New York Nov 26th. Met Hamilton Nyk Times. Called Banks. Boots. Not much difference in climate on coasts. Prepare for warm weather. Going either to Charleston or Texas.[7]

New York to 4th Dec. When embarked on steamer *North Star* and was at sea running southward until morning of 13th when arrived in Ship Island Harbor.

Saturday Dec 13th. Left Ship Island 2 o'clock for New Orleans. In mud off Bar S.W. Pass several hours. Pilot boat dancing on waves took up at River.

> *The next two pages are largely illegible but there appears to be mention of General Banks' dealings with incompetent officers. The last entry is not dated.*

[*Undated*] A Battle—Then like ravenous wolves in a gloomy fog, blind to danger the combatants, the rough arms and enemies march up to imminent death.

Who can describe in words the havoc, who the deaths of that fearful day, or who can furnish tears equal to the disaster.

They rush in and pour a round with arms close joined....

This ends the last of Hills' war journals that are known to exist.

> *Hills' activities from December 14, 1862, to May 1864 can be pieced together largely through to the Gunn Diaries, period newspapers, and the passes and artifacts he collected through the remainder of the war. His arrival in New Orleans was noted in the December 16 issue of the* Daily Delta:

Personal—Among the arrivals at the St. Charles Hotel, we notice the name of Lieut. Col. D. H. Strother, of Gen. Banks' staff, who is widely known as a pleasing writer under the nom de plums of Porte Crayon. F. H. Schell, reporter of Frank Leslie's Illustrated Newspaper; A.G. Hills, reporter of the *Boston Traveller*,[8] and Alfred C. Hills, reporter of the New York Herald. We hope these members of the fraternity will find their visit to the South a pleasant one.

9. A.G. Hills' Third Journal and His Return to New Orleans

> *A ship's pass from June 1863 indicates that his wife Sarah was with him this time but there are no other mentions about her in the journal, and she doesn't appear to be on the ship that took Hills and his other reporter friends back to New Orleans in the first place.*

By early December the group was already heading to Baton Rouge in search of action, but soon made its way back to New Orleans. It was during this expedition that Hills was commissioned a first lieutenant in the 4th Louisiana Native Guards, a colored regiment raised in New Orleans. The 4th did not see combat at Port Hudson while the 1st and 3rd regiments did. By the first assault Hills had resigned his commission.

The last entry describes what I believe is an attack at Port Hudson, possibly the demonstration of Banks' troops against it on March 14th since it most closely corresponds to Hills' last recorded journal entry. It is possible he had seen enough, much more carnage than during the attack on New Orleans the previous April, and decided to cover the war as an editor of the *Era* for the remainder of his stay in Louisiana. If Sarah had any influence on his actions during this stay he never wrote about it.

He returned to New York with Sarah in June but came back to New Orleans once again later in the year, probably alone. The exact date was not recorded. From the documents he had in his possession it appears he decided to cover the January 1865 amphibious assault on Fort Fisher at a minimum.

Pass for Hills' to go to New York with his wife.

10

The Reports for the *Boston Journal*

The following reports are more descriptive than the entries in the journals Hills wrote on his first trip to New Orleans, but the journals provided some of the information that appears in the reports. Hills had time to collect his impressions of the battles to allow for even more attention to detail. Some of the illegible entries in his journals have been covered in these reports.

The reports have been arranged in the order in which they were found, mostly in chronologically order although some may have duplicate coverage of some events.

This first report is of an engagement of the U.S. Steamer *Montgomery* off the Texas coast in early April 1862. When the vessel returned to the Mississippi on April 12, Hills obtained information regarding the *Montgomery's* actions at Fort San Louis Pass near Galveston, which resulted in the burning of a Confederate schooner and the capture of some of her crew. Despite the buildup of forces for the New Orleans attack, blockading southern ports was still a priority.

Bold Strategy of a Rebel Schooner Under the Guns of Fort San Louis and Confederate Soldiers Captured by the U.S. Steamer Montgomery

By the arrival of the U.S. Steamer "*Montgomery*," Lieut. Comdg. Charles Hunter, at the Head of the Passes on the 12th inst. I have obtained full particulars of the affair in which the vessel was recently engaged to which I briefly alluded in my last letter. The bold and sagacious character of the proceeding entitled it to a prominent place in the record of the rebellion of which it will form one of the most interesting chapters.

The "*Montgomery*" was cruising down the coast of Texas on the 5th inst. When about thirty miles below Galveston and near Pass San Luis, a schooner was discovered lying inside the shoal, under the protection of a battery on the point over which floated the confederate flag. Capt. Hunter at once decided to capture the vessel at any risk, and leaving his anchored his steamer within four miles of the schooner, he proceeded to convert her into a resemblance of a merchant steamer. The guns were drawn in, the port holes closed, and the gun on the forecastle covered up with a canvass. The crew with the exception of some dozen men who were disguised as common sailors were sent below, an English ensign set at the peak, a secession flag at the fore and a burgee, with the name of the mortar schooner "*Adolph Hugel*"[1] which the captain had presented to Captain Hunter, was hoisted

[2]

at the main. A swivel gun was fired as a signal for a pilot, which not being regarded by the enemy, at the expiration of two hours another shot was fired. Soon after a life boat containing ten men was seen to put off from the shore, and having passed through the breakers, it hauled up, the occupants appearing to be in consultation about proceeding to the steamer. The swivel was again fired, which seemed to decide the conference, as the boat came out and alongside, the captain, a pilot, and a young Texan who was introduced as Lieut. Edwards, stepped on board. In the meantime arrangements had been made to give the rebels a proper reception. The marines were drawn up in the ward room, and Acting Master Fletcher, introducing himself as Capt. Smith of the English steamer "*Adolph Hugel*," from Hall via Nassau, with a cargo of arms, ammunition and salt, invited them down to take some refreshments. Nothing suspecting, the two men descended to the gun deck when, catching sight of the battery they instantly realized the trap into which they had fallen, and exhibited signs of a weakness in the knees. Before they had time to fully realize their position Capt. "Smith" informed them that they were prisoners of war on board the United States Steamer "Montgomery." They received the intelligence with fattening heads, and acknowledged with as much grace as possible under

[3]

the circumstances, that the trick was well played. Edwards proved to be a Lieutenant in Capt. Ballou's company of the 6th Regiment Texas volunteers, commanded by Col. Bates. His company of one hundred men were stationed at Fort San Luis, and his captain, who was on a visit in the country had ordered him, in case he was attacked not to fire away any ammunition as *they had but a small quantity and that was of an inferior quality.* The men on the boats were privates in Capt. Ballou's company, and being ordered on board they were all detained as prisoners. The life boat fell into its rightful owners, it having been stolen by the rebels when they seized the coast survey schooner "_____² King." Edwards who is a son of a gentleman of wealth in Galveston was greatly surprised when instead of being placed in double irons and put in confinement, he was invited into the ward room to mess with the officers. It was ascertained that the fortifications commanding the pass consisted of one shore battery of two eighteen pounders, and another in the rear and above the first, in which were mounted six small howitzers.

To capture the schooner, boats were obliged to pass within two hundred yards of the battery; nevertheless it was decided to cut her out if possible. Accordingly the captured life boat in charge of Acting Master Thomas Pickering, and the captain's gig in charge of Master's Mate Barston with a force of eighteen men, were

[4]

sent in. On reaching the point they were hailed by a sentinel, and answered "all right." This did not evidently satisfy the sentry who fired his musket ball passing through the side of the boat. None was injured and the boats pulling alongside, the officers took possession of the vessel without opposition. The (ship) was found to be the schooner "*Columbia*" containing two hundred and seventy-five bales of cotton, and was intending to run the blockade for Kingston. Efforts were made by the captors to get the vessel out, failing in which, it was decided to burn her. Before firing her, a sailboat was discovered coming out to the schooner, and men being secreted behind the cotton bags, they awaited her approach. As the boat came alongside a man, who proved to be the captain of the Columbia, sang out "Take that line forward on the port side." The order was obeyed and as soon as the boat was alongside Acting Master Pickering called out "Boarders Away." The men responded when the captain cried out "Boarders! What Boarders? This is not my vessel." But it was too late; the boarders were upon him and secured all who were in the boat, including five passengers who were bound for Kingston. The vessel was then set on fire and the captors with their prisoners started for the steamer. Finding it hazardous to attempt to get the sailboat through the breakers,

[5]

The prisoners were detained till the schooner was burned to the water's edge when they were allowed to make the best of their way back to land, and the expedition returned to the steamer which they reached about seven on the next morning! If all the confederate officers are of the same way of thinking as Lieut. Edwards, they are certainly sick of the war, for in conversation with him one day he said he would willingly give five years of his life to see the trouble ended. The "*Montgomery*" has heretofore suffered from the inefficiency of her commander, but this expedition of Lieut. Hunter will ensure the steamer and her officers honorable mention in the history of the war.

> *This article may have been the first of the series of articles of "Agaius," written on sheets 4' × 13", much smaller than all the others. One titled "Seeking Information Under Difficulties" follows, and is not the same as another article transcribed later.*

Recollections of the Siege of Forts Jackson and St. Phillip and the Capture of New Orleans

Our correspondent Agaius furnishes the following items condensed from voluminous reports of scenes and incidents which he witnessed during the siege of the defenses of New Orleans, and after the capture of that city.

Seeking Information Under Difficulties [1]

My experience in obtaining information from the squadron during the siege would of itself furnish material for a long chapter. As the correspondent of the Journal I was uniformly received with courtesy by the officers of every ship I visited, but I was especially indebted to Capt. Guest of "*Owasco*," for the loan of a small boat, which in the hands of myself and the correspondent of the New York Times came to be known throughout the squadron as the "Press Gig." During the bombardment our dingy might have been seen flying from ship to ship, now struggling against the strong current, which had a tendency to develop the muscle of the occupants. Boarding a gunboat returning from an engagement with the enemy; again drifting down the line of mortars, while the shot and shell from the rebel batteries fell thickly about our frail bark, and screamed in the ears of her occupants too audibly for comfort or security. We felt it however to be well-nigh as hazardous to board the large ships, past whose sides the rapid current often swept at the rate of five knots, as to lay out under fire.

> *The following series of reports from one single comprehensive letter covers the heart of the New Orleans battle. A.G. Hills, along with along with Henry Winser of the New York Times, occupied a small boat*

nicknamed the "press gig" that rowed between attacking U.S. Navy ships to gather information about the battle. Other times he was allowed access high aboard warships to gain a birds-eye view of the battle. There was a lot of activity occurring simultaneously, and all phases of the action could not be covered by one correspondent. The battle described happened after the bombardment of Forts Jackson and St. Phillip. The Union fleet was on the move to pass the forts without first capturing them. Heavy smoke on the river made target selection difficult at best. Hills describes the sanding of the decks of the ships to improve the footing of the sailors and rebel intelligence as the fleet moved upriver. After the passing of the forts and their eventual surrender Hills describes the effects of the mortar bombardment and the reasons behind the surrender. As a reporter he seeks the reason for the defeat from the rebel press and details the personal cost of the victory while visiting the hospital at Pilot Town down the river.

U.S. Steamer *J.P. Jackson* off New Orleans April 30, 1862

After a roving existence of five months in the Gulf of Mexico, during which I have endeavored to keep the readers of the Journal informed of all that has transpired in connection with the movements of the land and naval forces engaged in the suppression of the rebellion, I find myself at length at the threshold of the city against which the resistless power of the federal government has been steadily and resolutely directed. The duty of recording the movements of the blockading fleet, the capture of the Confederate vessels, and the trifling engagements in which our cruisers have been engaged, was easy in comparison with the gigantic task of collecting from the mass of notes which I have taken, a concise and perspicuous narrative of the thrilling events which have culminated in the reduction of the rebel fortification of the lower Mississippi, and the capture of the Great Cotton Metropolis of the bogus Confederacy. One cannot be expected to perform impossibilities and if I fail to notice the gallant conduct of individual ships, their commanders and officers or to record incidents which, though of importance, are overtopped by the grand spectacle,
[2]
it will not be from any intention to overlook the merits of deserving men who have favored me with their experience or to omit the slightest circumstance which has contributed to the grand result, but rather from a lack of opportunity to witness every scene in this stirring tragedy of which I have been a vigilant spectator, and time to call them from the overstocked pages of my diary of each day's events. Not being ubiquitous,

it cannot be expected that I shall be present at the pulling down of the rebel flags on the Custom House and Mint at New Orleans while witnessing the evacuation of the forts by the confederate troops. As the correspondent of the Journal, I have been received numerous attention from the officers of the several ships, and every possible facility in the way of obtaining information, still without boat which through the generosity of Capt. Guest of the *Owasco*, I have used in company with Mr. Winser of the Times, I should have had to depend upon flying reports the details of which in times like these have to be taken with more than average allowance. Throughout the bombardment the "Press Gig," as our boat came to be
[3]
familiarly known through the squadron, might have been seen flying from ship to ship, now struggling against the rapid current to board some gun boat just retired, with her decks scarred and bloody from an engagement with the enemy and again drifting down the line of mortars, her occupants watching the effect of the firing on the vessels, while the shot and shell of the enemy whistle in unpleasant proximity to their respective persons. My aquatic experience has convinced me of one thing, sir; that it is much easier to go down with stream than to pull up against it les the rower have never so much muscle. The Mississippi is not only a river of ungovernable strength but of magnificent distances, and when, on the evening after the fleets passed the forts, in which at the time were momentarily expected to surrender, the mortar flotilla which furthermore I found a habitation and a home was born. Slowly down to its anchorage off Pilot Town, I could not but repeat my declination of numerous invitations to run the gauntlet of the forts, that I might have witnessed the progress of the Union fleet up the river, and the astonishment of the proud people of New Orleans of its appearance off their city.
[4]
But fated as I was to remain in the rear, it has not been without its advantages. I have the satisfaction of accompanying the van of the Union Army of Occupation up the Mississippi, of witnessing the humiliation of a defiant and baffled foe; of visiting the fortifications over which the star spangled banner again floats and of judging from observation the effects of the bombardment to which they were subjected. It has been my privilege to witness the evacuations of Forts Jackson and St. Phillip by the misguided and deluded soldiers of the southern Confederacy, to converse with the victims of a cunning and unscrupulous pit of traitors, and to gather from them and their late stronghold abundant material for the edification and instruction of the loyal people of New England. The sudden departure of

the vessel by which I sent my last letter compelled me to cut short my account of the bombardment of the forts, and to omit altogether my
[5]
description of the action which will forever be known as the most daring and severe and resulting in the most brilliant achievement of the American Navy.

It was said of Flag Officer Farragut, before the final action that "he had his hobby" that he considered wooden sides superior to brick walls. I do not pretend to say, in fact I disagree altogether with the assumption of the brave and active commander-in-chief, for whom I entertain the highest respect, but after the brilliant success which has crowned his labors I must confess that a strong force of steam vessels moving past a casemated fort offers an uncertain target to the most skillful artilleryman. The success of the expedition is however do as much to its coolness, perseverance, and indomitable resolution displayed by the commanders and men under his command, as to its bold and able men.
[6]

The Plan for the Advance of the Squadron

For several days prior to the action, Flag Officer Farragut held frequent consultations with the commanders of all the ships in the squadron relative to the plan of making the final attack upon and passage of the forts. The main question discussed was whether to proceed against them in daytime or night, upon which there was a difference of opinion. The majority were in favor of a night attack as presenting less damage to the men and ships. There was no expectation of surprising the enemy, whose silence for thirty-six hours before the action was sufficient proof that he was reserving his fire for the anticipated approach of the fleet, but the darkness was calculated to distract the aim of the rebels, and so it proved. The idea of attempting to reduce the forts by cannonading was abandoned, and the plan adopted to force a passage and push on to the city at once, in order to cut off reinforcements and supplies, as the surest way to possess the forts, while the presence of our fleet above the forts would enable Butler to land his troops and if necessary proceed against fort St. Phillip under cover of the gunboats.

On the 20th (instant) the flag officer issued an order for the squadron to advance on the night of the 22nd, but one or two ships were not in fighting trim, and to the great disappointment of all, the attack was not made. Officers and men were impatient at the delay. They had nerved themselves for the hazardous trial, and stacked their lives upon the issue. The rebel flags had flung defiance in their faces, and the hissing missiles of the enemy had whistled about their heads full long enough. Ten o'clock

the hour fixed upon for the advance of the squadron approached, and yet no signal had come from the
[7]
flagship. Anchors were hove short, decks white washed to light up the ships which were to pour their broadsides into the rebel stronghold. The fires were raked open, and from the surcharged boilers the steam came hissing with impatience. The gruff order of the boatswain, "up all hammocks," was an indication that the fleet was about to get underway; but still no lights apparent at the missing peak of the *Hartford*. Stillness reigned on the river, broken only by the deep boom of the mortars, as they busted the flickering globes up into the heavens and down upon the beleaguered garrison when secure behind their casemates awaited the coming foe. Suddenly from out of the darkness which enveloped the river and the forts, not a zone of lunar lights which moving rapidly towards the fleet, disclosed another of the weak inventions with which the enemy harassed us. As the fire raft rounded the point and came into the broad stream, its resinous flames darted upward lighting the placid surface of the river, the ships, and the foliage as it drifted towards us. The bells of the squadron rang out the alarm, and instant an hundred boats put off to meet the blazing rebel. A heavy volume of smoke
[8]
rolled sluggishly upward from the raft, casting a sable canopy over the river, and rendering the scene at once grand and appalling. Two or three steamers on guard, that night ran boldly upon the wicked craft, crushing it beneath their tons, while the sailors with their buckets deluged and extinguished the flames. Sent singly and our boys wanted no better fun than to fight the fire rafts, but had the rebel commander been harmonious in their defense, and shrewd enough to chain several of them together and stretched them across the river they would have thrown our ships into inextricable confusion and compelled them to drop down the river. Seeing that the fire rafts were quickly disposed of one after another, the enemy set adrift a dark raft of heavy logs, which swept across the chains of the *Hartford*, creating momentary confusion, resulting in a serious accident. In the attempt to get it clear of the ships by passing our chain, the capstan revolved with lightning rapidity, knocking down and injuring six men.
[9]

The Passage of the Forts

I acknowledge myself unequal to the task of describing even what I witnessed on the morning of the 24th, when the squadron forced a passage up the river under a shower of iron hail, such as no fleet has ever before encountered. Words are but tame impotent symbols of the events, and as best can convey but a faint idea of the appalling nature of the action.

[10]

The moon was first rising as the fleet got underway. Fort St. Phillip opened up every battery and the gunboats gallantly replying quickly disappeared amid the darkness. Soon the large ships were lost in the impenetrable smoke of battle relieved only by the sharp flashes of fire as the action became general. As the ships brought the broadside guns to bear, they vomited their contents upon the rebel forts, which disputed every inch of their progress. The scene becomes grand, awful, appealing as first we could distinguish the fire of the forts, and the heavy reports of the broadside batteries, but soon all is mingled in a prolonged roar, as of heavy thunder. Clouds of smoke are borne away by the still morning breeze, and we catch glimpses of the stars and stripes borne aloft amid the din of battle. The old flag never looks so beautiful as now. The cheers and shouts of our brave sailors reach our ears,

[11]

mingled with crashing of timbers as the rifled shot of the enemy bore their way through the wooden walls of the ships, the fleet passes on and immediately encounters the rebel gunboats, and then comes the most fearful scene of the action. We see nothing up the river but smoke and conflict mingled with the shouts of the victors and the shrieks of the dying. All is chaos. The current carries down the wrecks of the battle, dead bodies, shell boxes, splinters, and logs set adrift. Now three gunboats coming from the smoke one after another, and drifts down the current, pursued by the screaming rifled shot of the enemy. The *Winona* Lt. Commander Nichols formerly attached to the Navy Yard in Charleston, ran up close to

[12]

the guns of St. Phillip where she was exposed to the murderous fire from the guns in battery of the fort. He sheared off into the stream when the guns of Jackson were trained upon him. With the fire of both forts concentrated on his ship, Capt. Nichols, finding his men were being sacrificed without the possibility of getting through returned with a loss of three killed and six wounded, and five shot in his vessel. One shot killed and wounded every man at the rifled gun. One man was cut completely in two and knocked overboard. The killed were Alexander Tyler, boatswain, _____[3] Brown, ordinary seaman, and Charles Desney ordinary seaman. Among the severely wounded were Leonard Minnot, Michael Holland and George Thomas.

[13]

At 5 o'clock the *Harriet Lane* and the other steamers he attached to

the mortar flotilla having performed their duty, gracefully returned from the position where they poured an enfilading fire of shrapnel upon the exposed ramparts of Fort Jackson. Commander Porter set up three rockets as a signal for the mortars to cease fire and an exultant shout broke forth along the line of schooners. "They fought like brave men and well," and piled the ground with rebel slain and after a protracted bombardment of six days and five nights they were not loathe to suspend their labors. But their rest was of short duration. The rebels fought with the desperation of despair and nothing daunted by the loss of their prey, immediately set about for a renewal of the conflict. A powerful ironclad battery called the *Louisiana* which was brought down from New Orleans a few days before the action sustained the fire of the ships, the shot which glanced off from it, and left it the formidable opponent uninjured. The rebels endeavored to arm it with cannon from the fort, but the bombs fell too thickly about it, and they were baffled in their efforts. As soon however as the mortars ceased firing they erected
[14]
a derrick, and began to transfer guns from Fort Jackson to the battery. This fact being reported to Commander Porter, he ordered the flotilla to open fire upon, and in a moment the air resounded the deep boom of the mortars, which hurled their destructive missiles upon the heads of the enemy.

The morning's rosy light dissipated the gloom which had shrouded the river and turning from the conflict still waging above the forts. I attempted to gather some tidings of the fray. The sand decks of the *Harriet Lane* were saturated with the blood of two of the victims of the slaughter. She had been struck twice, one shell hit the sail on the bridge, where Commander Porter and Lt. Commander Wainwright were standing, and cutting off a piece about 4 inches long sent it whissing through the body of one sailor, killing him almost instantly, a second shot carried away the leg of another who was serving the after port gun.
[15]

Sinking of the Ram Manassas

About 8 o'clock in the morning a suspicious looking craft drifted down the east side of the river, exciting by her strange movement the fears of the timid, and curiosity of all. She looked like an enormous turtle, or as one of the sailors said, "like an old right whale." She had two smokestacks, one of which had been knocked askew by a shot. A volume of smoke poured out of a port hole in her bow, which was soon followed by a sheet of flame. It did not require much observation to satisfy us that the black unwieldy hulk was the notorious ram *Manassas*, and the once dreaded, now maimed and harmless rebel, became a target for the mortar men, who fired their long thirty-two's at her as she passed. She was boarded by Mr. Morris, Masters Mate of the *Horace Beals*, who secured the log slate which was written up to 8 o'clock the previous evening. She sunk about four miles below the forts. Soon after, another rebel steamer drifted by the fleet. It drifted passed and brought up on the bow at SW Pass. [16]

"The Forts Have Surrendered to the Mortar Fleets"

Such was the announcement which reached our ears on the morning of the 28th, from the trumpet of Capt. Guest of the *Owasco*, who came down to Pilot Town to bring the gratifying intelligence. We had seen the *Owasco* approaching with the stars and stripes displayed fore and aft, and long before she reached the bayou off which the Sea Foam, my temporary home, lay at anchor, we anticipated her mission. She passes the sloop of war *Portsmouth* and communicated the glad tidings, the sailors respond to the order, "Cheer Ship," and the air resounds with the shouts of the jubilant crews. The news of the surrender spread through the fleet of mortar vessels and supply and ordinance ships, and one after another they take up the shout, until the reeds and cane breaks echo the loud huzzas. The news is electrifying and flies with lightning rapidity, from ship to ship. Then our hearty hand shakings, vociferous cheers, mutual congratulations, exultant shouts throughout the fleet. In the ecstasy of delight men suddenly generous, and offer to give away all their clothes, the elongated countenances of the desponding relax into smiles, the officers of an English man of war below us, on learning the news, are heard to declare "We shall all have to turn farmers now, what is the use of wooden ships when you have such vessels as the *Monitor*, or Forts when you can pass them in this way?" [17]

All the bunting is got and flung to the breeze. Secession flags captured by blockading vessels are displayed in their appropriate place beneath the stars and stripes, and the fleet suddenly assumes a holiday appearance, Fourth of July, Seventeenth of June, Twenty-second of February[4] all mingled in the twenty-eighth of April, 1862. Now for the forts; But how shall we get there. Our gig is not a steamer, nor our muscles a steam engine.[5] We must bide our time and take the first vessel bound up. We have not long to wait. The steamer *J.P. Jackson* is on the point of starting and captain Woodworth generously offers us a passage and a home on his steamer as long as we choose to remain. On board the *Jackson* I meet an old friend and skillful seaman in the person of Sailing Master Dearborn, who has

carried the ship up and down the hazardous stream ever since the commencement of the siege, during which the Jackson has done good service not only in towing the mortar vessels and transports; but in fighting the rebels. Now we are underway. The current seems stronger than normal so impatient are we to heed the sacred soil of Dixie. A vague rumor reaches us that four ironclad gunboats from Mobile have come down to Ship Island and commenced shelling the troops encamped there. The report was unfounded though with their long range pieces the enemy may at any time harass the army of Butler. Captain Woodworth orders the engines of the Jackson "open her wide and give her all the steam you can," and on she leaps against the tortuous current. We pass the old position of the mortar fleet, and the squadron, now exercising a wholesome restraint over the traitors and protecting the Union people of New Orleans. At their anchorage in Oyster Bay, the troop ship *Mississippi, Matanzas, Great Republic* and the *Henry Lewis* are disembarking troops to garrison the forts. The New England boys have seen no fighting yet but
[18]
a more difficult and delicate task is before them. We take no heed of the thatched cabins on the banks of the river, or the secesh cattle, whose fellows have furnished many a dish of "sirloin rare" and "well done" during the siege. All eyes are directed at the forts. We approached the point below Fort Jackson, when the rebels felled the trees to obtain a wide range for their guns, and St. Phillip with its long low ramparts bristling with an array of dark muzzles which no longer gape angrily as we near them, is the first fort opened to our view. As we round the point the crouching walls of Fort Jackson half hid in its slough, it's stinging cannon so lately irate and boisterous, now meek and bashful, with their faces to the wall, lies before us. The "bars and stars" which so long flung defiance in the face of the besiegers has given place to the proud emblem of a broad nationality, and on both forts, the star spangled banner hangs drooping to the masts, as if considerate of the feelings of the vanquished foe, and waiting for them to take their departure, before unfolding its bright colors over its scene of triumph.

Visit to Fort Jackson

Immediately after the arrival opposite the forts, our steamer was moved back down the river to tow up a troop ship, and leaping into our rig, we pulled up to the landing of Fort Jackson. A sergeant of the Confederate Army made fast the painter, and climbing over a pile of sandbags which were brought down from New Orleans during the fight to repair the damage inflicted by our shells, we picked our way over the wreck of demolished barracks and blockhouses, through a slimy turpentine slough, along a

[19]
narrow levee, with barrels of tar and rosin on either side, the remnant of the stock from which the rebels drew their fuel for their fire rafts; and reaching the mote, we are ferried across a green and stagnant ditch in a barge which has usurped the place of the wooden bridge leading to the fort. The ground around the fort is flooded and we now see whence came the columns of water and mud which bellowed the descent of our bomb. At the entrance we met commanders Porter and Smith and Col. Jones of the 26th. Commander Smith looks none the worse from his conflict with the ram, and the indominable Porter, master of the stronghold which he labored so long and zealously to reduce, justly claims for the mortar flotilla the honor of the victory, and points exultingly to the fissures in the walls, the ruined citadel, the barbette guns dismounted, the gaping pits. On the ramparts, glacis, and within the fort; its crumbling roofs of casemates shattered by the terrible shock of the bombs, as evidence of the accuracy and aim and destructive fire of the mortars. The interior of the fort, the casemates and the parapet, exhibited the effects of the bombardment, and the desperate struggle of the enemy to prevent the passage of the squadron. Powder, shot and shell, muskets, rifles, equipments, were scattered about in reckless confusion, while trophy hunters were searching every nook and corner for mementos of the siege. The
[20]
arms and accoutrements of the garrison were left in perfect order, no attempt having been made to destroy any of the public property. Eleven guns were dismounted during the bombardment. The citadel was a mass of ruins and several of the casemates were rendered untenable. About eight thousand bombs were thrown by the flotilla during the siege, at least eighteen hundred of which fell within the fort. Only two simple wooden buildings were left standing outside the fort, besides the hospital, which was riddled by the fire of Fort St. Phillip the night the fleet passed up. There was about sixty days provisions in the fort when the rebels evacuated.
[21]

The Mutiny in Fort Jackson —
Desertion of Three Hundred Men

The sudden and unexpected change in the spirit of the commander of Fort Jackson arose from the demoralization and desertion of a large portion of his command. After the fleet had passed the forts and proceeded up to New Orleans, the troops who "fought as brave men long and well" for the defense of the city, became disheartened, and exhibited signs of insubordination. They saw the ships in the rear of St. Phillip landing troops, and all agree in saying they were resolved not to remain in the fort simply to defend a swamp, and be butchered by the overwhelming force advancing against them. Those of the soldiers with whom I conversed were not at all complimentary in their reference to the officers, whom they accused with cowardice, and said that they never exposed themselves to our fire except when its necessity was imperative. While the men were serving the barbette guns, under the terrible explosion of the bombs, the officers were securely in the casemates, from one to the other of which they moved as the bombs fell above them. Col. Higgins formed an exception to this sweeping change of pusillanimity, and when a private accused the officers with cowardice, a sergeant stepped forward and declared emphatically that a braver man than Ned Higgins did not exist. Gen. Duncan too was not wanting in pluck, for the soldiers say that even after the ships passed he declared he would slaughter every man before he would yield, and die himself in the trenches. The refusal of the commander to surrender finally led to open

[22]

revolt, which broke out among the garrison on the day previous to the surrender. Led on by a man familiarly known as Harry, a tall brawny Green Mountain boy, who being in New Orleans at the commencement of the war, was like thousands of others, forced to go to prison or starve. Three hundred men headed by this Harry refused to fight and through their officers reported their determination to the commander. Col. Higgins ordered the officers to put down the mutiny and attempted to quiet the men by telling them that reinforcements would soon be down and that Beauregard would come in person to command them, also that he could not surrender till he heard from New Orleans. But the disaffected soldiers led on by Harry took possession of the keys of the magazine, spiked all the guns bearing on the land side; filled their barracks with provision, and with their arms and clothing marched out of the fort on the evening of the 27th. The men who deserted were volunteers, principally from the parishes in the vicinity of New Orleans, and taking the "shell road" with epithets more expressive than refined towards their officers, they returned to their homes. With his force thus reduced it would have been folly for Gen. Duncan to have held out longer. He was cut off completely from the city; all the approaches to the fort from outside were cut off by our mortar vessels, and though he had sixty days provisions in the fort; still its reduction was only a question of time, and our fleet could afford to wait much longer than he could for the surrender,

[23]

which all felt must come sooner or later. But for the mutiny in Fort Jackson, we might still be below the forts. The feeling among the men in St. Phillip appeared to be much the same. They had made up their minds not to fight any longer after the fleet passed. The Delta says that by some traitorous means its reporters communicated to the garrison that the city had surrendered, that further resistance would be unavailing and that if the conflict was continued and the garrison captured they would all report to the Sword.

The Iron Clad Battling Louisiana *Blown up by the Rebels' Diabolical Attempt to Destroy the Union Steamers*

Pending the negotiations for the surrender of the forts, one of the utmost dastardly acts of war the rebels have been guilty during the rebellion was committed by the officers of the Confederate navy. While the conference of the commanders of the mortar flotilla and the forts, was going on in the cabin of the *Harriet Lane*, and while the flags of truce were flying on Forts Jackson and St. Phillip and the Steamer Lieut. John K. Mitchell and Lieut. A. F. Warley, both of whom were formerly officers in the U.S. Navy, having first collected the arms and accoutrements from the several steamers captured by Commander Porter, and placed them on board the Iron Clad battling *Louisiana*, set here on fire. This fact was reported to Commander Porter, and also that the battery was drifting down upon our steamers. He inquired of Col. Higgins if she had powder in her, to which he replied that he didn't know, that he was not responsible for the acts of the Naval Officers. The battery which mounted sixteen guns of heavy caliber and cost a million and a half of dollars to construct,

[24]

drifted down opposite St. Phillip, when the guns began to discharge from the intense heat, and in a few minutes she blew up with a tremendous explosion and disappeared altogether. One man was killed and a gun dismounted in St. Phillip by the fall of one of the iron bars which formed her roof. The battery was 140 feet long, 25 feet high, with slanting lids had four engines and two propellers, and was constructed very much after the model of Foote's gunboats. She was perfectly shot-proof, the heavy broad sides which our ships pound into her, made no impression, and had she come down among the mortar flotilla after the fleet past the forts, she would have proved a formidable opponents. Our officers were however prepared to receive her and if she had ventured below the forts, the *Westfield*, *Clifton*, and *Jackson* were to have steamed boldly upon her and crowded her ashore. On the morning of the action, Lieut. Dixon's Company of artillery were transferred to St. Phillip to *Louisiana* to work the guns, but the battery was not placed in a position to be of much service.

Three Rebel Steamers Captured

After the conference on the *Harriet Lane* had ended the flag officer was hauled over, the crew went to quarters and the steamer put underway and went up the river along the forts, where three rebel steamers the *Landis, Burton and Defiance* which escaped destruction of the fleet, were lying under the river bank. They were still in possession of the enemy, and had the Confederate flag flying. A rifle shot was fired from the *Harriet Lane's* Parrot gun, and the Secesh rags came

[25]

came down instantly. Lieut. Commander Wainwright went onboard demanded their unconditional surrender, and received the swords of the rebel officers, among them Commander Mitchell, Lieut. Comm J. McKinson, A. F. Warley and Lieut. MC Whyttle who were implicated in the cowardly act of blowing up the *Louisiana*. They sent a message to Commander Porter, saying they did not suppose the battery would drift down upon our steamers, but their infamous conduct was not excused and they were conveyed on board the steamer *Clifton* where they have since been kept close prisoners of war and fed on Philips rations. The *Defiance* was a gun boat and carried one rifled gun. She was partially sunk but has since been raised and is now doing good Union service in towing our store ships upriver. Before the rebels left her, they destroyed all her glass, mutilated the furniture, threw a large quantity of arms overboard which has furnished piscatorial occupation for our sailors who have fished up a large number of muskets and cutlasses. The *Landis* and *Burton*, are lofty river steamers (tugs), the latter suffered terribly in the action of the 24th. Her pilot was found dead in the wheelhouse, her Captain was wounded and the steamer riddled through and through with shot and shell.

[26]

How the Rebels Account for their Defeat

The significant remark of Gen. Duncan during the conference on board the *Harriet Lane*, disclaiming all connection with the officers in command of the confederate gunboats, is the key to the failure of the rebel plans of defense which had been matured, and which failed through the cowardice or neglect of the naval officers to perform their part in the programme. Upon the commander of the *Louisiana* rests the heaviest responsibility. The Delta of May 1st, referring to the matter says the first of the causes of their defeat was the want of command, organization and energy in their squadron. The commanders refused or failed to watch and defend the chains they think would not have been cut away if the gunboats had taken the place they were directed to take in order to protect it. The

Louisiana with its powerful battery was rendered of no use by the refusal of her commander to place her in a position where she could be effective. After the chain was cut several of the hulks were filled with combustible materials (which a rebel soldier informed me) and have been set on fire when our fleet approached by means of a battery at Fort Jackson. In a note to McIntosh, the commander of the *Louisiana*, Gen. Duncan says the lower schooner
[27]
will be lighted by firing her from a row boat from Fort St. Phillip at early dusk, and as this one dies away the next one will be fired and so on, all night. But the electric apparatus did not work effectively, and the fleet passed under cover of the darkness. The battery has since been found and is in possession of Lieut. Comdg. Woodworth of the steamer *J.P. Jackson*. "The Delta says that as long as the duty of keeping the river lighted was confided to the forts, it was promptly and regularly done, but when the ships undertook it, it was grossly neglected, and on the night of this passage of the enemy it was entirely omitted."

The following letter which I have been permitted by Commander Porter to copy from the original in his possession, while it pays a flattering compliment to the mortar flotilla by admitting the effect which this fire produced on the fort, also leads to the conclusion that the unfortunate McIntosh was not alone responsible for the non–execution of the pre–concerted plan of defense.
[28]

Fort Jackson La
April 22nd, 1862

Captain,

Your note of this date relative to the steamer Louisiana, the forwardness of their preparations for attack, the disposition to be made of her and received.

It is of vital importance that the present fire of the enemy should be withdrawn from us, which you alone can do. This can be done in the manner suggested this morning, under the cover of our guns where your work on the boat can still be carried out in safety and security.

Our position is a critical one, dependent entirely upon the powers of endurance of our casemates, many of which have been completely shattered and are crumbling away by repeated shock and I respectively but earnestly again urge my suggestions of this morning upon your notice. Our magazines are also in danger.

Very respectfully your obt serv
J.K. Duncan[6]

Capt. J.K. Mitchell
Comdg. Naval Forces
Lower Mississippi River

[29]

It was a part of the plan of defense to set adrift a large fleet of fire rafts as soon as soon as the squadron began to move up the river, but fifty-five rafts which had been ordered were not completed and a large amount of turpentine and rosin which the rebels expected to obtain from Mobile, was not forthcoming. I have no means of judging how many fire rafts were burned during the grand attack, but from what I have seen I imagine their stock of this means of defense to have been low. One raft remains unscorched after the action. 21 laid below Fort Jackson and was partially filled with wood, barrels of tar and loose cotton. The only ship which from first to last sustained any injury or was in eminent danger from the fire rafts was the *Hartford*, which was set on fire by one of them pushed against her by a rebel steamer.

[30]

As I stated in my last letter, the enemy was perfectly aware of the object the reconnaissance of the Coast Survey Officers, as is proved by a telegraphic dispatch which Gen Duncan sent to Gen Lovell, on the 14th, the original of which was found in Fort Jackson. It runs this: "the enemy has triangulated the points below, and put up signal flags, preparatory to placing his mortar boats. <u>We will remove them tonight if possible.</u>" He did so as I stated.

The sharp shooters who were encamped in the woods below the woods, where the Lieut. Bruce, discovered the remains of their camp, claimed to have killed two of men in the launches on the 14th and Gen Duncan the false report worth telegraphing to the Commander and Chief.

The sharp shooters appear to have performed another equally brilliant exploit, namely, seven of our men, who have not as yet been reported as missing. On the 15th (Capt.) Mullen their commander telegraphed to Quarter Master D. Bidwell as follows: "Quitma says got about seven of them — one big officer; had been drowned out of the swamp, and was moving above fort." This may however refer to the recapture of some of their deserters.

[31]

The rebels had a telegraphic operator named Stickney at the "Jump," who kept Gen. Duncan fully informed of all the movements of our vessels from the time they made their first appearance within sight of that point. He evidently occupied an exposed position where he was in danger of discovery by our ships, for on the 14th, Gen. Duncan telegraphed to him as follows:

"Endeavor to run your line into some concealed shelter where you can telegraph in security to yourself. If a strict watch be kept, you can see the approach of the enemy and keeping clear of boats inform me imme-

diately." Duncan wanted Stickney to inform him of every vessel that passed, and to take particular notice, in order that he might enumerate the whole if necessary.
[32]

The same officer announced that "the boys got another rap at them yesterday, knocking over some five or six from a launch." If by this message, Capt. Mullen wishes the world to believe that five or six Union men were rolled out of a launch, all I can say is that we "doubt it in that light."
[33]

The Abandonment of Fort Livingston by the Rebels

In the midst of the rejoicings of the brilliant victory on the river comes the unexpected and gratifying intelligence that Fort Livingston at the entrance to Barataria Bay had been abandoned and that the old flag again floated over it. The first report of the event reached me in a hurried note from an officer on board the U.S. gunboat *Kittatinny*, Capt. Lamson of Beverly, Mass, who shares in the honor of the capture. You will probably receive minute details of the affair from the correspondent of the *Journal* on board the *Kittatinny*, but as the mortar flotilla had a hand in the massive affair I will venture to anticipate his report. The *Kittatinny* had been blockading off Barataria Bay some ten days when on the 27th of April the mortar schooner "*Henry James*,"[7] Capt. L. W. Pennington, one of six vessels which Commander Porter dispatched to blockade Bastian Bay and the rear approaches to Fort Jackson, to prevent supplies from reaching the besieged garrison, was carried by the current away from her station, down to within a few miles from the fort. I can best
[34]
describe what followed by including my report with snatches of braggadocio in which a mercurial correspondent of the *Picayune,* indulged in a letter written only eighteen days before, that their hundred "brave and gallant Louisianians" under command of Col. Paul E. Thiard, a young Creole, took to their heels and fled at the approach of a single bomb schooner. The rebels were "spoiling for a fight" for he says "although panting for an attack we have no prospect of a fight at this post. He hears "that an attack is being made upon Forts Jackson and St. Phillip." The concussion of the bombardment subsequently broke the glass and rattled the crockery at Fort Livingston, and the approach of one of those same "bummers" alarmed the bold soldiers of the Confederacy. This victim of cacoethes scribendi,[8] begs his dear Pie, "not to sink all the Yankee gunboats. It would be unfair. Our boys are anxious for a brush, and if Gen. Lovell will only spare some four or five and send them here, I pledge my word that there will be as

fine a display of courage and gallantry, as ever was witnessed on this continent! Brave words. But at sight of one of these puny vessels, backed by a volunteer commander from the "Hub of the Union,
[35]
the courage of the Soldiers of the Pelican State, oozes out of their heels, they blow up their magazines and beat an inglorious retreat. There are, he says, some three hundred Louisianians, forfeited almost, in a fort on a barren island. The general himself takes no heed of us. But their day has come, and then seeing upon it, there will be a hard fought battle and many a laurel won." It seems by the officers of two Federal schooners carried by accident within sight of the rebel garrison, who a few days before indulged in a hearty laugh when "a puny vessel bore in sight, and the impudent Lincolnites saluted us at a distance of three miles with two shells!" They had powder to spare and made no response to the demonstration of Commander Woodhull of the U.S. ship *Connecticut*. He tried the range of his Parrott gun on the fort. "Such fellows" says the "special" of the Picayune, "will never disable our dreams." But if there is any attempt calculated to "affright the souls of fearful adversaries, "it is the huge mortars that have laid Fort Jackson in ruin.

The fort was abandoned on the morning of the 27th of April, and Capt. Lamson of the *Kittatinny* seeing a flag of truce immediately dispatched a boat and took possession of the fort. The Stars and Stripes were hoisted over by Masters Mate J. H. Gregory who is a native of Marblehead, Mass. The rebels lost during
[36]
the siege fifteen killed and thirty seven wounded. In St. Phillips ten men were killed and five wounded. Lieut. Comdg. C. F. McIntosh of the ironclad battery *Louisiana* had an arm shot off and both legs broken.

The loss on our side as far as they have been reported are as follows: *Hartford* 3 killed, 10 wounded; *Brooklyn* 9 killed, 26 wounded; *Pensacola* 2 killed, 33 wounded; *Richmond* 2 killed, 4 wounded; *Mississippi* 2 killed, 6 wounded; *Cayuga* 6 wounded; *Sciota* 2 wounded; *Katahdin* none killed or wounded; *Varuna* (sunk) 3 killed, 9 wounded; *Winona* 3 killed, 5 wounded; *Itasca* 4 wounded. The Mortar Flotilla lost one man killed and one wounded the first day of the bombardment, and had five wounded in the subsequent days.
[37]

The Wounded Hospital at Pilot Town

On the evening of the day on which I dispatched my letter by the "*Dan Smith*." I went on shore at my old quarters at Pilot Town, and visited

the Naval Hospital where all the wounded during the bombardment were conveyed before the final action. Several gunboats had by turns been employed in their duty; among them the *Katahdin* Lieut. Comdg. Preble, who when not under fire was actively engaged in fighting fire rafts and other important duties. Entering the largest of the buildings, which had been comfortably filled up with bedsteads found in the deserted dwellings of the fugitive Secessionists. I met Dr. Wales the resident surgeon under whose skillful attention our brave sailors are rapidly recovering. To whom I am indebted for the following list of the wounded then in the hospital. Michael Brady, carpenter, bomb schooner *Norfolk Packet*, slight wound in leg by explosion of a shell; John Moir, sloop of was *Oneida*, slight contusion of thigh; J. A. Miller, seaman, *Oneida*, left hand amputated; Patrick Flynn, bomb schooner *Maria J. Carlton*, simple fracture of leg; George Scott, *Oneida*, slight wound of knee; Richard Graham, *Oneida*, slight contusion of thigh; Charles G. Murphy, *Oneida*, slight contusion of foot; Ernest Smerbing (?), schooner *Maria J. Carlton*, contusion of chest; Edward Perry, *Oneida*, slight contusion of foot; Joseph Judd, sloop of war *Iroquois*, gunshot wound in knee; John J. Wim, *Oneida*, leg and arm shot off, in critical condition; Dennis Disney, sloop of war *Hartford*, injury of lungs; George H. Miller, *Hartford*, slight fracture of arm; William English,
[38]
gunboat *Miami*, slight contusion of hip; Thomas Travers, gunboat *Winona*, contusion of head; William Wood, *Winona*, contusion of head; Michael Holland, amputation of leg; Leonard Winnot, *Winona*, gunshot wound of chest; George W. Huston, steamer *Harriet Lane*, amputation of thigh; John Hancock, a seaman on the sloop of war *Portsmouth*, who had a leg shot off in the action on the 24th, died after entering the hospital and was buried at Pilot Town.

I went through the wards and conversed with several of the poor fellows, who lay stretched on beds of pain. It was a sad spectacle calculated to awaken the most obdurate heart to sympathy. One complained that he got nothing to eat, deprived suddenly of his rations, he felt the last of his grog and "salt horse," but the surgeon knew what was best for him, and fed him sparingly. The most remarkable case was that of Mim the Quartermaster wounded on the *Oneida*. A young, athletic man who lost his left leg and left arm, he bore his sufferings with the fortitude of a hero. Constitutionally superior to the ever acute suffering he appeared cheerful and talked of going down into the other wards to open a prayer meeting among his fellow sufferers.

Charles O. Rogers was a publisher for the Boston Journal, *probably A.G. Hills' boss. The following was likely the first sent by A.G.*

Hills back to the Boston Journal *after the passage of the forts, and describes the battle and eventual surrender of New Orleans.*

Letter to Charles O. Rogers, April 28, 1862

Mississippi River April 28, 1862
To Charles O. Rogers
120 Washington Street Boston

The Sabastopol of Mississippi fallen. Fort Jackson and St. Phillip surrendered Commander David D Porter Union Mortar Flotilla. Squadron of Flag officer Farragut at anchor off city New Orleans in possession U.S. Forces. Stars and Stripes wave over Custom House, great stronghold rebellion ours, and Succession has received death blow. The twenty-eighth of April eighteen hundred sixty two will forever be a red letter day in history of the great southern rebellion.

We have passed through stirring
[2]
scenes, and witnessed thrilling events within the last ten days. Brave hearts have met determined and unscrupulous foe, and have vanquished him. The Confederate flags which have flaunted defiance in face of gallant defenders of glorious old ensign of Union, trails in dust at feet of conquerors and the Stars and Stripes float over the great cotton Memphis of the south. The enemy made bold and desperate resistance but has at length surrendered the defenses of New Orleans to the rightful possessors.

Forts Jackson and St. Phillip have sustained a protracted siege, the greatest naval engagement in the history of our Republic has been fought and a brilliant victory one. Immortal honors avail the heroes who have achieved the triumph.
[3]
On morning of 18th inst mortar flotilla commenced bombardment of Fort Jackson, supported by gun boats of Flag Officer Farragut's Squadron. Jackson and St. Phillip return fire in a series of sharp engagements occurred during the day. The second division of mortar vessels Lt. Commanding Queen stationed on the east bank of river, and first, Lt. Commanding Queen and third, Lt. Commanding Bruce on the west bank, distance one and two thirds miles from Jackson. The schooners *TA Ward* and *George Mangham* of Queens Division were struck by the enemy shot and one man killed. Forenoon and position too hot, Commander Porter ordered them rear of third division. Hostilities ceased at sun set and
[4]

Bombardment reopened morning 19th, continued day and night til morning 24th. Second day schooner *Maria J. Carleton* sunk by rebels, and mortar fire as going down. Sloop of *Oneida* struck by three shot, disabling after pivot gun, wounding nine men. Next day shell past through her smoke stack, cut off arm and leg of John J. Mim signal quarter master of *Brooklyn* and exploded under stern, still alive in hospital at Pilot town. Total casualties in mortar flotilla one man killed, six wounded. Exposed to terrific fire from both forts all through bombardment. *Iroquois, Oneida, Owasco* distinguished for bravery.

Night of 20th chain across river cut by gunboat *Itasca*, Lt. Commanding Caldwell of Boston, assisted by *Pinola*, Lt. Commanding Crosby.
[5]
Hulks drifted down. River clear obstructions. Except fire rafts — inoffensive, harmless, good sport for sailors extinguishing flames. Sent down almost every day and night. Rebels held fire both forts from four o'clock 22nd till advance.

Three and half o'clock morning of twenty-fourth, squadron got under way for grand attack and passage of forts. Signal lights at once made St. Phillip, answered Jackson and terrific fire opened on fleet by light of fires on shore. Ships and gunboats moved two lines. First division ships under Farragut on *Hartford*, and second division gunboats under Fleet Captain Bell engaged Jackson, Second Ships and five gunboats, Bailey of *Colorado*, steamers of mortar flotilla under Morris at St. Phillip. *Pensacola* and Commander Porter enfiladed Jackson. Fleet encountered fearful fire both forts. All but three gunboats (*Itasca, Winina, Kennebec*[9] passed up) ran gauntlet. As soon as
[6]
Union fleet passed line fire of forts, pouring in broadsides to both encountered Confederate navy. Magnificent spectacle, mortars belching, ships and forts tremendous cannonade. Ram *Manassas* bumped *Mississippi*, which single-handed vanquished her, Commander Warley late USN prisoner, ram sunk below forts. Terrible engagement above forts. *Hartford* set on fire by raft. Extinguished, lost two killed, eight wounded, all our ships suffered more or less. Alden of *Richmond* behaved great gallantry, dropping down after passing and pouring in another broadside. Eleven confederate steamers destroyed, U.S. Steamer *Varuna* sunk by enemy loss of three killed, seven wounded. At Quarantine Station, fleet took five hundred Confederate prisoners. Found large supply of coal. Buried dead and Farragut with all large ships and gunboats, save two pushed on to New Orleans. After passage of squadron Porter demanded unconditional surrender of forts, rebels fired on flag of truce, replied Col. Higgins, Commander

[7]
said terms inadmissible. Enemy employed 24th dismounting guns from Jackson on floating ironclad 16 gun battery, and four steamers left by our fleet as passed. Mortar flotilla retired to Pilot Town under cover of steamers under Porter. Small force of gunboats — to protect their formidable craft. No further demonstrations by rebels. Sunday Porter made another demand for surrender. Enemy still obstinate. Replied respectfully saying had not received official information. N. O. in possession U.S. forces and until did could not think surrendering.

On night before surrender three hundred of men in Jackson spiked guns and deserted. Next morning commander offered to surrender and conference held on board *Harriet Lane* when articles of capitulation signed.
[8]
New Orleans taken possession of by Flag Officer Farragut on 24th. American flag hoisted on Custom House and mint.

May 3rd, 1862

Butler's troops landed on 1st May, and invested city. Hear that they had mob yesterday and troops shot several of rioters.

> *The next report seems to be incomplete, focusing primarily on the actions of the USS* Mississippi *before actually combating the ram* Manassas. *Mr. Hills had a sketch of the CSS* Manassas *drawn just before the ram blew up. As Mr. Hills was not known to produce his own drawings, the sketch may have been made by William Waud, famous artist of the war, and there are multiple references to Hills' interaction with Waud in his journal.*

The *Mississippi* and the Ram *Manassas*

The prominent part which the frigate *Mississippi* played in the action of the 24th, as the destroyer of the notorious ~~ram~~ entitles her to special mention. As an illustration of the spirit which animated her commander and its officers and crew I must refer to an incident which transpired during the hour when the squadron, all in column and ready to move, were waiting for the signal from the flagship. The officers were sitting over their coffee in the ward-room chatting and cracking jokes as composedly as if they were sipping over one of Mrs. Haven's round tables; Commander Smith was pacing the quarter deck with his accustomed air of meditation, when her crew walked aft, and preferred a request to "splice the main brace, a term which for the benefit of this reader not versed in the vernacular of a man-of-war, applies to the extra rations of grog which the sailors usually

receive before or after the performance of extraordinary duties, and on occasions of rejoicing, as after the recent victory when the "main brace was spliced" fore and aft. Their request was not granted on this occasion, Commander Smith telling the men "we'll have no Dutch courage[10] tonight; we'll go into this thing with clear heads and sober senses," and so they did. Her men were served liberally
[2]
with hot coffee, and when they met the enemy they fought the better from having abstained from liquor. The *Mississippi* advanced in the column pitted against Fort St. Phillip, sailing Master King to whom I am indebted for the particulars of the movements on the spanker boom holding on the mizzen mast and curving the ship up by the forts and through the maze of rebel steamers. The ship had scarcely passed the line of the casemate fire of Fort Jackson when she grounded, and remained ashore about ten minutes, exposed to the barbette guns of both forts, and fire rafts on either side of her. The scene at this time was grand and yet terrific. The *Mississippi* was working both broadsides, and the other ships were pouring grape, canister, and shrapnel into these forts and steamers, which returned the fire with effect. In the midst of all this a solid forty-two pound shot, one of seventeen missiles which took effect in the *Mississippi*, came in between decks, and smashing mess chests and everything else in its course, passed through a solid bulk head into the engine room where Mr. Bartleman the first assistant engineer had a hair breadth escape from instant death. Another shot severed two mizzen stay, one demolished a boat and the hammock netting on her portside, and still another shot struck the ship without loss of life.

> *The next report includes the actions of the USS* Kineo *during the battle but also describes some of the damage to the forts from the bombardment of the mortar fleet. Some portions also allude to the number of New Englanders in New Orleans before the war, underscoring the population diversity of New Orleans, not seen in any other southern city.*

Letter from the Mississippi River

> US Gunboat Kineo
> Mississippi River
> May 5th, 1862

I joined the steamer this morning off Pilot Town, Lieut. Comdg. George M. Ransom, having kindly offered me a passage to New Orleans, and as the steamer is now underway, and some twenty-four hours will elapse before we reach the city, I propose to sketch the incidents which occur and the impressions I receive during my second passage up the Mississippi from its principal mouth, the South West Pass.

Picking Up Boats

Approaching the steam frigate *Mississippi* which, with her sister ships of the Union squadron, is now in full and undisputed possession of her aqueous namesake as far up as Carrollton. The order is given to "slow down," and instantly the jar of the propeller subsides, and the steamer, heading the current, holds her own, Capt. Ransom with trumpet in hand, mounts the aft rail and hails the *Mississippi* to learn if Commander Smith — every porthole broadside, bow and stern whose noble ship, bristles with cannon, among them the 32's of the ill-fated *Varuna*— has any message for the Flag Officer. The gallant commander replies from the hurricane deck that he is hurrying up as fast as he can, and as soon as he has finished coaling, we are confident that he will hasten to join the squadron, and move on to Baton Rouge,

[2]
Natchez, Vicksburg, and Memphis; or to proceed to the support of the Mortar Flotilla in their attack on Fort Morgan.

The *Kineo*, as well as many other gunboats in the squadron has lost her boats, some from collisions in which they were ground into splinters, and some from the perforation of shot and shell. The more fortunate commanders sympathize with the boatless steamers, and direct them to the bayous and secluded points on the river, where previous to the action; all the boats that could be spared were moored for safekeeping. Gen. Butler even offers Capt. Ransom his pick from the numerous launches with which he was provided to land his troops. The *Kineo* shoots ahead and across the Pass to a bayou, where a pilot's house has been converted a small hospital where the *Owasco* and other steamers stored their launches, spars, and rigging before going into action. Lieut. McKenzie is sent in to "fake his pitch." "All is fair in love," and so in war. The end justifies the means; boats are indispensable and they must be had by *hook* or by crook. But the *Owasco* has lost all the boats with which she started from Pilot Town before the fight. She escaped even a scratch during the bombardment, while drawing the fire of the forts from the mortar fleet, but going to New Orleans after the capture of the city, she collided with the *Brooklyn*, whose commander I am constrained to say, behaved most ungenerously towards Capt. Guest, who lost not only his boats, but his foremast and six of men narrowly escaped drowning.
[3]

Lieut. McKenzie returns empty-handed, reporting that the only boat to be had was too long and too heavy for our davits. Capt. Ransom being anxious to secure anything in the shape of a boat sends back and has her brought alongside. She proves to be a better boat than the one lost, and is hoisted at the same davits. Boats are at a premium now; the "Press Gig" even having been reclaimed and is now doing duty as launch cutters and gig to the *Owasco*.

"*Steady's the word*" and the *Kineo* pushes her prow against the waters which are rushing all the way from the falls of St. Anthony, the Rocky Mountains, the Alleghenies, and the great rain shed of the Valley of the West, down to the Gulf. From this point to the Head of the Passes the trip is devoid of interest, if we except the sight of huge amphibious denizens of the cane break, which lie basking in the sun, and the lonely graves of some unfortunate sailors who, stricken by the dreaded epidemic of the tropics, repose within their narrow beds enclosed with rough pickets to keep off the herds of cattle which graze along the banks.

Cubett Again

I have once referred to a suspicious character, an Englishman named Cubett, who lives at the Head of the Passes, and the sight of his shanty on the starboard bow as we enter the main river reminds me that among the documents found in the quarters of Duncan at Fort Jackson was a letter, which convicts Mr. Dick S. Cubett of being a traitor of the deepest dye. While the
[4]
Federal fleet were here, he professed to be loyal in order to obtain information respecting the movements of your vessels, he volunteered statements in reference to the strength and position of the enemy, taking good care nothing which he said should militate against the rebels whose confidence he boasted of enjoying. By his open and apparently truthful manner he succeeded in ingratiating himself with the Flag Officer, and subsequently when Gen. Butler wanted a guide for a reconnaissance in the rear of Fort St. Phillip, Cubett was employed to pilot the party. The letter to which I refer was written just before the affair between the Manassas, Richmond and Vincennes last autumn and contained the announcement that the Federal ships were here and only waiting for some gunboats to arrive, when they were to have paid a visit to the forts. This he learned from Capt. Pope, who told Cubett he was at liberty to go and not return. He thanked Capt. Pope, promised to remain withal, and not communicate with the enemy, on which conditions he was allowed to remain. He went on to say that they were going to send spies as soon as the nights got dark; that there

was a man on board one of the ships who had been to New Orleans twice, and volunteered this remark "there are some d__n traitors in the city." Commodore Hollins desired him to remain here, and he expressed his willingness to obey his orders, but no d__n Yankee

could drive him away. The letter informed the rebels that our ships were building a triangular battery at the point, and that
[5]
when the *Ivy* (CSS)[11] came down and peppered them, they stopped that game. He would fight for the country that gave him bread, and preferred a request for two barrels of flour, at the same time saying that if his niggers employed in the fort wanted shoes to give them some and make them work. He closed his letter with the request that it should be burned. This rebel general neglected to do, and falling into the hands of Commander Porter the other day, he sent an officer to arrest the traitor, but Mr. Cubett was non est inventus.[12] Should he be discovered he will likely grace a cross bar in some elevated and conspicuous place as a warning to all traitors. There is every reason to believe that Cubett was in communication with the enemy during the whole time that our squadron was assembling here, through the telegraph operator stationed at the "Jump," who informed Gen. Duncan daily of all the movements of our vessels.

Head of the Passes

This point, whence the Mississippi branches off into the Delta, will necessarily occupy a prominent place in the history of the expedition as the rendezvous of the Union fleet prior to their advance up the river. It was here that the ships were put in fighting trim. From here it was customary to send a picket guard of three or more gunboats, to drive back the rebel steamers whose black smoke was seen daily, curling above the woods, as they attempted to crawl out to view our movements, and as quickly retired upon advance of our guard boats, keeping at a provokingly safe distance from their pursuers.
[6]
Here the mortar flotilla received their cream colored coat; and were converted into veritable "mud sills," which so fittingly rebuked the reproachful epithet which Senator Chestnut of South Carolina applied to the brave men who fought them so well. But the "bummers" are no longer here, they sailed this morning for Ship Island, whence they will shortly proceed to try their range on Fort Morgan. The reports from the mast head "there's a steamer coming around the Point, Sir! There's two steamers coming down Sir," is no longer heard as was customary before the squadron advanced on its victorious expedition and we steam up the river unmo-

lested by rebel sharpshooters, fire-rafts, or even the semblance of a confederate gunboat. A grateful shower has cooled the arid air, and as we approach the "Jump" the scene grows familiar from long and exciting experience.

We run close to the banks of the river, now and then catching glimpses of red boxes marked "10 sec," which time the fuses burned that exploded the eleven inch shells they contained, and which came drifting down the tide after each sharp engagement between our gunboats and the enemy. The great highway of commerce is open again, and smacks, their owners no longer terrified by Federal blockaders and displaying the "stars and stripes," are borne by the current down to their old fishing grounds. The navigation of the river is now free up to New Orleans, and if there were no
[7]
other impediments, vessels might go to the city, load with cotton and sugar and depart. Unfortunately the rebels have burned the supply of the staple there was in New Orleans when our fleet appeared, and it will probably be some time before any is sent down from the river country.

Now we pass a sunken hulk, one of several which Capt. Guest of the *Owasco* destroyed on the day of the surrender of the forts, and on either side of the river are fire-rafts, some charred and blackened, others complete and uninjured, full of wood and barrels of tar and turpentine, which the rebels failed to get off on the night of the memorable action. Mostly white objects scattered along the shore and bunches of cotton which have drifted down from the rebel steamers destroyed by our ships. The enemy relied upon cotton bales to protect their machinery, boilers and magazines.[13] But all before the undaunted band of loyalists who were pitted against them.

The sun goes down in a blaze of glory — 'tis a southern sunset — and now as we pass the locality where so many vivid impressions have been given and received, we set in the twilight and scan each well known shrub and tree, and point out the places where the
[8]
shot and shell of Jackson and St. Phillip raised water spouts, around our busy, daring gunboats.

There are now no deadly projectiles screaming about our ears; no sharp crack of rifles from over the Chapparel, no gloomy clouds of resinous smoke to warn us of danger from fire rafts, and while the lamps are lighting I lay down my pencil to admire the tranquil scene. "Grim visage war has smoothed his ruffled front," and we may study the picture at our leisure.

Taking a Tow

Nine hours from Pilot Town to Fort Jackson and distance of about 25 miles. Slow traveling you will say; but if you have a five knot current

against you, and a gun boat, like all the rest of her class, cannot make over nine knots, under the most favorable circumstances and deduct two hours for stoppages, you will not be surprised that we have made so little progress. Our last detention was to take in tow the Schooner *Wilder*, of which you have heard before. This vessel lay at anchor just below the forts with a load of ordinance stores for the squadron and Capt. Ransom, knowing that the material was wanted above, promptly fastened to the schooner which a proves a drag to the *Kineo* and will prolong our passage at least eight hours. This is one of the very agreeable experiences of you correspondent
[9]
will do the justice to believe is most anxious to reach the scene of the present operations of Gen. Butler, especially as he is a bearer of dispatches to him.

The Scene of the Grand Action

We are now in the midst of darkness, deep as that which shrouded the river on the eventful morning of the 24th of April when brave men faced death in its most fearful form. Imagination lends its aid and we catch the very spirit which animated the gallant defenders of the bright flag under which they fought. On our left as we proceed stands Fort Jackson, whose grim sentinels, now silent under the vigilant guard of Union Soldiers, so lately poured their murderous fire upon the federal fleet. To the right, and ahead the long low outline of the ramparts of St. Phillips are defined by the light of a Union campfire. Our nearness to the formidable batteries, which but yesterday were charged with destruction to loyal men forcibly impresses us with the fearful position of the fleet in the tragedy of which your correspondent was a spectator at a safe distance; and we shrink from the contemplation of that morn of terror and dismay; of "death shots falling thick and fast," of timbers rent asunder; the vivid flashes of sulphurous fire; horrid wounds, decks slippery with the gore of the dead and dying; the appalling shrieks of the wounded and the ghastly features of friend and foe, lit up by the lurid glare of battle. No historic pen or artistic pencil can
[10]
portray the realities of that eventful morning. The fleet advances, working slowly and cautiously past the barrier, by which the enemy thought to arrest its progress. One after another the Federal gunboats and ships pick their way through the difficult gaps in the obstructions below the forts, and with their guns trained sharply forward, the men at quarters in silence, gunners with lock string in hand; the officers with perception sharpened

by the intense anxiety of the hour, they advance on their hazardous mission. On a raft under cover of the bank below St. Phillip, a man is stationed whose duty it is to signal the approach of the hostile fleet, by discharging a rocket, but his heart fails him; he is New Englander from the "Pine Tree State," and rather than light the match which was to have warned the rebel garrisons, he deserts his post and hastens to escape.

The special duty assigned to the division to which the *Kineo* is attached is to engage St. Phillip. Led on by the gallant and intrepid Bailey in the *Cayuga*, the division nears the sullen batteries, their defenders wrapped in slumber. The *Varuna* shoots past unheeded, and encounters a fleet of rebel gunboats, who officers and men charged with lighting up the river for the work of death are reposing in fancied security. But the forts discover the approaching squadron and springing to their guns from the darkness they pour a terrific fire of shot and shell upon our lofty ships and puny gunboats, now appearing strikingly diminutive from the removal of their masts and all necessary gear. They are stripped like the pugilist for the encounter, and when they "strike out" with their eleven inch pivots, the enemy finds to his dismay that they are not so

[11]

insignificant as they appear. They rebels light their "port fires," and by the blue glare, those who can stop to look see the spectral forms of the traitors as they maneuver their guns. Ahead and on either hand appear fire rafts, and iron clad batteries, and steamers which, caught napping, now cough and puff in their efforts to awake and receive the coming foe. The ships pour forth broadside after broadside, but their fire like that of the forts is too high, and the shot and shell pass over the heads of the rebels. The mortars, which have kept up a steady fire at long intervals all night, now open their wide mouths in rapid succession, and hurl their potent agents of death upon the misguided. Soldiers, who stand at the barbette guns, and fight bravely amid the shower of iron hail which rains upon them.

Meanwhile, the *Kineo* is in a critical position. In passing the barrier, the *Brooklyn*, shearing to deliver a broadside into Fort Jackson, runs smashing into her, carrying away her head and bowsprit, and swinging alongside crushes her port waist-boat; slants her deck beams, and wrenches her entire frame. By this unfortunate accident the *Kineo* is forced for a moment out of her position in the column. A panic breaks out among the men forward, some of whom rush aft and cry out to Capt. Ransom "she's sinking Sir, she's sinking." The position of the ship calls for prompt action, and the order is given by the captain "stop her, back her." The men rush for the life buoys, but the coolness of the officers and the report from the engine room that the ship is

[12]
not sinking restores order; the men promptly return to duty; amidst a galling fire from both forts; and the *Kineo* quickly rejoins the column in her original position. She passes close under the guns of St. Phillip, a thirty-two pound shot from which enters the engine room, slightly wounding Mr. Craig, Senior Engineer, and striking an iron bulkhead falls at his feet. The scene becomes grand and appalling. At every shot fired white clouds of smoke rise, which merging form a dense canopy over the river, relieved only when the jets of flame which dart out from casemate, parapet and port hole. The spirit which animates the scene is thrilling and not to be described. The roar of the cannonade, the blaze of fire rafts, and the flashes of lightning which light up the scene occasions a spectacle which must be witnessed to be realized. In the midst of the action the *Kineo* still pressing on, receives a solid shot from Fort St. Phillip, which strikes the pivot gun making a deep indentation in the solid metal, glances and shatters the slide, partially disabling he piece. The shock of the impact bursts the shot, the fragments of which spread death and destruction among the crew. One man is instantly killed and his body blown away, seven men are wounded, some seriously, and the deck is covered in gore. With eight men dead and wounded, and as many more removing them to the ward room, which on board the gunboats supplies the place of the cock-pit in times of action, the pivot gun is left with only four men. But
[13]
nothing daunted the survivors keep up their fire. Mr. Colburn, the officer of the division, assisted only by Thompson, the captain of the guns, the powder boy and two others continue to work the piece, and keep up a steady fire on the rebels. The next experience of the *Kineo* is to escape an immense fire raft which comes floating down. The officers of the mosquito navy have awakened to their duty, are now struggling to escape up the river by embarrassing the Federal fleet. The *Kineo* escapes the raft and meets the rebel steamer *McRae*, which is mistaken for the *Iroquois*. The guns are trained upon her, but before her real character is discovered the order is given to cease firing. The mistake is made by the whole fleet, nearly everyone who notices her, later, her for the *Iroquois*. The commander of which held his fire supposing her to be his sister ship the *Oneida*. Just as the day is breaking, an old captain of the forecastle, calls the attention of Capt. Ransom to the fact that the smokestack of the strange craft is aloft the main-mast, on which he immediately puts the helm about and pours a fire from all his guns into the rebel, doing fearful execution. The *Kineo* passes on followed by the *Richmond*, and Capt. Ransom hails Capt. Alden with "That fellow has not yet struck," but the latter in the heat and fervor of the action does not

understand him and replies "What's that you say, Ransom, do you see the stars and stripes above the forts? Three cheers!" and swinging
[14]
his hat, he shouts exultantly. The men throughout the fleet take up the cheer, and from ship to ship comes the inspiring huzzas. One after another they run up the old flag, which waves proudly amid the din and smoke of battle. The little *Kineo* which has worn one ensign throughout the action, displays another at her smokestack half as large as herself.

The ships pass out of the line of fire. The *Mississippi* returns and Capt. Smith invites Capt. Ransom to accompany him in pursuit of the "ram" *Manassas*. He joins him, and the two steamers head down the river directly at her. The "ram," which all the while has been chasing our ships, now running into and sinking the *Varuna*, making a pass at *Wissahickon*, and dodging the large vessels, at sight (of) the old flag ship of Commodore Perry, and the hero of the Mexican War, turns her head to the bank and beats an inglorious retreat. A scuttle on her turtle back is thrown open and her crew, fleeing in consternation, leap out and escape to the woods under a brisk fire from the *Mississippi* and *Kineo*. The latter makes preparations with a boat and hawser to take the ram in tow, but the *Mississippi* claiming her prize, comes between the two; informs Capt. Ransom that two gunboats below are showing the white flags, and asks him to take
[15]
possession of them. The *Kineo* promptly proceeds to execute the order of her superior and encounters the *McRae*, backed up by two other gunboats. While the ships were passing the rascals struck their confederate flag and showed the white feather; but on the approach of the *Kineo* alone and unsupported, themselves covered by the guns of both forts, they open a heavy fire, which compels the *Kineo* with her disabled gun to head up stream. She gives the *McRae* one broadside with telling effect, and proceeds upriver, while the *McRae* and her villainous consorts remain under the protection of the forts.

The squadron having passed on to New Orleans, leaving the *Wissahickon* and *Kineo* to guard the Quarantine Station until Gen. Butler lands his troops, the two vessels are in constant expectancy of an attack from the *McRae*, *Resolute*, and two other rebel steamers. In the afternoon one of the latter approaches to the assistance of the *Resolute*, which is on shore just outside the point below the Quarantine, and within range of the fort. Our two gunboats immediately run down to engage the enemy, who as usual backs down. And why should he not? He witnessed the scene of the morning. He saw fourteen Federal ships pass the forts, and eleven of his steamers on fire; blown up and

[16]
destroyed. But the *Kineo* availed herself of this opportunity and throwing an eleven inch shot into the *Resolute*, the latter was rendered worthless, and burned the next day. She was one of the finest of the rebel steamers, and said to have been worth seventy-five thousand dollars.

"Brought To" by St. Phillip

While I have been endeavoring to bring the reader to a nearer view of these memorable events, our steamer has made considerable progress up the river. Before reaching the forts, we were passed by a large black steamer, which we recognized at once as the "*Tennessee*," late rebel, now doing loyal service for the Union. We have often seen her at a distance when, before the reduction of the forts, she was wont to come down from New Orleans, flaunting the confederate flag, and hovering about Jackson and St. Phillip; and now as she passes us with troops from Ship Island, going to reinforce Gen. Butler, we take a nearer and more satisfactory look at her. She is one of the few rebel steamers which escaped the general destruction by friend and foe on the 24th, and proves a valuable acquisition to the squadron. She was at anchor on our starboard bow as we approached St. Phillip, and a blank shot from the lower battery of the fort, warned the *Kineo* to slow down. All vessels passing the forts are hailed to ascertain their character, and our ship having a clean record is allowed to proceed. Night is now
[17]
upon us, shutting out the beauties of "Dixie Land," and while the *Kineo* is breasting the current, I consult my note book for items of the all prevailing topic.

A Second Visit to the Fort

My first visit to Fort Jackson was in the twilight on the day of the surrender, to which event I have not done full justice. My inspection of the ruined fortress was necessarily hurried, as there was no telling how soon Commander Porter whom I desired to see might slip away down river. A sleepless night passed in a sanguinary conflict with the long billed phlebotomists which literally swarmed about my berth on the *Harriet Lane*, and I left the steamer in the gray of morning, glad to escape the tormentors who had robbed me of "nature's sweet restorer," and excited my destructive propensities to a degree truly alarming. The mosquitoes of the Mississippi are *traitors*, and whether they have sworn allegiance to the Southern Confederacy or not, to the mind of your correspondent they are more powerful allies of the rebels than all the fire rafts with which they sought to destroy the Union fleet. My compliments to Monsieur Mosquito, and I shall refer to his case non.

[18]

Dropping down to the forts in our dingey, I witnessed the embarkation of the rebel soldiers who, having been paroled, were conveyed to the city in the captured steamers *Burton* and *Landis*. They were a motley crowd as they stood along the levee and around the hospital, waiting to be taken off; and looked more like a band of emigrants just from Cork than like Soldiers. The order was given for them to go on board the steamer *J. P. Jackson*, and each one seizing his knapsack, bundle or bag which contained his scanty outfit. The vanquished and dispirited crew quit the vermin invested fort where for eight months they waited in suspense for the Yankees whom they thought to drive out of the river. They were an ill-mingled set, scarcely two being dressed alike. There wore black pants and grey, felt hats and muddy colored coats, and vests made of carpeting with plaids wide enough to satisfy the castle of the most dashing swell. Some looked sober; some looked glad; some looked sullen, others sad, and all appeared to realize they humiliating position in which they were placed. The original garrison consisted of the companies B, D, E, and H of the First Regiment Louisiana Volunteers, the St. Mary's Cannoneers, the Allen Guards, and a company of sappers and miners, in all about six hundred men. Of this number between three and four hundred deserted, and after wandering about the swamps all night, two hundred

[19]

and sixty delivered themselves up to the *Kineo*, and were transferred to the custody of Col. Jones of the 26th Mass. Regiment stationed at Quarantine.

After seeing the rebel soldiers safely on board the *Burton*, we returned to Fort Jackson and made a closer inspection of that work. The rebels left their compliments to their successors in the form of inscriptions on the guns, two of which ran as follows: "We fought, but fought in vain, but Beauregard will come with us again." "Hot-shot and shell for you d__d Yankees." They gave the "Yanks," as they call us, hot shot and shell, one of which the *Kineo* carries in her hull, but their furnaces were battered down during the bombardment, and they were driven from their barbette guns on the morning of the grand advance. They made a gallant advance, but the Confederate flag was hauled down at both forts, at two o'clock and forty-eight minutes on the 28th, and at 3–15 the "stars and stripes" were hoisted by Comdg. Renshaw of the *Westfield* on Fort Jackson, and Lieut. Comdg. Nichols of the *Winona* at Fort St. Philip. Upon entering the fort I met my old companions in Fort Massachusetts. The 4th Massachusetts Battery Capt. Manning, three detachments of whom with Co. B 2nd Mass.

Cavalry and three companies of the 30th Mass. Regt. of infantry were the first Union troops to occupy the captured forts; forts are at present garrisoned by the 26th Mass. Reg. Col. Jones.

The damage which the fort sustained
[20]
during the bombardment, cannot be overestimated, but the best evidence of the success of the Mortar Flotilla is found in the report of the officers of the Coast Survey, who have made a careful inspection of the fort and on a large plan which I have seen marked the spot where the bombs fell. If you will dip a sponge in ink and touch it lightly to a sheet of paper you will get a very good idea of the appearance of the chart, which is thickly dotted with the shell-box marks. Eleven hundred and thirty seven fell on the dry land within the line of the fort, and it is estimated that 3300 fell within a radius of 350 yards of the center. The mortars had the range so accurately when they commenced firing that the second bomb fell within the fort. Gen. Lovell who with his staff was on a visit to the fort at the time, picked up the shell, took it to the blacksmith who broke the fragments into small pieces, and the rebel officers carried them to New Orleans to distribute among their friends. One day the officers of the fort were sitting at dinner when a shell came down through the casemate, mixing bricks and mud with their soup and wine (it they were so fortunate as to have it). Not relishing this kind of condiment the officers dispersed each taking his corner, and waiting in an agony of suspense for the missile to explode. The bomb for once proved ineffective, and rolling off the table quietly "held its own." During the passage of the fleet a country volunteer, who had charge of a battery of casemate guns, which were throwing hot shot, being afraid of overshooting the
[21]
vessels, depressed his guns, and was working vigorously when an officer complained that his shot were falling short. He didn't discover his mistake 'til he heard a hissing in the water below, when to his mortification he found that his shot were rolling out of his gun and dropping into the moat, while he was blazing away with his hay wadding alone. He endeavored to retrieve his error, and was pouring a galling fire into a distant target, when he was again reprimanded by his senior, who discovered that the excited artillerist was firing into one of the chain hulks on the opposite side of the river.

The fort was shaken to its foundation by the force of the bombs, and not a single casemate remains uninjured. The roof of one was broken through in three places, and masses of brick and mortar were knocked down by the bombs falling on top. The outside walls contain fissures four inches wide, and the ramparts were so much cut up that in the intervals when the fire of the mortars slackened, men ventured out and repaired them with sand bags, to supply which a steamer was kept running to and from the city hall. By the reports of the commanders of the several divisions of the flotilla I learn that about 7,500 bombs were fired, of which number it is compiled that 1080 exploded

[22]

in the air. Deducting these and the number which fell within the fort, and there remains about 3000 which fell in the mote and the marsh outside the work. In passing, I cannot refrain from paying a deserved tribute to the cool determination Commander Porter and the officers of the flotilla who, have by their spirit, judgment, and intrepidity won the approbation and confidence not only of the Flag Officer, but of every impartial observer of their conduct.

The Graves of the Rebel Dead

After satisfying my curiosity by an inspection of the interior of the fort, I ascended the ramparts and bent my steps towards some new-made graves on the land side. I had not proceeded for, when my progress was arrested by a swarm of angry bees, whose hive had been demolished by one of our shots or shells. Their store of honey was scattered in every direction, and the busy creatures, still in arms against the invaders, stood guard over their ruined fortress. Making a detour to avoid the enemy, I passed to his rear, and reached a secluded spot, where I found two graves, into which, amidst the shower of iron hail which fell about them, the rebels had hurriedly thrown their ill-fated companions. The air was rank with noisome vapor, and I instinctively compressed my olfactorys. Whether they were "darkly at dead of night," or in the glare of noon-day, none could tell. A shingle placed at the head of each

[23]

Bore the simple record of their names; the company to which they belonged and the date of their death written in pencil:

"A. Walley
St. Mary's Cannoneers
April 24, 1862"
F.F. Hoyle
St. Mary's Cannoneers
April 18, 1862

The latter fell on the first day of the bombardment; the former during the action with the fleet.[14] There were other graves beyond but time pressed and I willingly hurried away to other and more agreeable scenes.

Fort St. Phillip

Crossing the river on the *J.P. Jackson* I paid my respects to Major H.O. Whittemore in command of the Union garrison of Fort St. Phillip. I am particular to give the initials of Capt. Woodsworth's steamer last, by omitting it, she should be confounded with the rebel steamers *Jackson*, *Stonewall Jackson*, with Fort Jackson, Jackson's Square, Jackson's Statue, and the old hero himself, who, if were to return to his old battleground, would find the tables turned at English Turn, and the traitorous sons of the soil which he defended against a foreign foe, playing the part of Pakenham[15] to the victorious defenders of the Union which he fought to establish. Crossing the deck of the steamer *Landis*, crowded with 220 prisoners taken on the *Burton*, *Landis* and *Resolute* the previous day, and who a few hours later were conveyed

[24]

to New Orleans, in charge of Lieut. Lea of the steamer *Harriet Lane*, I stepped ashore. The first familiar form which I encountered was that of Brig. Gen, Phillips, who had been assigned to the command of both forts. The general wore the same quiet and unassuming air with which I have seen him, wading through the sands of Ship Island. If anything he was more demonstrative and indulged in a moiety of congratulation at the success which had attended the expedition. I recalled his prophetic words to the soldiers on the *Constitution* on her first trip out. "You'll have a good deal of hard work, and but little fighting to do" and again at Ship Island, when the 26th were firing at target. "Do your best boys," said he, "this is all the fighting you'll have to do." Verily, the navy has caught the bird, and the army is holding it, as I predicted would be the result of the "special service" of the New England Division. Gen. Butler and his troops have however a delicate and important duty to discharge, and the assignment of the Massachusetts lawyer. The military marshal of Baltimore to the Department of the Gulf shows the wisdom of the selection.

Agaius

In the rush of events which have crowded themselves upon your correspondent, it has been impossible for me to watch the movements of the Massachusetts troops with that closeness which they deserve, and the thousands of their friends — readers of the Journal — desire.[16]

> *In the next report A.G. Hills describes the humor involved when raccoons got a bit too close to the ships of the mortar flotilla. They were likely a happy diversion from the standard bill of fare of government issued provisions.*

Spectators of the Bombardment

The siege was not without its amusing incidents. Not only the men at the mortars but the coons on shore became accustomed to the deafening roar of the bombardment, and while the former, working watch and watch, threw themselves upon the deck, and fell asleep on being relieved, the shaggy denizens of the chaparral, came fearlessly down to the river's bank, within an oar's length of the vessels and gazed in mute astonishment at the novel scene. Occasionally the sharp crack of a musket put an end to the reflections of these spectators, whose next appearance was on the dinner table in the cabin of the ward room or in the mess pan of the blue jackets. Occasionally in the heat of battle, when the shells of the enemy were flying over the hen coop of the steamer Jackson, a bold chanticleer stretched up his neck and crowed most excellently. The Romans were warned of danger by the cackling of geese, and though chanticleer was a loyal Baltimorean, there were grave suspicions that he intended to warn the rebels of the fate which awaited them.

Even though the American Civil War may be considered the first "modern" war, there was still some reverence for the Sabbath, but the reverence for this day did not stop the armies from fighting. It appears that A.G. Hills was a bit taken aback by the savagery on what was observed as a sacred day back home.

How the Sabbath of the Siege Was Observed

The third day of the bombardment fell on Easter Sunday, and such a Sabbath! Never shall I forget the reflections suggested by the scenes which that day witnessed. It was unlike any other Sunday, and its observance was strangely in contrast with the peaceful character of the Christian Sabbath. It succeeded the first nights bombardment, throughout which the mortars had kept up their incessant thunder. A few hours before daybreak a smart shower of rain fell. It was the first and only "damper" which occurred during the siege, and when at six o'clock it ceased, the sun beamed forth upon the placid surface of the river, which was riffled only by the splashing of the propellers and the plunge of the hissing projectiles which the rebels hurled at our venturesome gunboats. There was a slight movement in the atmosphere, which swept the sulfurous clouds from the mortars down the river, enveloping the squadron for the first time in the smoke of battle. The air was more rarified than on the previous days, and the bark of the huge war dogs had a sharper tone which fell with painful distinctness and rapidity on the ear. Six bombs leap into the air in as many seconds, and

from the crosstrees of the *Richmond* we watch them, as now they burst high over the heads of the rebels, emitting a cloud of intense smoke, not larger than to the eye than the puff from a Meershaum; now plunging into the mote around Fort Jackson, and dashing the water up in columns higher than the Confederate flag-staff, they glistened in the bright sun light, or bringing their huge bodies
[4]
in the glacis, explode and fill the air with clouds of yellow dust. One shell falls inside the fort, near the main entrance, cuts a rebel soldier in twain, and forms the rite of sepulcher by burying beneath a mound of earth which has been thrown up to protect the magazine. Go then a week after and the humid air will testify to the truth of this singular statement. It was an unwelcome shaft that so hurriedly buried its victim, but no doubt the traitors involuntarily thanked us foe completing the work of death and relieving them from the hazardous task of bringing their dead under the shower of hail that was rained upon them on that Sabbath morning.

But take another and more inspiring view of the scene, one that revived memories of other times and places; that carried us in imagination to the day when the nation shall rejoice in the declaration of peace and the glad shouts of rejoicing shall be heard from hill, valley, and plain. Throughout the squadron "eight bells" is reported so the commanders who answer "make it so" and instantly as if by magic all the bells in the fleet small and great toll off the hour of eight A.M. The next moments, and old Quartermasters punctual to a tick, run up the star spangled banner. The bright folds of the old flag waving from the peak of forty ships, no sooner arrests the siege, than the ear catches the strains of music mingled with the distant roar of the guns of St. Phillip. The band of the *"Mississippi,"* the only one in the squadron is assisted by
[5]
the "bummers" and rebel artillery are "stealing the thunder" with which our old favorite of the B.B.B.[17] annually entertains the multitude who flock to the Common on Independence Day. The tune is popular with us just now, but I fear the traitors by this "time" complain of the "measure" of the music to which they are compelled to listen. We like it however; it suits us and consequently is just what we want. "Logic," you will say "worthy of Jack Birusby." The scene is inspiring, quickening the pulse and awakening feelings to which most of us have been strangers.

Hours later and a scene more in consonance with the day, is witnessed on board the frigate *Mississippi*, which I believe is the only ship in the squadron to hold religious services. The flag — we know but one now — is spread over the capstan; the gunning is spread over the quarter deck;

the Marines in full dress are drawn up; the sailors in neat white shirts and blue pants arranged on one side, while on the other are assembled the officers of the ship. A choir composed of members of the band and sailors form one end of the hollow square, and in the center stands Commander Smith and his clerk. The latter conducts the simple service, rendered deeply impressive by the awful adjuncts which mingle with the prayer, and voices of the singers. There is not a pale face or a shrinking nerve among the worshippers, brought nearer to the stern realities before them by the solemn service in which they participate. They will face the coming danger with stouter hearts and stronger wills for their days service.

The Confederate attempt to restrict access up the Mississippi through the use of a chain has been well documented. In this report AG explains how the Confederate strategy failed and what he would have recommended to make it more effective.

A Plan for Obstructing the Mississippi at the Forts; Found Among the Papers Left in Fort Jackson and Pronounced Impenetrable by the Most Skillful Officers of Our Squadron

On the right bank of the river opposite for St. Phillip I moon a gigantic raft. This raft is submerged with the exception of a few sticks simulating a pile of drift wood. To this raft is attached four feet below water a chain stretching across to Fort Phillip and there also made fast four feet below the surface of the water. This chain is composed of long bars of iron. Say two or three rail road bars welded together, shackled by a single link working in swivel eyes; the end of the box being forged round with a head. Perhaps a better plan would be to turn over the ends of the bars with an eye piece and insert a link by a wrist pin. Either device would prevent tension and admit of such curvature of the chain. This chain is rendered *imperfectly buoyant* by attached logs. Until the raft is set free, the chain lies fifty or sixty feet below water so as not to interfere with navigation or drift. When the hostile squadron is just abreast the fort the raft is checked down the stream gently and set free without a jar after the chain has been strained to the utmost. Once set free the rafts, and its radius-vector will carry all before them. The momentum will be perfectly irresistible. The obstacle to the progress of the vessels, being invisible will be unsuspected, and they will be pinned to the left bank under the guns of the fort before they know what is the matter.
[2]
To cut the chain at a depth of six or nine feet would be a most difficult

undertaking. Nor can it be forced by sudden impact like a chain fast at both ends. To get out of the pound (would) be a very difficult manner. Especially if the raft was provided with a spur to enter the bank, or slyly druped and anchored. I concluded that the ascending fleet, or such portion as shall come within the sweep of the raft will be captured or destroyed. To prevent the possibility of any other vessel ascending a second raft attached to the first by a similar chain might be moored above the first on the same side and follow it along the bank until its chain was stretched taut across the river. The only precaution requisite would be not to check the second raft until the first had effected its landing. Again it might be found more expedient and certain to start an independent raft from the left bank, made fast a little above Fort Jackson. This would secure any vessels which have passed in the gap, by hugging the right bank on which might have subsequently come up. It is possible, nay probable that I have overestimated the destructiveness of my chain raft. But this is obvious that whilst guarded by this simple apparatus, a hostile fleet can never pass the forts at a hard gallop. I have also a scheme for a fire boom to be used in connection with the above, or separately, which will be gladly communicated to Col. Hebert or Capt. Duncan, but which as well as the present is to go no further without my consent.

> *The primary focus of the next article is the reported actions of Beverly McKennon, commanding the CSS* McRae *above the forts during the battle, against one of his crew. McKennon's own report mentions this action as a false charge that caused him to be held in prison instead of exchanged. It is possible that Hills' report was the cause of this prolonged imprisonment. There is no record for the source of Hills' information. The article was apparently unfinished.*

The Loss on Both Sides

It is impossible to arrive at a correct estimate of the loss of the rebels in the action between our fleet and their steamers. Hundreds were drowned, a large number were killed, wounded and taken prisoners and many succeeded in getting in on shore, and escaping under cover of the woods. The action was a scene tumult, darkness, and death. The carnage on some of the rebel steamers was fearful, and one of the confederate officers, not content with the nerve which our ships made with his crew, actually killed his steward,[18] who had failed to awake him at the approach of the squadron, and set fire to his ship and abandoning her leaving his wounded to perish in the flames. This man is Beverly Kennon, formerly an officer in the U.S.

Navy, and no doubt considered a very chivalric gentleman among his class. Humanity reprobates this infamous act, and the odium of history awaits his name. The rebels lost in Fort Jackson during....

> Members of the press corps had opportunities to board individual ships to report on the battle, but this would put them at direct risk to enemy fire. Some resorted to the "Press Gig," which was a small boat that traveled between Union ships for up-to-date battle reports, powered by the correspondents themselves. It is no wonder that reports were so hard to read after all this physical activity.

Seeking Information under Difficulties [2]

My experience in obtaining information from the squadrons, in visiting the forts and finally after a succession of drawbacks in reaching New Orleans has not been productive of the most pleasing reminiscences of the great expedition. As the correspondent of the Journal I have uniformally been received with courteous attention by the officers of the squadron, who have afforded me every possible facility to obtain reliable intelligence, still without the "Press Gig" as the boat which Capt. Guest of the "*Owasco*," kindly loaned me came to be familiarly known throughout the squadron. I should have remained in ignorance of many important matters connected with the expedition. Throughout the bombardment the "Press Gig" might have been seen flying from ship to ship, now struggling against the rapid current to board a gunboat just retired from an engagement with the enemy, her decks scarred and bloody; and again drifting down the line of mortars, her occupants watching the effect of the firing on the vessels, while the rebel shot and shell whistled in unpleasant proximity to their respective persons.

> Reports of the surrender were apparently delayed due to a failure of communication regarding vessels leaving the battle area to carry news reports. Also, although the reception of Union occupation forces was primarily ill received, some southerners were eager to cheer their occupiers and may have suffered for their enthusiasm.

The Surrender of the City

You will have learned through other sources the particulars of the surrender of the city which from the difficulties I experienced in ascending the river; I was unable to send by the dispatch steamer which carried the

intelligence north. And here let me say by way of accounting for my failure to forward my reports that the officers of the steamer on which I chanced to be when the *Cayuga* left, as well as several other vessels in the squadron, received no information of her intended departure. The neglect of the Flag Officer to give seasonable notice of her sailing, not only deprived the representatives of several leading journals from sending their dispatches, but hundreds of men in the squadron, who were most anxious to communicate with their families informing them of their safety. The departure of the steamer in the manner described has led to frequent animadversion against those whose duty it was to inform all the ships in the squadron of the intended departure. But in order to make my record of the capture
[2]
and surrender of the fortifications and the city complete it is proper that I should state that about one o'clock in the afternoon of the 24th, Flag Officer Farragut dispatched Captain Bailey under a guard of Marines with a demand upon the mayor and council for the unconditional surrender of the city, the hoisting of the United States flag on the Custom House, Post Office and Mint, and the state flag of Louisiana should be hauled down from the city hall. Upon landing Captain Bailey was met by an excited and tumultuous crowd, who gave vent to their indignation in the council in provocations, applying the most opprobrious epithets to the officers and Marines, and insulting then in the grossest manner. No notice was taken of these manifestations of displeasure, and Captain Bailey proceeding to the city hall followed by the insults of the mob had an interview with the Mayor, who in answer to his demand replied Gen. Lovell was in command here, and that he had no authority to act in military matters. Gen. Lovell having been sent for refused to surrender the city or his forces, accompanying his refusal with the statement he should evacuate the city, withdraw his troops, and have the civil authority to act as they might deem proper. The result of the interview having been communicated to Flag Officer Farragut, he addressed a communication to the Mayor stating that he came here to reduce the city in obedience to the laws of the United States, and while he guaranteed
[3]
the security of the citizens in their persons and property, he reiterated the demand for the unconditional surrender of the city, substitution of the Federal for the confederate flags over the public buildings belonging to the United States. He requested the Mayor to exercise his authority in quelling disturbances and restoring order, and called upon the citizens to return to their vocations, concluding his communication by declaring his intention to severely punish any person who should commit gross outrages as armed

men firing upon helpless men. Women and children, for expressing their pleasure at witnessing the old flag, an outrage which was committed by a party of rebel dragoons who dashed among a crowd of union people on the levee, and discharged their revolvers at them for waving their hats and handkerchiefs while the ships were passing.

This ends the reports of A.G. Hills during the New Orleans Campaign of 1862 for the Boston Journal. His articles of the campaign were published in the Boston Journal under the signature "Agaius." All of his journals and reports transcribed for this book remain in the family for preservation. I will of course continue to seek out his articles from other editions of the Journal as well as his editing venture with The Era in New Orleans.

When I started writing Hills' story I had no idea just how well known he was in the journalistic community. Even before the war he had gained a respectful reputation for his work around Boston, but his reports and ventures during the war made him a bit of a celebrity. When he traveled from port to port his arrival was noted in the paper. His postwar activities were also reported, even those concerning his well-being. Hills made many friends in high places and served on committees aimed at progress. One can only speculate what more he would have achieved if hadn't passed away so soon.

Sadly, Hills' name and the names of most of his correspondent friends do not appear on the War Correspondent's Memorial at Crampton's Gap in Maryland. He certainly worked with some of those who have been recognized. Perhaps Hills' early passing before the monument was built was a factor in the decision to leave his name off, but I believe he deserves to be there. He served the Boston Journal well, though obviously in a less violent region than his contemporary Charles Coffin in the eastern theatre of the war. Thankfully, through his journals and reports, his legacy has been preserved.

Albert Gaius Hills Timeline

Below is a timeline that tracks some of the events of Hills' life as well as his movements during the Civil War to aid in understanding his journal.

August 26, 1829	A.G. Hills was born.
1850	Listed in U.S. census as a sailor.
May 29, 1853	Married Sarah Kenfield.
December 23, 1853	Graduated from Mercantile Academy in Boston.
1860	Listed in U.S. census as a reporter.
March 6, 1861	Attended Lincoln Inaugural Ball at Mount Vernon Hall in Boston.
August 21, 1861	Left Boston Harbor on the mail steamer *Constitution* to cover New Orleans Campaign. Began first journal.
December 4, 1861	Arrived at Ship Island.
December 19, 1861	Left with expedition to Pensacola.
December 23, 1861	Returned to Ship Island.
January 6, 1862	Left on another expedition on USS *Massachusetts*.
January 8, 1862	Returned to Ship Island.
February 1, 1862	Left on steamer *Santiago de Cuba* for Key West.
February 3, 1862	Arrived at Key West.
February 25, 1862	Left for Havana on steamer *Sophronia*.
March 1, 1862	Left Havana and arrived back at Key West same day.
March 26, 1862	Left Key West on expedition of the Gulf to Tampa, Apalachicola Bay, Pensacola, and Mobile Bay.
April 1, 1862	Arrived at Head of Passes on steamer *Connecticut*.

April 18, 1862	Witnessed bombardment of mortar fleet of Forts Jackson and St. Phillip.
April 27, 1862	Began second journal.
May 1, 1862	Arrived at New Orleans to report on the surrender.
May 7, 1862	Left for New York on USS *Rhode Island*.
November 20, 1862	Began third and last war journal.
December 4, 1862	Left New York on steamer *North Star* with other reporters for unknown destination.
December 14, 1862	Arrived in New Orleans.
February 1863	Began work as editor of the *Era* with A.C. Hills.
February 15, 1863	Commissioned 1st Lieutenant in 4th Louisiana Native Guards.
May 18, 1863	Resigned commission.
June 26, 1863	Returned to New York with his wife, Sarah, on the steamer *Morning Star*. Sarah had arrived sometime before but apparently not during the December trip.
August 17, 1863	Sailed from New York to New Orleans on the *Morning Star*.
November 17, 1863	Became qualified registrar for New Orleans.
December 23, 1863	Travelled to St. Charles Parish and returned at an undisclosed date.
January 9, 1864	Sailed for Havana on the *Morning Star*.
January 29, 1864	Signed loyalty oath to the U.S.
March 1864	Ended editorial partnership of the *Era* with Alfred C. Hills.
April 1864	Headed up the Red River to visit Headquarters Department of the Gulf.
April 4, 1864	Assigned to jury duty.
May 23, 1864	Left for New York.
January 1865	Acquired map of assault on Fort Fisher, North Carolina.
January 1867	Sailed to Europe to sell prints of Marshall's engraving of President Lincoln.
June 24, 1879	Died of Bright's Disease in Boston. Buried in Mount Auburn Cemetery, Cambridge, Massachusetts.

Notes

Chapter 1

1. Benjamin Read, *The History of Swanzey, New Hampshire, from 1734 to 1890* (Salem, MA: 1892).
2. William Sanford Hills, *The Hills Family in America* (New York: 1906).
3. The Universalists were Christians believing in the final restitution of all souls. (Read, *History of Swanzey*, p. 182).
4. Hills, *The Hills Family in America*.
5. In Hills' later journal describing his travels to Europe he included at least ten pages that described his father's harsh treatment at the hand of relatives, including having to sleep outside and being confined "under the steps."
6. This was verified by a handwritten note from his physician that was kept by him and the family for almost 160 years.
7. *St. Albans Advertiser*, August 21, 1877.
8. This was probably one held in Boston, but the site does not appear to remain in existence.
9. Black Republicans were an element of the party that sought black equality. They were especially despised by the South during the years of Reconstruction. Among Hills' possessions were autographs and letters of Black Republicans such as Carl Schurz and William Lloyd Garrison.
10. The New Orleans Campaign kicked off in November of 1861. President Lincoln wondered why it hadn't begun sooner. Troops had to be diverted from other potential campaigns, and ships had to be collected (and some modified) for the assault up the Mississippi to the south's largest city. It was April 1862 before everything was ready, allowing southern forces time to improve fortifications and naval resources.
11. Charles Carleton Coffin was also a correspondent for the *Boston Journal* under the byline of "Carleton," covering the Union advances on Forts Henry and Donelson before returning east to cover eastern battles such as Antietam, Fredericksburg, Gettysburg, and the Wilderness. He was one of the more famous correspondents of the war. Like A. G. Hills, he is buried at Mount Auburn Cemetery in Cambridge.
12. Thomas Butler Gunn Diaries, 1861–1863 (Missouri History Museum, http://wwwmohistory.org/, 2011).
13. Gunn Diaries.
14. A drink consisting of whiskey, lemon peel, and hot water.
15. The Gunn Diaries provided much of the information regarding the interactions of the press corps that left New York for New Orleans in November 1862.
16. This term refers to an unconventional or vagabond life compared to that of a Gypsy.
17. Even though this group enjoyed a better diet than their military companions, Hills weighed only 149 pounds.
18. General Grover was also a source of mail for the correspondents, according to the Thomas Butler Gunn Diaries. Brigadier General Cuvier Grover was in command of the 4th Division of Banks' XIX Corps and was a veteran of the Peninsula and Second Manassas battles.
19. Samuel B. Holabird was a Brevet Brigadier General serving in the Depart-

ment of the Gulf as Chief Quarter Master. The authorization Hills had was on the Office Asst. Quarter Master letterhead.

20. "Revolt in the Corps d'Afrique," *Civil War Times Illustrated*, May 1985.

21. A.G. Hills and A.C. Hills were not related.

22. Thomas Butler Gunn Diaries.

23. The Gunn Diaries propose that negative reports of General Banks' staff resulted in the demise of the *Delta* and the rise of the *Era*. While serving as officers in the 4th Louisiana Native Guards both A.G. and A.C. Hills were "detailed" to serve as editors for the *Era*. It is highly probable that neither engaged in any training, let alone combat. The commissions may have given them easier access to information and an advantage over their competitors.

24. "Mutiny in the Army," *Civil War Times Illustrated*, July 1985. The colonel of the regiment treated his troops cruelly and was nearly killed by them.

25. General Order No 14, Department of the Gulf, New Orleans, February 7, 1863. This order set the guidelines for the removal of officers from command. While there is no information that ties Hills to this order for resigning his commission, it could have been used for justification. It could just have easily been the result of an administrative decision by General Banks. There was no military necessity for either A.G. Hills or A.C. Hills to become an officer in the United States Army. Their duties as officers and as editors of the *Era* certainly overlapped for General Banks' purposes as military governor.

26. Assistant Paymaster Frederick Calvin Hills was imprisoned in Columbia, South Carolina, before being transferred to Libby Prison in May 1863 to be exchanged. He was paroled a few days later and was almost immediately assigned to the USS *DeSoto*, on which he served until 1864. His original orders were to report to New Orleans (following a well-deserved leave) to Rear Admiral Farragut for duty on the steamer *John P. Jackson*, but he ended up on the *DeSoto*. July 1863 was one of the few months that A.G. was not in New Orleans, so a reunion would not have been possible. The *DeSoto* was eventually quarantined in Baltimore that year due to a Yellow Fever outbreak, and Hills was eventually discharged in December. F.C. Hills lived until 1898 and was buried in Boston. The February 3, 1863, edition of the *Richmond Examiner* covered the story of the capture of the *Isaac P. Smith*, and A.G. somehow managed to get a copy of this southern paper.

27. Unfortunately, the article does not indicate whether A.C. Hills was arrested or whether A.G. Hills' resignation from the army is related to the incident.

28. According to a U.S. Treasury report from 1868 a payment of $987.25 was made to A.C. Hills and A.G. Hills toward the original claim.

29. It is a tribute to the Hills widows that they were able work together to reach an amicable solution after nearly twenty years had elapsed.

30. This edition of the *Savannah Republican* also contained the obituary of Edward Everett, famous orator, educator, and politician. Hills had met Everett on several occasions.

31. *New York Herald-Tribune*, July 8, 1865.

32. *New York Commercial Advertiser*, July 5, 1866.

33. Hills kept these letters and they are still preserved by his descendants.

34. *Boston Journal*, September 9, 1870.

Chapter 2

1. Northern strategy to deny southern ports of any imports, in order to gradually suffocate the Confederate war effort.

2. In Hills' journals he refers to retaking federal property such as the U.S. Mint and Customs House.

3. David D. Porter, "The Opening of the Lower Mississippi," in Robert U. Johnson and Clarence C. Buel, eds., *Battles and Leaders of the Civil War*, Vol. 2 (Secaucus, NJ: Castle, 1982), pp. 23–24.

4. Ezra J. Warner, *Generals in Blue* (Baton Rouge: Louisiana State University Press, 1964).

5. Hills listed this battery as the 5th Massachusetts.

6. Johnson and Buel, eds., *Battles and Leaders*, Vol. 2, p.74.

7. The *Manassas* had been engaged by Union ships in October 1861 near the Head of Passes, and although she was damaged she left an impression on the federal ships as a vessel to be respected.

8. The "List of the Officers of the Mortar Flotilla" and "Fleet Under the Command

of D.S. Farragut" were among the effects of A.G. Hills passed down through his family.

9. Period maps show Pass à Loutre between Bay Honde and Blind Bay. It was the entrance closest to Ship Island.

10. The Head of Passes is the point on the Mississippi where the river branches out to connect to the Gulf of Mexico. It is considered the mouth of the Mississippi River, according to the Army Corps of Engineers.

11. According to Hills' 1855 copy of the U.S. Coast Survey map, Pilot Town is just upriver of the mouth of the Southwest Pass.

12. "The Jump" is located near present day Venice, Louisiana, where the river breaks to the West Bay and into the Gulf. The landscape looks much different now than it did in Hills' day. Much area has been filled in since the Civil War. The use of the Jump as a telegraph station is noted in Hills' journal.

13. A common practice in the Civil War was to sink old or obsolete vessels in shipping lanes to block or obstruct the passage of enemy ships. This restricted the points where ships could pass up a river or enter a harbor, allowing defenders better opportunities to target their fire on attackers while still providing a point for friendly shipping to pass.

14. The reader should be aware that there were multiple ships named "Jackson" in the New Orleans Campaign. The *J.P. Jackson* was a Union vessel while the *Stonewall Jackson* and *Jackson* were Confederate. At times Hills left off the "J.P." when mentioning the Union vessel.

15. English Turn is the last bend of the Mississippi River that turns eastward before approaching New Orleans.

16. Colonel Jon T. Hoffman, *USMC: A Complete History* (Westport, CT: Hugh Lauter Levin Associates, 2002).

17. Butler issued a proclamation announcing the surrender on May 1. Hills acquired a copy that was printed in the offices of the *New Orleans Delta*. The *New Orleans True Delta* refused to print the proclamation and saw its publications suspended on May 2. It was back in business the next day.(Department of the Gulf General Orders 17 and 18.)

18. The *Pocahontas* was serving in the Atlantic at this time. The *Richmond* may have been the true identity of this vessel.

19. The Seventh Vermont was charged with repairs to Fort Pike. The Eighth New Hampshire took command of Fort Wood. The gunboat *New London* was commended for its service in taking control of the forts.

Chapter 3

1. In *Bohemian Brigade: Civil War Newsmen in Action* by Louis Starr (Madison: University of Wisconsin Press, 1987) there is a reference to Henry Winser's paddling some 50 miles in a "leaky dugout" on the Mississippi River to get battle reports during Farragut's New Orleans Campaign. The "leaky dugout" is the same "press gig" described by Hills, who deserves equal credit for this devotion to his paper and, frankly, to Winser's *New York Times* covering the reports of the battle.

2. Hills mentions his expenditures in his journal entries as well as in a couple of pages separate from the journal which I have not included in the transcriptions.

Chapter 4

1. Hills used this term to describe southern forces or citizens. It may be used interchangeably with "Confederate" or "rebel."

Chapter 5

1. Fortress Monroe was a U.S. installation guarding the Chesapeake Bay at Old Point Comfort. Historically the site was known for its defensive potential since the settlement at Jamestown, but the fortifications referred to during the Civil War began in 1819 and were completed in 1834. Unlike some other Union forts in confederate territory, Fortress Monroe remained in federal hands throughout the war.

2. Not to be confused with the warship of the same name, this ship carried mail from the Isthmus of Panama to San Francisco before the war.

3. The USS *Kingfisher* was a barque purchased by the U.S. Navy in 1861. She joined the Gulf Blockading Squadron during the New Orleans Campaign but was grounded and abandoned in South Carolina in 1864.

4. Hills' ship headed north at the onset, likely to collect supplies and Maine troops. As if on a weekend pass, he returned to Boston by train and spent some last hours

with his wife Sarah, then took another train to Baltimore to rejoin his ship. This was likely the first time A. G. had ever spent much time away from home.

5. General Benjamin Butler led Union land forces assigned to capture New Orleans and became the military governor until relieved in December 1862 following a very controversial command. He later commanded the Army of the James in Virginia and was again relieved, this time for incompetence.

6. Spirits.

7. The USS *Minnesota*, later grounded during the Battle of Hampton Roads against the CSS *Virginia* on March 8, 1862. She was a part of the North Atlantic Blockading Squadron and survived the war.

8. The USS *Colorado* joined the Gulf Blockading Squadron but was too heavy to cross the bar and enter the Mississippi River. She later participated in the bombardment of Fort Fisher in January 1865 and survived the war.

9. General Wool was one of the senior officers in the U.S. Army at the onset of the Civil War. A veteran of the Mexican War, he assured Union control of Fortress Monroe and served admirably until his retirement in 1863.

10. The *Daylight* was assigned to the North Atlantic Blockading Squadron, serving extensively in the waters of Virginia and North Carolina.

11. The steamer *John P. Jackson* served in the Gulf Blockading Squadron and was one of the vessels towing mortar schooners into position for the bombardment of the forts on the Mississippi River. She later participated in the Mobile Bay battle of 1864.

12. USS *Brooklyn* joined the Gulf Blockading Squadron and was prominently engaged in the attack on New Orleans. She served with distinction in battles on the Mississippi River and the assaults on Fort Morgan in 1864 and Fort Fisher in 1865, also surviving the war.

13. Hills was teased more than once regarding his seasickness.

14. Although this was the first instance when Hills knew where the fleet was going, General Butler, Commander Porter and Flag Officer Farragut certainly knew their destination and final objective.

15. Hills' effects included a U.S. Coast Survey map from 1855 of the mouth of the Mississippi and an 1859 map of Texas.

16. Pensacola.

17. New England Division.

18. Not all of these regiments landed in New Orleans.

19. Biloxi and Pensacola.

20. Unknown vessel.

21. Mississippi City lies on the coast just west of Biloxi.

22. Charlestown, MA.

23. Ship Island lies off the coast of Mississippi south of Biloxi. Confederate forces eventually occupied the island after the secession of Mississippi, but gave it up to Union forces in September of 1861. The island was used as a Union staging area for the attack up the Mississippi to take New Orleans as well as for raids along the Gulf Coast.

24. The word here is illegible, but would have described Hills' terrible struggle with seasickness.

25. Seminole War era fort, 1838.

26. Both off Key Biscayne Bay.

27. This poem may be attribuited to A.G. Hills, and although he is listed wth the occupation of sailors in the U.S. 1850 census, he must not have spent significant time at sea.

28. Chandeleur Island is just south of Ship Island.

29. Named for the president of the Central Georgia Railroad, the *R.R. Cuyler* served in the Gulf Blockading Squadron and survived the war.

30. USS *Massachusetts* served as a store ship for the war.

31. This is the gunboat *Florida*, not the commerce raider by the same name. It was later named the *Selma*.

32. The U.S. steamer *Henry Lewis* was assigned to the Gulf Blockading Squadron in the latter half of 1861. She participated in the Biloxi expedition of December 31, 1861. According to Hills she was transferred to the U.S. Army and served as a troop transport.

33. USS *DeSoto* served in the Gulf Blockading Squadron. Hills' brother Frederick Calvin served on the *DeSoto* after his exchange in 1863. A yellow fever outbreak in 1864 required a period of quarantine for the rest of the war.

34. USS *New London* served in the Gulf Blockading Squadron and supported the raid on Biloxi at the end of December 1861.

35. All three of these rebel gunboats opposed the Union advance up the Mississippi River. The *Calhoun* had been active at the

Notes — Chapter 5

Head of Passes as early as October 1861 and was captured off the Southwest Pass on January 23, 1862. The *Oregon* assisted in the Confederate evacuation of Ship Island in September 1861. The *Oregon* and the *Pamlico* were ineffective in slowing the Union advance and both were eventually scuttled by their crews in April 1862 to prevent capture when New Orleans surrendered.

36. Hills may be referring to the 1860 Arctic Expedition led by Isaac Israel Hayes. A list of the crew for the USS *DeSoto* dated April 1863 in Hills' records does not contain a member by this name at any rank.

37. USS *Kinio* (*Kineo*) was assigned to the Gulf Blockading Squadron and patrolled the Mississippi River, participating in numerous battles through the end of the war.

38. The *Rachel Seaman* was assigned to the Gulf Blockading Squadron and survived the war.

39. USS *New London*.

40. This is probably a reference to Confederate forces in general. A rebel privateer of this name was lost in August of 1861, so if this is a ship reference the name is in error.

41. This minié ball was likely a stray round from target practice, although Ship Island was not immune from rebel attack, as Hills noted in a later journal entry while the Union fleet was moving up the Mississippi.

42. The *Grey Cloud* was a Confederate transport active in the Biloxi area. She was captured by Union naval forces in July 1862.

43. The *Pampero* was a supply ship for the Gulf Blockading Fleet for the war's duration.

44. The *Water Witch* served in the Gulf Blockading Squadron starting in 1861, and had been involved in the river battle at the Head of Passes later that year against the rebel ram *Manassas*. In 1864 while operating off the coast of northern Florida she was surprised and captured by a Confederate boarding party. She was burned by her new possessors later that year to prevent recapture.

45. USS *R.R. Cuyler*.

46. The *South Carolina* served in the Gulf Blockading Squadron for the first half of the war and the Atlantic Blockading Squadron for the remainder.

47. The *Wissahickon* served in the Gulf Blockading Squadron and participated in the New Orleans Campaign as well as the campaign against Vicksburg. She later served in the South Atlantic Blockading Squadron and participated in bombardments against Forts Wagner and Sumter.

48. The *Baltic* was a transatlantic liner that was used as a transport during the war.

49. The *Potomac* was a pre-war frigate that was used as a stores ship for the Gulf Blockading Squadron.

50. The *Huntsville* was part of the Gulf Blockading Squadron until an outbreak of yellow fever on board in 1864 forced the ship into quarantine.

51. The supply served with the Gulf Blockading Squadron as a transport and supply ship for the war but did capture one rebel ship on its own.

52. A slang term apparently used to describe a group of refugees reaching the ship Potomac.

53. The *Niagara* served in the Gulf Blockading Squadron through 1863, and then sailed to Europe to track Confederate vessels being built there. She survived the war.

54. Although primarily a supply ship, the *Rhode Island* nevertheless captured rebel shipping in the Gulf and the Atlantic. She also towed Union ironclad vessels, including the *Monitor* when it sank off of Cape Hatteras in late 1862. The *Rhode Island* later participated in the bombardments of Fort Fisher in 1864 and 1865.

55. Officers.

56. Confederate General Braxton Bragg.

57. 6th and 75th New York Regiments.

58. However many times I've looked at this passage the word I always see is "pants." The "Billy" referred to here is William Wilson, commanding the 6th New York Infantry Regiment. Wilson was highly respected by the correspondent corps and is also mentioned in the Gunn Diaries from the end of 1862 in New Orleans.

59. Protected fort entranceway.

60. This may be a reference to the parade ground.

61. Contrabands were escaped slaves. Union ships lying off Confederate held ports or fortifications were magnets for escaped slaves. Many also sailed to Ship Island after it was occupied by Federal forces.

62. Santa Rosa Point.

63. Frederick Phisterer, *New York in the War of the Rebellion* (Albany: Weed, Parsons, 1890).

64. Left blank for an expletive.

65. This is a term Hills used to describe his misery during sea travel.

66. The *Preble* joined the Gulf Blockading Squadron in mid–1861. She was accidentally destroyed by fire in April 1863.

67. Construction of the circular Fort Massachusetts on Ship Island commenced just before the outbreak of the Civil War. The fort remains today despite the effects of time and gulf storms.

68. Horn Island Pass, between Horn and Petit Bois islands.

69. USS *New London*.

70. Rebel schooner.

71. Unknown vessel.

72. The *Fearnot* was a coal and supply ship assigned to the Gulf Blockading Squadron.

73. Brigadier General Phelps.

74. Rebel schooner *Captain Spedden*.

75. USS *Richmond*?

76. The *Mercedita* was assigned to the Gulf Blockading Squadron in early 1862. She participated in the attack on St. Vincent's Island near Apalachicola Bay in March 1862. Late in 1862 she was transferred to the South Atlantic Blockading Squadron. At the end of January 1863 she was attacked by Confederate warships in the harbor of Charleston, SC. She was rammed and left to sink as the rebel ships accepted the paroles of the officers and crew. Making hasty repairs, the crew made way to safer waters and eventually returned to blockading.

77. The *Winona* was assigned to the Gulf Blockading Squadron in early 1862. She was part of the fleet that ascended the Mississippi River to New Orleans but hit a snag near the rebel forts and remained below them as the fleet moved on. She later saw action against Vicksburg and Port Hudson. In 1864 she was reassigned to the South Atlantic Blockading Squadron.

78. This ship is likely the *Sagamore* which was attached to the Gulf Blockading Squadron at the end of 1861. The *Sagamore* and the *Mercedita* landed sailors who captured Apalachicola, Florida, on April 3, 1862. She served much of the war around Florida.

79. Island off the Mississippi coast east of Ship Island.

80. Grant's Pass is between Dauphin Island and the Alabama mainland. An attack on Mobile through Grant's Pass would avoid Fort Morgan.

81. Petit Bois Island is off the Mississippi coast and east of Horn Island.

82. This is an unknown vessel. There was a Union steamer by this name serving in the Atlantic Blockading Squadron, but it had not been commissioned by this date in Hills' journal.

83. Steamer *Henry Lewis*.

84. Unknown vessel.

85. The *Kittatinny* was assigned to the Gulf Blockading Squadron at the very end of 1861 and was part of the fleet that captured New Orleans in April 1862. She served in the North Atlantic in 1863 and returned to the Gulf in 1864 to finish out her service.

86. French vessel.

87. The true identity of this ship is in question. There was an HMS *Black Prince* completed later in 1862, but I have found no U.S. Navy ships by this name. It may have been a merchant vessel, or Hills may have mistaken the name, although it does appear twice in the journal.

88. Brigadier John Wolcott Phelps was the Union commander of Ship Island. Later, at New Orleans, he organized Negro troops, an act denounced by the Lincoln administration. As a result he resigned his commission and later turned down an opportunity to be a major general in command of colored troops when the administration reversed course and recruited colored troops.

89. Unknown vessel.

90. Unknown vessel.

91. The *Portsmouth* was assigned to the Gulf Blockading Squadron and was with the fleet that captured New Orleans. It served near New Orleans for the remainder of the war.

92. Unknown vessel.

93. Unknown vessel.

94. Unknown vessel.

95. Rebel work vessel from Mobile.

96. The *Santiago de Cuba* was sent to Havana in November 1861 to intercept rebel blockade runners. She was evidently a fast ship since she was tasked with chasing rebel commerce raiders as well. In late 1864 and early 1865 she participated in the attacks against Fort Fisher.

97. This was not a direct family member, but the Hills family is distantly related to the Gorham family from Massachusetts.

98. The *Oriental* was rented by the U.S. Army as a troop transport. In May 1862 she

ran aground near Pea Island in the Outer Banks of North Carolina.

99. Unknown vessels.

100. The *Kanawha* was assigned to the Gulf Blockading Squadron and survived the war.

101. The identification of this vessel is unclear. A rebel vessel by this name was captured in 1863.

102. These four ships were part of the mortar flotilla that bombarded Forts Jackson and St. Phillip. Although modified to accept mortars, they were not defenseless. The *Matthew Vassar* actually captured blockade runners on the East Coast and when assigned to the Gulf Blockading Squadron.

103. Navy records report the *Roanoke* was assigned to the defenses of the Hampton Roads area in Virginia.

104. The *Pensacola* was assigned to the Gulf Blockading Squadron in early 1862. She ascended the Mississippi River past the forts and was present at the surrender of New Orleans. She remained to defend the position for the remainder of the war.

105. The *Hartford* became the flagship of the Gulf Blockading Squadron in early 1862. With Farragut on board she passed the fire of the forts to New Orleans. She fought against the defenses of Vicksburg and Port Hudson and eventually at the Battle of Mobile Bay in 1864, where Farragut was credited with the "Damn the torpedoes, full speed ahead!" command.

106. The names of these mortar schooners do not match exactly Hills' list from page 18. The *Adolph Hughes* should be the *Adolph Hugel*, the *Oliver Brach* could be the *Oliver Lee*, and the *George Nahaw* the *George Mangham*. The *G.A. Ward* is likely the *T.A. Ward*. The other vessels for this entry are unknown.

107. This was a rebel ship recently captured off Atchafalaya River and renamed the *Isabella*.

108. The *Montgomery* served on blockading duty in the Gulf from mid–1861, then joined the North Atlantic Blockading Squadron in 1864. She later participated in the bombardments of Fort Fisher.

109. Unknown vessel.

110. Probably 47th and 90th New York Regiments

111. This was probably not a warship, serving as a supply vessel to the Gulf Squadron.

112. The gunboat *Owasco* was assigned to the Gulf Blockading Squadron. In preparation for the attack on New Orleans her duty was to tow mortar vessels upriver, a task later performed in support of attacks against Vicksburg. She served in the Gulf and off the coast of Texas for the last two years of the war.

113. Unknown vessel.

114. Unknown vessel.

115. Unidentified vessels.

116. This was a term given to describe a schooner in the mortar flotilla, generally kept behind during a naval advance. These had all been modified for the purpose of carrying mortars to bombard fortifications.

117. Unidentified vessel.

118. Unidentified vessel.

119. The steamer *Philadelphia* served primarily in the North and South Atlantic Blockading Squadrons.

120. The *Richmond* served in the Gulf in the latter half of 1861, and fought against the Confederate ram *Manassas* and other vessels near the Head of Passes in October. She suffered severe damage when attacking the rebel defenses of Pensacola in November 1861. She was repaired in time to accompany the Union fleet against New Orleans and later battled against Vicksburg, Port Hudson, and finally Mobile Bay in 1864.

121. The *Columbia* was a rebel blockade runner captured by the *Santiago de Cuba* in August 1862.

122. The *Sophronia* was a mortar schooner that participated in the bombardment of the forts protecting New Orleans and later against the Vicksburg defenses. In 1863 she was transferred to the Potomac River flotilla.

123. The *Nonpareil* appears in several journal entries but its description is unknown.

124. The steamer *Harriet Lane* was part of the relief expedition to Fort Sumter in April 1861 that turned away when it heard of the fort's fall. She was the flagship of Commander Porter and the mortar flotilla that bombarded the river forts. She took part in the capture of Galveston in October 1862 and was there when the Confederates counterattacked the city on January 1, 1863. In that battle she was captured by Confederate forces and suffered heavy casualties in the process.

125. The *Magnolia* was a rebel steamer captured by the *Brooklyn* and *South Carolina* in February 1862. She was later fitted to join

the Gulf Blockading Squadron against her former owners.
126. Added by author.
127. Unknown vessel.
128. The steamer *Westfield* joined the fleet ascending the Mississippi River against the rebel forts and supported the mortar flotilla. She skirmished with rebel vessels on the river before the mortar bombardment. After New Orleans fell she saw service at Vicksburg and Galveston. At Galveston she was present at the initial capture of the city as well as the Confederate attack that took it back. She was damaged in the attack and was destroyed to prevent her capture.
129. The steamer *Clifton* joined the Gulf Blockading Squadron just before the attack on the river forts below New Orleans. She also saw action against Vicksburg and Galveston and was captured by Confederate forces at Sabine Crossroads in 1863.
130. Unknown vessel.
131. Fort Jefferson, Dry Tortugas.
132. The *Oneida* was assigned to the Gulf Blockading Squadron in 1862 and fought in the river battle below New Orleans in April 1862. She served on the Mississippi River against Vicksburg, participated in the battle of Mobile Bay, and performed blockading duties in the Gulf for the remainder of the war.
133. The *Nightingale* served in the Gulf throughout the war as a supply vessel.
134. Added by author.
135. Unknown vessel.
136. The *Mohawk* served in the Gulf until she was sold in 1864.
137. Fort Zachary Taylor, Key West.
138. The *Katahdin* was part of the Union fleet that passed the Mississippi River forts in April 1862. She later took part in battles against Vicksburg and Baton Rouge. She finished the war attached to the Gulf Blockading Squadron.
139. Unidentified vessel.
140. The *Eugenie Smith* was captured by the Union ship *Bohio* at the mouth of the Mississippi.
141. The *Ethan Allen* patrolled the Gulf from 1861 to 1863 to enforce the blockade. She served in the South Atlantic Blockading Squadron for the remainder of the war.
142. Unknown vessel.
143. Parentheses by Hills.
144. The *Tahoma* was assigned to the Gulf Blockading Squadron for the duration of the war.

145. The *Bainbridge* was an older vessel of the fleet when the war began. She served in the Gulf of Mexico against blockade runners and also protected shipping lanes to Panama. In August 1863 she capsized in a storm off Cape Hatteras with only one survivor.
146. Walkula.
147. The *J.C. Kuhn* was assigned to the Gulf Blockading Squadron supplying ships on the Mississippi River and in the Gulf.
148. St. Vincent and St. Georges.
149. The *Marion* joined the Gulf Blockading Squadron in mid–1861.
150. No roster book was found in any of Hills' records.
151. Unknown vessel.
152. The *Maria A. Wood* was a sailing vessel assigned to the Gulf Blockading Squadron for the war's duration.
153. The *Vincennes* was one of the older ships in the U.S. Navy at the outbreak of war and had been just about everywhere. She was assigned to the Gulf Blockading Squadron in 1861 and participated in the battle near the Head of Passes with the CSS *Manassas*. She ran aground and would have been scuttled, but the explosives used failed to ignite. She was soon refloated and served on blockading duty nearby for the rest of the war.
154. The *Mississippi* was part of the Gulf Blockading Squadron that participated in the passing of the Mississippi river forts and surrender of New Orleans. She was the heaviest ship to pass the bar at the Southwest Pass. She remained near New Orleans until May 1863 when she was attacking Port Hudson and grounded. She was destroyed by her crew to prevent capture.
155. Left blank by Hills.
156. The *Iroquois* was assigned to the Gulf Blockading Squadron in 1862 and was part of the fleet that captured New Orleans. She accepted the surrender of Baton Rouge in May 1862 and fought against the Vicksburg batteries. In 1863 she was assigned to the North Atlantic Blockading Squadron.
157. The *Varuna* was assigned to the Gulf Blockading Squadron in early 1862. She was part of the fleet that engaged the rebel forts on the Mississippi River and was the only vessel sunk due to enemy fire during the battle.
158. The *Kineo* was assigned to the Gulf Blockading Squadron and fought in the battles for New Orleans, Vicksburg, and

Port Hudson, as well as blockading Gulf ports.

159. While Hills was heading up the Mississippi with the Union fleet an expedition was being launched against Biloxi and Pass Christian, Mississippi, primarily by the 9th Connecticut. General Butler praised the action of this regiment and others in General Order Number 10. It is very curious that this story was not mentioned at all by Hills.

160. Hills used this phrase on a few occasions. It indicates the frequent alarms on ship for the crews to get up and begin firing mortars at Forts Jackson and St. Phillip or prepare to run past the forts entirely.

161. Unknown vessel.

162. The bark *Horace Beals* supplied ships of the mortar flotilla that bombarded the river forts in April 1862. She later supplied vessels in the bombardments of Vicksburg and Port Hudson in 1863 as well as others in the Gulf Blockading Squadron.

163. The *Mohican* served primarily in the Atlantic Blockading Squadrons and participated in the bombardment of Fort Fisher during the attack in 1865. Other sources place this ship near Fort Pulaski in Georgia in April 1862.

164. Hoyt was probably Captain Stephen Hoyt, Chief Engineer on the *J. P. Jackson*.

165. The *Orvetta* was a mortar schooner participating in the bombardment of the forts below New Orleans and later at Vicksburg. The *Arletta* was a mortar schooner present at the bombardment of the forts below New Orleans and later at Vicksburg. Later in 1862 the *Arletta* was transferred east to the North Atlantic Blockading Squadron.

166. The schooner *Dan Smith* was part of the mortar flotilla bombarding the forts below New Orleans and the defenses of Vicksburg in 1862. She was then transferred east, patrolling the rivers draining to the Chesapeake Bay and supporting the South Atlantic Blockading Squadron.

167. Hills may have meant the ship *Great Republic*, a transport listed in one of Butler's General Orders.

168. The *Idaho* was a Union troop transport. The *Bowsprit* was likely a transport as well, but I could not make a confirmation.

169. Blanks left by Hills.

170. The *Sachem* was present in Hampton Roads for the battle between the *Monitor* and the *Virginia* but still made it to the Mississippi River to join the expedition against New Orleans. She also saw action against Vicksburg and Port Hudson.

171. The *Pinola* and *Itasca* successfully broke the chain by the forts on this night. The *Pensacola* was not part of this mission.

172. The gunboat *Itasca* served in the Gulf Blockading Squadron throughout the war and was part of the fleet that captured New Orleans.

173. Unknown vessel.

174. Left blank by Hills.

175. The *Sciota* was assigned to the Gulf Blockading Squadron and was with Farragut at New Orleans and saw action at and below Vicksburg in 1862. She collided with a Union steamer on the Mississippi River in 1863 and sank but was raised and repaired. She saw action off Galveston and at the battle of Mobile Bay in 1864 where she struck a torpedo and sank again.

176. The *Norfolk Packet* was a mortar schooner with the fleet that bombarded the river forts below New Orleans and later saw action against Vicksburg. In 1863 she was transferred to the South Atlantic Blockading Squadron.

177. The *Bliar* and *Hallet* are unknown vessels, and do not appear on the list of ships that Hills included in his records.

178. The Confederate gunboat *Morgan* saw service in the area around Mobile during the war. She participated in the Battle of Mobile Bay in 1864 and managed to escape capture when the defenses fell. She remained on duty until the end of the war.

179. The *Gaines* was based out of Mobile and patrolled the Gulf until she was sunk in the Battle of Mobile Bay in 1864.

180. Hills later reported that news of this attack was an unfounded rumor.

181. The steamer *Matanzas* was probably a converted passenger vessel.

182. The *South America* was to be part of the "stone fleet" sunk in December 1861 in Charleston Harbor, South Carolina, but ended up as a wharf on Tybee Island Georgia. Either Hills' refers is in error or he refers to a different type of ship with the same name. This was not unusual during the Civil War. *Harper's Weekly*, January 11, 1862.

183. The *Miami* served with the fleet assigned to capture New Orleans and protected the mortar flotilla. She participated in the campaigns against other Confederate river defenses and later transferred to the eastern theatre of war.

184. This is the *Maria J. Carlton* of the

mortar flotilla. She was sunk on the second day of the bombardment of the forts below New Orleans.

185. Unknown vessel.

186. As the New Orleans Campaign came to a successful conclusion with the capture of that city, some expected the Union fleet's next move would be against the defenses of Mobile Bay.

187. While there was a Federal vessel named the *Union* in the Gulf Blockading Squadron in 1863, it appears to have been in the Atlantic Squadron in 1862. Hills may have confused this vessel with the *Harriet Lane*, which did receive Confederate officers for surrender.

188. It is not clear which ship Hills is referring to here. None of the vessels in the battle match these initials.

189. General Beauregard.

190. The *Burton* (or *W. Burton*) was an unarmed rebel tender assigned to the CSS *Louisiana*. She surrendered to the Union fleet on April 28.

191. *Harriet Lane.*

192. The *Landis* was an unarmed tender for the CSS *Louisiana*. She surrendered to the Union fleet with the *Burton* on April 28.

193. The *Defiance* was the only rebel gunboat to escape damage or capture during the river battle above Forts Jackson and St. Phillip. She was destroyed by her crew to prevent capture when New Orleans surrendered.

194. The *Pinola* was assigned to the Gulf Blockading Squadron in early 1862 and with the *Itasca* broke the chain below the Mississippi River forts on April 20 to allow the Union fleet to pass on April 24. She was with the fleet at New Orleans and later in the year ran past the Vicksburg defenses. She served on blockading duty in the Gulf for the war.

195. Point à la Hache.

196. USS *Connecticut*.

197. Presumably Magnolia Plantation near Point à la Hache.

198. Hills probably means Fort St. Leon, located at English Turn.

199. *Harriet Lane.*

200. Slaughterhouse Point is a reference dating back to French occupation. It was later known as Algiers.

201. The *E. Wilder Farley* was a Union troop transport.

202. Located in Algiers.

203. Customs House.

204. The steamer *Sallie Robinson* was captured by the Union Navy in New Orleans. She was later used as a transport for Union troops.

205. *Harriet Lane.*

206. Presumably this means "up and deserted."

207. Stars and Stripes.

208. Picayune.

209. Algiers.

210. Assumed to be *Wissahickon*.

211. "*Pen*" and "*Penco*" both used for USS *Pensacola*.

212. Farragut.

213. This appears to be a reference to the CSS *Louisiana* and the *Manassas*.

214. The CSS *Governor Moore* was owned and operated by the State of Louisiana and commanded by Lt. Beverly Kennon, a former U.S. Navy officer. During the river battle of April 24 the *Governor Moore* was primarily responsible for destroying the USS *Varuna* but suffered heavy casualties from the rest of the Union fleet. After being severely damaged she was destroyed by the remnants of her crew.

215. Quarantine Station was located on the east bank of the Mississippi north of Fort St. Phillip and opposite the Confederate Camp Lovell. The site is near Ostrica, Louisiana, today.

216. The *Tennessee* was a captured Confederate vessel.

217. Unknown vessel.

218. The *Diana* was captured when Union ships came to New Orleans. She was taken into Union service but was recaptured by rebel forces in March 1863 near the mouth of Bayou Teche. In April she assisted Confederate ground forces not far from here but was destroyed to prevent her capture when land forces withdrew.

219. The Chalmette Regiment was raised for local defense and made up of nearly all foreign-born men. The commander, Colonel Ignatius Szymanski, was actually from Poland rather than Portland. The regiment was surrendered and later paroled. The "drowned out" description may refer to terrain along the Chalmette line. Colonel Szymanski survived the war.

220. It is believed that "K" refers to Confederate Colonel Skimansky.

221. This may be J.F. Otis, editor of the *Daily Picayune*. He was from Boston but remained in New Orleans when the war started.

222. The *Cayuga* joined the Gulf Blockading Squadron in March 1862 and was active in the New Orleans Campaign. She was still on the Mississippi in August to shell Confederate positions at Donalsonville, Louisiana, and captured blockade runners in the Gulf. She survived the war although some of her crew were captured ashore at Sabine's Pass, Texas, in April 1863.

223. Unable to pinpoint location of this camp presumably near New Orleans.

224. The *Sea Pennell* and *Whit.* may be southern vessels captured or docked at New Orleans.

225. The *Tennessee* was being used to bring in troops, possibly from the Connecticut regiments according to this entry.

226. Handkerchief?

227. Not entirely certain about this meaning, possibly "head, heart, hands, feet," or some other body part. This may be a 19th century "flasher" account.

228. Unknown reference.

229. Leon.

230. The *Calhoun* was a rebel privateer captured by the USS *Colorado* in January 1862. She joined the Gulf Blockading Squadron that March and served very well as a blockader.

231. Unknown vessel.

232. If this refers to a specific tobacco company I have not been able to verify it through other sources.

233. Presumably this refers to prisoners from either the CSS *Louisiana* or *Manassas*, or both.

234. The steamer *City of New York* was part of Burnside's Hatteras expedition in January 1862. It was grounded and eventually sank. It is possible that the ship Hills refers to is either a schooner of the same name or an incorrectly named vessel.

235. "Nis" and "Thy" may be a reference to one or two names of confederate prisoners. If these are Confederate Navy officers they do not match the names of the senior officers.

236. The rebel steamer *Whiteman* was captured by the USS *Calhoun* on Lake Pontchartrain on May 6. Hills attributed the capture to the USS *New London* which was with the *Calhoun*.

237. This is an unknown vessel, but it is possible that Hills meant the *Eliza and Ella*, a vessel known to carry mail from Ship Island. The *Eliza and Ella* made it back to Ship Island in an unseaworthy condition after suffering damage at Horn Island. She had left Ship Island on May 7 with ten thousand letters for soldiers' and sailors' families back North.

238. I believe Hills was trying to say that the road to the fort was covered by shells as a pavement.

239. Warrington and Woolsey were towns on Pensacola Bay that contained support structures for the U.S. Navy at Fort Pickens. Warrington still exists.

240. Woodworth.

241. Hills used many abbreviations in his journals. This is probably Apalachicola, located to the east of Pensacola.

242. Information.

243. Fort Gaines protecting Mobile Bay

244. This was an exceptionally difficult portion to decipher. There appears to have been serious thought given to attack Fort Morgan, Pensacola, or Apalachicola. Fort Morgan wasn't taken until August 23, 1864, but Pensacola was occupied in May 1862.

245. It is very likely that Hills was able to speak to the prisoners on the Rhode Island on the trip to Fortress Monroe. One might wonder why he didn't clarify, while he had the chance, the story of Kennon's mistreating his crew during the river battle.

Chapter 6

1. This same Lieutenant Warley commanded a Confederate landing party that occupied Ship Island in July 1861. Peggy Robbins, "When the Rebels Lost Ship Island," *Civil War Times Illustrated*, January 1979.

2. The CSS *McRae* was assigned to the defense of the Mississippi and blockade runners in 1861 and fought at the Head of Passes in October that year. In the river battle above the forts on April 24 she was badly damaged but managed to stay afloat to take Confederate wounded to New Orleans from the forts. She sank on April 28 at New Orleans.

3. The *Stonewall Jackson* was part of the rebel river defense fleet. After ramming the *Varuna* she was chased by the USS *Oneida* and ran aground.

4. The *General Breckinridge* was a rebel river defense vessel that fought in the battle of April 24 but was abandoned and destroyed by her crew.

5. The *General Quitman* was a gunboat

operated by the state of Louisiana. She participated in the river battle of April 24 and like so many other rebel warships after the battle was burned by her crew to prevent capture.

6. The *Warrior* was one of the river defense vessels engaged in the battle of April 24. Heavily damaged by the USS *Brooklyn*, she was grounded, burned, and eventually destroyed.

7. Another river defense vessel, the *Resolute* was part of the rebel fleet engaged on April 24. She was abandoned flying the white flag but not destroyed. When several Confederate crewmen from the *McRae* tried to get her underway she was fired on by the Union fleet and so severely damaged that she was destroyed to prevent capture.

8. The *General Lovell* was also a river defense vessel that was part of the rebel fleet on April 24. She was abandoned and destroyed by her crew to prevent capture.

9. Tugboat.

10. The *Star* was destroyed during the river battle above the forts.

11. The *Belle Algerine* was a tugboat that worked to support Forts Jackson and St. Phillip before the river battle of April 24. During that battle she was used to push fire rafts downstream but suffered damage in the process. When she got in the way of the *Governor Moore* she was sunk by that vessel.

12. Although Hills does not say so specifically, Water Street in Boston is very near the residence of his father, Luther Hills, indicating a reunion. A.G. Hills does not describe how he reached Boston from Fortress Monroe at Hampton Roads.

Chapter 8

1. All of these rules or regulations have been taken from the General Orders of the Department of the Gulf issued during Butler's tenure in command, particularly numbers 28, 40, 48, 50, 55, 60, 73, 75, 76, 87, and 105.

2. Although the identity of this paper is not certain it is likely either the *New York Times* or *New York Herald* since that is the origin of the expedition for Hills in November 1862.

3. The *Essex* served on the Tennessee River and against Fort Henry early in 1862. She ran past the Vicksburg batteries later in July, eventually being retrofitted in New Orleans in September. After Hills' trip the *Essex* was part of the expedition that captured Port Hudson. She remained on river service for the remainder of the war.

4. Lt. Col. O.W. Lull, 8th New Hampshire Infantry.

5. Gunn Diaries.

6. According to the Gunn Diaries, the group of reporters living at the St. Charles Hotel spent much time loafing when there wasn't much going on at the front line. They passed the time seeking information from officers at the Army of the Gulf Headquarters and drinking.

Chapter 9

1. Gunn Diaries.

2. No longer in existence, the Astor House was considered a fine hotel. It was located on Broadway between Vesey and Barclay streets in New York City.

3. Left blank by Hills.

4. General George B. McClellan, former commander of all Union armies. Scott may be retired General Winfield Scott, McClellan's predecessor.

5. The *North Star* was a passenger ship that had made the trip from Panama to New York.

6. A passenger ship named the *Northern Lights* had made the trip from Panama to New York in June 1862.

7. As with the 1861 New Orleans Campaign, there was some secrecy involved when naval expeditions left northern ports.

8. Hills was still associated with the *Boston Journal* at this time.

Chapter 10

1. The *Adolph Hugel* was assigned to the mortar squadron that bombarded Forts Jackson and St. Phillip and remained below the forts after their surrender. When the decision was made to move upriver against Vicksburg instead of the forts surrounding Mobile, she joined other mortar vessels for the attack. Later in 1862 she was transferred with other mortar vessels to the James River in Virginia to support McClellan on the Peninsula. She served the remainder of the war in supporting the Union armies in Virginia and defending Washington, D.C.

2. Left blank by Hills.

3. Left blank by Hills.

4. The Fourth of July reference is obvious. "Seventeenth of June" refers to Bunker Hill Day in Massachusetts, and February 22 is George Washington's Birthday.

5. Hills' "press gig" partner was Henry Winser of the *New York Times*.

6. Also found in Johnson and Buel, eds., *Battles and Leaders*, vol. 2, p.101.

7. This should be the *Henry Janes*. The *Henry Janes* participated in the bombardment of Forts Jackson and St. Phillip. She shelled Vicksburg in June 1862 and served in the Gulf Blockading Squadron until 1864. She was transferred to the North Atlantic Blockading Squadron for the rest of the war for duty as an ordnance vessel.

8. Irresistible urge to write.

9. The *Kennebec* was assigned to the Gulf Blockading Squadron by February 1862. She participated in the attack against Forts Jackson and St. Phillip on April 24 but became tangled in the rafts of the chain obstruction along with the *Itasca* and *Winona*. Unable to pass, she drifted downriver and away from the range of the guns of the forts. The *Kennebec* remained in the Gulf throughout the war and joined the attacking forces at Mobile in 1864.

10. Courage inspired by the consumption of alcoholic beverages.

11. The *Ivy* served as a gunboat on the Mississippi River and was present at the battle at the Head of Passes in October 1861. While serving on the Yazoo River in May 1863 she was destroyed to prevent her capture.

12. "Not found."

13. These vessels were also known as "cotton clads."

14. This passage was lined through in pencil from the journal.

15. General Pakenham commanded the British forces in the failed attack against New Orleans in 1815.

16. Crossed out in pencil after Agaius' signature.

17. Boston Brass Band.

18. According to Kennon's report in *Battles and Leaders*, this report is false and may have increased his time of confinement. Kennon did not appear to know the source of this story and did not harbor an outstanding grudge.

Bibliography

Newspapers

Boston Daily Advertiser
Boston Herald
Boston Journal
The Era [New Orleans]
Fitchburg Sentinel
Harper's Weekly
New Hampshire Sentinel
New Orleans Bee
New Orleans Daily Delta
New Orleans Times-Picayune
New York Commercial Advertiser
New York Herald
New York Herald-Tribune
St. Albans Advertiser
Soldier's News-Letter [Ship Island, Harrison County, MS], Vol. 1, May 10, 1862.

Other Sources

Broome, Lt. Col. John. "My Own Account of the Fall of New Orleans." *Civil War Times Illustrated,* May 1987.

Census Reports of the United States, 1830–1920.

Davis, George B., Leslie J. Perry, and Joseph K. Kirkley. *The Official Military Atlas of the Civil War.* New York: Gramercy, 1983.

General Orders, Department of the Gulf. 1862-63.

Gunn, Thomas Butler. Diaries, 1861-1863. Missouri History Museum. http://www.mohistory.org/. 2011.

Hills, William Sanford. *The Hills Family in America.* New York: 1906.

Hoffman, Colonel Jon T. *USMC: A Complete History.* Westport CT: Hugh Lauter Levin Associates, 2002.

Index to Compiled Military Service Records. Official Army Register of the Volunteer Force 1861-1865. National Archives. Washington, DC.

Johnson, Robert U., and Clarence C. Buel, eds. *Battles and Leaders of the Civil War.* Vol. 2. Secaucus, NJ: Castle, 1982.

Long, E.B. *The Civil War Day by Day.* New York: Doubleday, 1971.

New York Passenger Lists, 1820-1957. United States Archives.

Nichols, James L. *Confederate Engineers.* Tuscaloosa, AL: Confederate Publishing, 1957.

Phisterer, Frederick. *New York in the War of the Rebellion.* Albany: Weed, Parsons, 1890.

Read, Benjamin. *The History of Swanzey, New Hampshire, from 1734 to 1890.* Salem, MA: 1892.

Robbins, Peggy. "Island in the Gulf." *Civil War Times Illustrated*, January 1979.

Still, William L. "Confederate Behemoth, The CSS *Louisiana*." *Civil War Times Illustrated*, November 1977.

United States. Department of the Navy. Naval History Division. *Dictionary of American Naval Fighting Ships*. Ed. James Mooney. Washington, DC: GPO, 1991.

_____. _____. _____. *Navy Chronology of the Civil War*. Washington, DC: GPO, 1966.

_____. _____. Naval War Records Office. *Official Records of the Union and Confederate Navies in the War of the Rebellion*. Volume 13. Washington, DC: GPO, 1901.

Warner, Ezra J. *Generals in Blue*. Baton Rouge: Louisiana State University Press, 1964.

_____. *Generals in Gray*. Baton Rouge: Louisiana State University Press, 1959.

Wert, Jeffrey D. "Mutiny in the Army." *Civil War Times Illustrated*, April 1985.

.

Index

Abcott, Lt. Col. 67
Adolph Hugel (or Hughes, Huger) 27, 62, 84, 129, 181
Agaius 22, 91, 116, 131, 165, 172, 187
Alden, Capt. 52, 64, 91, 150, 159
Alexandria, Louisiana 14
Algiers 39, 100, 103, 104, 184
Allen, Provost Marshall 106
Allen Guards 162
Amelia 79
American Telegraph Company 68
Anaconda Plan 23
Annable, Capt. 44, 61
Apalachicola 71, 73, 74, 180, 185
Apalachicola Bay 72, 73, 173, 180
Apalachicola River 73, 74
Arletta 26, 84, 183
Astor House 124, 186

Bailey, Capt. 33, 85, 102, 150, 158, 171
Bainbridge 67, 71, 72, 120, 182
Ballou, Capt. 129, 130
Baltic 52, 179
Baltimore 2, 21, 43, 44, 165, 176, 178
Bampton 76, 78, 80, 88
Banks, General 9, 10, 12–19, 38, 108, 118, 120, 123–127, 175, 176
Barataria Bay 34, 146
Barr, Henry C. 20
Barracuda 86
Barston, Master's Mate 130
Bartleman 79, 80, 152
Bastian Bay 146
Baten, Frank 44
Bates, Col. 129
Bates, Dr. 67
Baton Rouge 11, 108, 119, 120, 123, 127, 153, 176, 182
Bay Honde 177

Bealer, Dr. 69
Beauregard 66, 141, 162, 184
Bee, New Orleans 33
Bell, Capt. 79, 81, 150
Belle Algerine 115, 186
Belle Fontaine 47
Bellville iron works 100
Berry 52, 65
Berwick Bay 12
Beth, Frederick 99
Bidwell 145
Biloxi 9, 24, 27, 51, 54–57, 106, 178, 179, 183
Biloxi Bay 47
Bird, Francis 80
Black Prince 59, 61, 76, 180
Black Republicans 8, 175
Blake, John 62
Blanchard, Capt. 79, 86
Bliar 93, 183
Blind Bay 34
Blood, Capt. 44, 62
Boston 7–11, 21, 24, 37, 42–44, 59, 69, 80, 115, 123, 124, 172–174, 176, 177, 184, 186, 187
Boston Herald 16
Boston House 100
Boston Traveller 123, 126
Bowsprit 85, 183
Bradt, Dr. 42, 44, 48
Brady 51, 148
Bragg 30, 52, 107, 179
Brannan (or Brannon) 63, 64, 67
Brasher, Commander 72
Breckinridge 31, 113, 115, 185
Breese, Capt. 84, 85
Bridge, J.T. 20
Brigham, Billy 44
Bright's Disease 21, 22, 174

Broler, Lt. Comdg. 72
Brooklyn 29, 33, 45, 77, 88, 91, 100–103, 147, 150, 153, 158, 178, 181, 186
Broome, Capt. 33
Brown 86, 136, 154
Brown, General 63
Brown's Sappers and Miners 29
Bruce, Lt. 145, 149
Buchanon 51
Bullion 60
Bullovich 86
"bummer" 27, 31, 63, 66, 84, 89, 92, 94, 146, 155, 167
Burton 34, 95, 96, 104, 115, 143, 162, 165, 184
bushwhackers 11, 30
Butler, Capt. 61
Butler, Col. 51
Butler, General 8–10, 15, 24–26, 28, 29, 33, 34, 43, 45, 46, 55, 58, 59, 75, 76, 79–81, 85, 87, 90, 93, 103, 105, 107, 108, 118–120, 123, 124, 134, 139, 151, 153, 154, 157, 160, 161, 165, 177, 178, 183, 186
Butler, Lt. 56

C.O. Rogers 63
C.P. Miller 62
C.P. Williams 26, 84
Caldwell, Lt. 32, 150
Calhoun 26, 50, 105, 106, 178, 185
Camp Lovell 184
Cape Elizabeth 43
Cape Florida 48
Cape Hatteras 25, 45, 120, 179, 182
Cape Henry 45
Cape Sable 69
Captain Spedden 56, 180
Carrollton 102, 153
Carrysfort LeReef 48
Case Bay 43
Cat Island 45, 47
Cayuga 26, 33, 67, 101, 103, 109, 147, 158, 171, 185
Cedar Key 9, 69–71, 73
Chalmette 31, 33, 101, 102, 184
Chandeleur Island 47, 49, 178
Chandeleur Sound 69
Charlestown 47, 178
Charlotte Harbor 69
Chas. H.H. Savage 62
Chestnut, Senator 155
City of New York 105, 185
Clapp 68
Clapp, J.C. 117
Clapp, M.L.W. 124
Clerk, Capt. 43
Clifton 26, 67, 94, 142, 143, 182

Cloud 46
Cloue, Capt. 95
Coffin, Charles 8, 172, 175
Colburn 159
Collins, Capt. 62
Colorado 26, 29, 33, 44, 45, 74, 76, 78, 85, 92, 93, 104, 150, 178, 185
Columbia 64, 116, 117, 130, 181
Conlan, Sgt. 126
Connecticut 27, 29, 47, 50, 55, 60, 62, 68, 69, 71–73, 75–79, 84, 87, 116, 117, 147, 173, 184
Conner 99
Constitution 11, 37, 42, 44, 46, 49, 50, 62, 67, 68, 117, 165
Cook, Acting Master 116
Cora 68
Corinth 100, 106, 108
Corps d'Afrique 13, 120
Craig, Sr. Eng. 159
Crescent 60
Crosby, Lt. 32, 150
Cubett, Dick 154, 155
Customs House 102, 105, 133, 149, 151, 171, 176, 184
Cuyer 54

Daily Delta 4, 10, 15, 16, 118, 126, 142–144, 176, 177
Daily Picayune 4, 184
Daily True Delta 4
Dan Smith 27, 84, 147, 183
Darling, Capt. 84
Dauphin Island 106, 180
Davis, Capt. 44
Davis, Paymaster 102
Daylight 45, 178
Dearborn, Sailing Master 138
DeCamp, Capt. 95, 96
Deer Island 56
Defiance 31, 96, 104, 143, 184
De Kraffs, Capt. 52
Del House Key 70
Deming, Col. 107
Dennison, Capt. 45, 65
Depot Key 70
Desney, Charles 1136
DeSoto 3, 33, 50, 51, 176, 178, 179
Diana 33, 102, 115, 184
Disney, Dennis 148
Dixon, Lt. 96, 142
Dog Island 71–73
Douglass, Frederick 21
Duncan, Capt. 169
Duncan, General 30, 141, 143–146, 154, 155
Du Pont, Commander 72
Durivage's Cavalry 26, 28, 29

E. Wilder Farley 28, 29, 34, 98, 105, 184
Edwards, Lt. 129–131
Egmont Key 69
8th New Hampshire 25, 105, 106, 186
8th Vermont 25
Eliza Siler 106
Emancipation Proclamation 120
Emma 62
English, William 148
English Turn 33, 81, 97–99, 101, 165, 177, 184
Era 10, 12, 13, 15–17, 19, 22, 64, 121, 122, 127, 172, 174, 176
Essex 120, 186
Ethan Allen 69, 182
Eugenie Smith 69, 182
Evening Post 18, 123
Everett's Battery 28, 29

Fairbanks, Capt. 59
Fairfax, J.W. 16–18
Farr, Lt. Col 43
Farragut 9, 10, 24, 26, 30, 33, 35, 62, 77, 79, 81, 87, 92, 95, 96, 102, 106, 108, 134, 149–151, 171, 176–178, 181, 183, 184
Fearnot 55, 93, 180
Febigner, Lt. 74, 86
Felton, Lt. 77
Ferry, G.W. 20
15th Maine 26
5th Massachusetts Battery 42
50th Massachusetts 125
52nd Massachusetts 124, 125
fire raft 31, 32, 87, 88, 93–95, 115, 123, 135, 140, 145, 148, 150, 152, 156, 158, 159, 161, 186
1st Louisiana Native Guards 127
1st Maine Battery 26
1st New York 46
1st Vermont Battery 25
Fitchburg Sentinel 21
Flanders, B. F. 16, 19
Fletcher, Acting Master 129
Fletcher, Capt. 42, 45, 46, 49
Florida 49, 51, 93, 178
Flynn, Patrick 148
Foltz, Dr. 78
Foretop 37
Fornby 69
Fort Barancas 53, 54, 107
Fort Fisher 19, 122, 127, 174, 178–181, 183
Fort Gaines 54, 107, 185
Fort Independence 43
Fort Jackson 6, 9, 27, 30–33, 35, 81, 83, 87, 90, 91, 93, 94, 96, 98, 100, 103, 109, 132, 133, 136, 137, 139, 140, 142, 144–147,
149- 152, 154, 156–158, 161, 162, 165, 167, 169, 170, 174, 181, 183, 184, 186, 187
Fort Jefferson 182
Fort Livingston 34, 146
Fort Massachusetts 76, 162, 180
Fort McHenry 2, 44
Fort McRae 54, 74, 107
Fort Morgan 52, 54, 105–107, 122, 153, 155, 178, 180, 185
Fort Pickens 9, 52, 53, 63, 73, 74, 107, 185
Fort Pike 34, 60, 105, 106, 177
Fort Poinset 69
Fort St. Leon 105, 184
Fort St. Phillip 6, 9, 27, 30, 33, 79, 81, 83, 87, 91, 93–96, 98, 103, 109, 132–134, 136, 139–144, 146, 147, 149, 150, 152, 154, 156–159, 161, 162, 165, 167, 168, 174, 181, 183, 184, 186, 187
Fort Taylor 61, 63, 64, 68
Fort Warren 43
Fort Wood 106, 177
Fortress Monroe 9, 24, 25, 34, 42–45, 68, 76, 107, 177, 178, 185, 186
Fortress Morro 64, 65
41st Massachusetts 125
42nd Massachusetts 125
47th Pennsylvania 61, 62, 64, 181
14th Maine 26
4th Louisiana Native Guards 12, 13, 14, 127, 174, 176
4th Massachusetts Battery 25, 55, 60, 162
4th Vermont Battery 25
4th Wisconsin 26, 26, 28, 29
Frank Leslie's Illustrated 59, 78, 126
Freeman, Act. Master 56
French, C. W. 62
French, Capt. 115
French, Col. 46
Frye, Major 43
Fulcher, Fred 87

G.A. Ward 62, 181
Gaines 93, 183
Galveston 9, 37, 61, 120, 128–130, 181–183
Garrison, William Lloyd 20, 175
Garvy, Capt. 59
General Lovell 31, 115, 186
General Order No. 3 25
General Order No. 7 24
General Order No.8 27, 29
General Order No. 9 27, 28
General Order No. 10 183
General Order No. 14 176
General Order No. 27 119
General Order No. 28 119
General Orders Nos. 17 and 18 177
General Quitman 31, 115, 185

Index

George Greener 59
George Nahaw 62, 181
George Mangham 27, 149, 181
George Snow 63
Gibbs, Lt. 61, 64
Godfrey, Washington 84
Gorham, Ed 60
Governor Moore 31, 32, 109, 113, 115, 184, 186
Graham, Richard 148
Grand Key 48
Grant 115
Grant's Pass 50, 57, 94, 180
Graudrau, John 57
Graveline Bay 47
Great Republic 28, 93, 139, 183
Green, Capt. 103
Green, Henry 15
Gregory, J.H. 147
Grey Cloud 51, 179
Grover, General 11, 175
Guest, Capt. 79, 86, 92, 131, 133, 138, 153, 156, 170
Gulfport 24
Gun Key 48
Gunn, Thomas Butler 10, 11, 123, 126, 175, 176, 179, 186
Gypsy 55

H. Toone 94
Hahn, Michael 13
Hale, John Turner 69
Hallbrook, Maj. 106
Hallett 93
Hamilton 10, 123, 126
Hampton Roads 45, 49, 178, 181, 183, 186
Hampton Village 45
Hancock, John 148
Harper's Weekly 9, 183
Harriet Lane 26, 66, 84, 86–88, 94, 96, 98, 106, 107, 120, 136, 137, 142, 143, 148, 151, 161, 165, 181, 184
Harris, Major 44
Hartford 26, 32, 33, 62, 87–91, 100–104, 115, 135, 145, 147, 148, 150, 181
Harve de Grace 43
Hatteras 70, 84
Havana 14, 27, 38, 59, 60, 62, 64–67, 105, 116, 117, 173, 174, 180
Hayes 10, 68, 123, 179
Head of Passes 29, 30, 77–80, 92, 117, 173, 176, 177, 179, 181, 182, 185, 187
Heisler, Lt. 62
Hemony, George 125
Henry James 27, 146, 187
Henry Lewis 28, 50, 55, 56, 57, 59, 93, 139, 178, 180

Higgins, Col. 141, 142, 150
Higgins, L. F. 78
Hilbert, Chf. Eng. 62
Hills, A.C. 10, 13–16, 18, 122, 123, 174, 176
Hills, Frederick Calvin 3, 4, 7, 14, 176, 178
Hills, Luther 7, 8, 21, 22, 44, 186
Hill, Major 116
Hills, Sarah 4, 8, 15, 21, 22, 44, 79, 121, 127, 173, 174, 178
Hillsboro Key 69
Hilton Head 47
Holabird, Samuel 12, 16, 175
Holland, Michael 136, 148
Hollins, Commodore 60, 155
Hood, Capt. George 84
Horace Beals 27, 64, 80, 84, 85, 87, 88, 138, 183
Horker, Dr. 43
Horn, Dave 60, 67
Horn Island 106, 180, 185
Horn Island Pass 51, 57, 59, 180
Hotel Dearborn 21, 22
Howe, Capt. 61
Howe, Col. 16, 17, 124
Howell, Lt. 70
Hoyle, F. F. 164
Hoyt 50, 82, 104, 183
Hoyt, Capt. Stephen 16, 17
Huger, Capt. 114, 115
Hunter, Lt. 128, 129, 131
Huntsville 52, 55, 179
Hurlbut, General 18, 19
Huston, George 148

Idaho 34, 85, 183
Iroquois 26, 77, 79, 86, 88, 92, 95, 101, 104, 109, 148, 150, 159, 182
Isaac P. Smith 3, 14, 176
Isabella 62, 181
Isle au Briton 69
Itasca 26, 32, 88, 93, 147, 150, 183, 184, 187
Ivy 155, 187

J.C. Kuhn 72, 73, 182
J.P. Jackson 45, 76, 93, 97, 100, 101, 104, 107, 138, 139, 142, 144, 162, 165, 166, 176–178, 183
J.W. Hall 60, 62, 116
Jack, Capt. 80
Jackson 26, 109, 113, 114, 165, 177
Jackson Square 100
Jenks, Actg. Master 84
John Griffith 27, 86
Jones, Capt. 60
Jones, Col. 43, 45, 50, 52, 55, 61, 87, 94, 105, 140, 162, 163

Judd, Joseph 148
The Jump 30, 93, 145, 155, 156, 177

Kanawha 61, 62, 74, 75, 181
Katahdin 26, 68, 79, 84, 101, 102, 105, 147, 148, 182
Kennebec 26, 79, 81, 150, 187
Kennon, Beverly 102, 108, 109, 115, 169, 184, 185, 187
Key West 9, 25, 27, 37, 38, 49, 50, 58, 60–62, 64, 67–69, 71, 73, 85, 107, 116, 173, 182
Kineo 26, 50, 77, 79, 88, 152–154, 157–162, 179, 182
King, Master 152
Kingfisher 43, 51, 52, 54, 57–59, 67, 68, 177
Kingston 130
Kittatinny 26, 59, 76, 146, 147, 180

Lake Pontchartrain 34, 185
Lamond, Amos 126
Lamson, Capt. 146, 147
Landis 34, 96, 98, 104, 115, 143, 162, 165, 184
Langthorn, Amos 84
Laugthome, Capt. 62
Lea, Lt. 89, 96, 107
Lee, Acting Master 72
Lee, Tom 125
Libby Prison 3, 5, 176
Lidet, J.T. 120
Lincoln 105
Lincoln, President Abraham 4, 8, 20, 23, 48, 105, 173–175, 180
Locke 62
Louisiana 26, 31, 32, 108, 109, 114, 115, 137, 142–144, 147, 184, 185
Louisiana (steamer) 144
Lovell, General 145, 146, 163, 171
Lull, Lt. Col. 106, 120, 186

Magee's Cavalry 20
Magnolia 66, 68, 117, 181
Manassas 26, 31, 32, 91, 103, 104, 108, 109, 115, 137, 138, 150, 151, 154, 160, 176, 179, 181, 182, 184, 185
Manning 61
Manning, Capt. 42, 162
Manning's Battery 28, 29
Maria A. Wood 74, 182
Maria Carlton 26, 80, 148, 150, 183
Marion 73, 182
Marks, Capt. 63
Marshall, William Edgar 4, 20, 174
Mason and Slidell 48, 55
Massachusetts 56, 85, 173, 178

Massachusetts Legislative Committee on Railroads 21
Master's Mate 138
Matanzas 28, 29, 93, 103, 105, 139, 180
Matthew Vasser 26, 62
May Key 70
Mcanty, Lt. 125
McClellan 10, 23, 48, 76, 124, 186
McIntosh, Lt. 114, 115, 144, 147
McKean 55, 57
McKenzie, Lt. 153, 154
McKinson, Lt. Comm. 143
McRae 31, 109, 114, 115, 159, 160, 169, 185, 186
Meadinzer, Dr. 20
Medora 88
Mercantile Academy 8, 173
Mercedita 73, 74, 180
Merrimac 35, 48, 87
Miami 26, 94, 148, 183
Milan 59, 93, 95, 100
Miller, George 148
Miller, J.A. 148
Millwood, Capt. 44
Milston 59
Mim, John 148, 150
Minnesota 44, 178
Minnot, Leonard 136
Mint, U.S. 100, 102, 119, 133, 151, 171, 176
Mississippi 26, 27, 29, 32–34, 75, 76, 80, 84–88, 90, 93–95, 101, 103, 109, 120, 139, 147, 150–153, 160, 167, 182
Mississippi City 45, 47, 178
Mitchell, J. K. 131, 95, 104, 108, 109, 114, 142–144
Mobile 26, 27, 35, 45, 51, 52, 60, 72–75, 93, 94, 98, 106, 107, 122, 139, 145, 173, 178, 180–187
Mohawk 67, 182
Mohican 80, 183
Moir, John 148
Monitor 76, 93, 138, 179, 183
Montgomery 26, 50, 62, 84, 128, 129, 131, 181
Morgan 93, 183
Morning Star 174
Morris 50, 102
mortar flotilla 26, 27, 32, 35, 38, 39, 62, 68, 80, 84, 86, 87, 91, 93, 101, 106, 107, 133, 137–140, 142, 144, 146, 147, 149–153, 155, 163, 165, 174, 176, 181, 183, 184
Mosher 115
Mount Auburn Cemetery 22, 174, 175
Mount Vernon Hall 8, 173
Mrs. Mallory 67
Mulan 55
Mullen, Capt. 145, 146

Mumford, William 119
Murphy, Charles 148

Natchez 108, 153
New Bern 20
New Hampshire Sentinel 107
New London 50, 51, 55–59, 106, 177–180, 185
New York Commercial Advertiser 176
New York Herald 9, 126, 186
New York Herald-Tribune 176
New York Times 37, 123, 131, 177, 186, 187
New York Tribune 123
Niagara 52, 54–56, 61, 67, 68, 101, 107, 109
Nichols, Lt. Commander 95, 136, 162
Nightingale 67, 182
Nim's Battery 26
9th Connecticut 25, 27, 28, 29, 42, 43, 45, 46, 50, 55, 58, 59, 75, 76, 183
9th Michigan 27, 28
90th New York 62, 181
Nonpareil 66, 116, 181
Norfolk Packet 26, 80, 93, 148, 183
North America 28, 29
North Key 70
North Star 10, 123–126, 174, 186
Northern Lights 126, 186

Oak Island 54
Olerry, Col. 126
Oliver, Lt. 57, 58
Oliver Brach 62, 181
Oliver H. Lee 26, 84, 181
Oltmanus, Dr. 69
169th New York 126
Oneida 67, 86, 88, 98, 101, 109, 148, 150, 159, 182, 185
Oregon 50, 51, 60, 179
Oriental 61, 62, 66, 116, 180
Orvetta 27, 84, 86, 183
Osborne, Flag Lt. 62
Otis 103, 184
Owasco 62, 64, 68, 86, 92–94, 97, 103, 131, 133, 138, 150, 153, 154, 156, 170, 181
Oyster Bay 93, 139
Packer, Capt. 58
Pamlico 50, 60, 179
Pampero 51, 54, 55, 179
Para 26, 84
Parker, Lt. 49, 52
Pass à Loutre 29, 86, 103, 177
Pennington, Capt. 146
Pensacola 9, 26, 27, 35, 50–54, 59, 61, 74, 81, 85, 107, 173, 178, 181, 185
Pensacola 26, 29, 33, 35, 62, 64, 74, 76, 79, 88, 91, 92, 99–101, 103, 105, 109, 147, 150, 181, 183, 184

Perkins, Lt. 33
Perry, Commodore 160
Perry, Edward 148
Perryville 43
Petit Bois Island 180
Phelps, General 24, 25, 45, 50, 55, 58, 59, 180
Philadelphia 43
Philadelphia 116, 181
Phillips, General 165
Phillips, Lt. 51
Picayune Pier 100
Pickering, Acting Master 130
Piget, J. W. 20
Pilot Town 30, 77–80, 85–87, 92, 93, 103, 105, 107, 132, 133, 138, 147, 148, 150–153, 156, 177
Pinola 26, 32, 98, 109, 150, 183, 184
Pocahontas 33, 177
Point à la Hache 184
Pt. La Harota 98
Ponto fort 64
Pope, Capt. 154
Port Hudson 9, 11–14, 119–123, 127, 180–183, 186
Port Royal 47, 107, 116
Porter (David) 10, 23, 24, 26, 61, 62, 68, 84, 86, 87, 93, 94, 98, 106, 107, 117, 137, 140, 142–144, 146, 149–151, 155, 161, 164, 176, 178, 181
Porter, Capt. 100, 109
Portsmouth 60, 87, 88, 93, 105, 138, 148, 180
Post Office (New Orleans) 171
Potomac 51, 52, 54, 179
Powell, Capt. 52
Powers 10
Preble 54, 55, 74, 75, 84, 102, 148, 180
press gig 37, 38, 99, 131–133, 154, 170, 177, 187
Proctorville 34, 105
Pubter, Capt. 43

Quarantine Station 102, 113, 150, 160, 162, 184
Queen, Lt. 86, 88, 149
Quentin's Bayou 93

R.R. Cuyler 49–52, 60, 66, 67, 178, 179
Racer 27
Rachel Seaman 50, 51, 179
Ransom, Capt. 77, 88, 152–154, 157–160
Read's Cavalry 26, 29
Reaney 63, 67
Red River 14, 20, 35, 36, 96, 122, 174
Reinhart 61
Reliance 109

Renshaw, Capt. 94, 109, 114, 162
Resolute 31, 109, 115, 160, 161, 165, 186
Rhode Island 36, 52, 54, 55, 62, 63, 67, 104–107, 117, 174, 179, 185
Richelieu 11
Richmond 26, 64, 77, 80, 86, 88, 91, 92, 100–104, 106, 147, 150, 154, 159, 167, 177, 180, 181
Richmond Examiner 176
Rip Raps 44
Roanoke 62, 116, 181
Robertson, Acting Master 99
Rogers, Charles 63, 148, 149
Rogers, Major 43, 50
Rogers, William 84
Rogles, Maj. 124
Ruglesbe, Capt. 61
Russell, Lt. 74, 81
Russell House 38, 61–63, 69
Ryder, Act. Master 56

Sabine Crossroads 14, 182
Sable Island 93
Sachem 86, 88, 94, 183
Sacramento Union 9
Sagamon 57
Sagamore 72, 180
St. Alban's Advertiser 175
St. Andrews 73, 74
St. Charles 33, 102
St. Charles Hotel 10, 11, 100, 105, 126, 186
St. Charles Parish 174
St. Georges 72, 73, 182
St. Marks 71, 72, 73
St. Mary's Cannoneers 162, 164
St. Vincent 73, 74, 180, 182
Sallie Robinson 33, 100, 102, 184
San Louis Pass 128
Sand Island 75
Santa Rosa 52–54, 73, 74, 170
Santiago de Cuba 69, 72, 77
Sarah Bruen 27
Savage 65, 66, 88
Savannah 5, 47
Savannah Republican 19, 176
Sawtell, Major 43
Saxon 62, 63, 79, 87
Schell 10, 123, 126
Schurz, Carl 175
Sciota 26, 79, 90, 101, 147, 183
Scott, General 48, 124
Scott, George 148
Sea Foam 27, 62, 138
Sea Horse Key 70
Sea Pennell 104, 185
2nd Louisiana Native Guards 12

2nd Massachusetts Cavalry Battalion 25, 162
2nd Vermont Battery 25, 29
7th New Hampshire 67, 106
7th Vermont 25
75th New York 53, 54, 179
76th Colored Infantry 12
Shepley, General 26, 106
Ship Island 9, 24–28, 35, 37, 38, 45, 47, 48, 52, 54–56, 58, 61–63, 66, 68, 73, 75, 77, 79, 84, 87, 95, 97, 104–107, 116, 118, 120, 123, 126, 139, 155, 161, 165, 173, 177–180, 185
Shufeldt 65
6th Massachusetts Battery 25, 26
6th Michigan 25, 26, 29
6th New York 54, 179
6th Texas 129
Skimansky, Col. 102, 184
Slaughterhouse Point 99, 184
Slidell 101
Smerbing, Ernest 148
Smith, Lt. Albert 81
Smith, Allen 74, 108
Smith, Capt. 98, 109, 177
Smith, Commander (Melancton) 56, 61, 76, 84, 85, 140, 151–153, 168
Smith, Thomas 84
Soldier's Newsletter 35, 118
Sombrero Key 64
Sombrero Light 49
Sophronia 26, 64, 84, 173, 181
Soule 101
South America 94, 183
South Carolina 52, 179, 181
South West Pass 27, 29, 76, 78, 153, 177, 179, 182
Southern Republic 85
Southern Restaurant 11
Southern Sentinel 4
Squires, Capt. 96
Star 115, 186
Steel, Judge 70
Stellwagon, Lt. 73
Stevenson 115
Stickney 145, 146
Stillwell, Lt. 102
Stiner, W.H. 44
Stonewall Jackson 31, 32, 115, 165, 177, 189
Stono River 3
Strong, George, A.A.G. 25, 26, 28, 29, 87
Strother, Lt. Col. 126
Sumner, Senator Charles 20
Supply 52, 54, 60
Suwanee River 70
Sydney C. Jones 26

T.A. Ward 26, 80, 86, 88, 181
Tahoma 70, 71, 182
Tallahassee 71
Tampa 69, 73, 173
Tennessee 33, 96, 102, 104, 105, 161, 184, 185
Tenseta 62
Terry 104
Thiard, Col. 120
Thibodeaux 120
3rd Louisiana Native Guards 127
13th Connecticut 25
13th Maine 26
30th Massachusetts 25, 26, 29, 96, 97, 163
31st Massachusetts 25, 26, 29
Thomas, George 136
Thompson 159
Thornton, Lt. 62
Ticknor and Fields 20
Torbell 62
Tortugas 49, 67, 69, 117, 182
Tracy, T.G. 16–18
Travers, Thomas 148
Tucker, James T. 16
12th Connecticut 25, 28, 29, 46, 107
12th Illinois 43
12th Maine 26, 46
28th Massachusetts 46
21st Indiana 26, 28, 29, 103
26th Massachusetts 25, 26, 28, 29, 42, 43, 46, 48, 50, 51, 55, 57, 58, 59, 68, 75, 76, 140, 162, 163, 165
Tybee 47, 183
Tyler, Alexander 136

Varuna 26, 32, 101, 105, 109, 113, 147, 150, 153, 158, 160, 182, 184, 185
Vicksburg 24, 35, 119, 120, 153, 179–184, 186, 187
Vincennes 74, 75, 154, 182

W.B. Eaton 69
W. Burton 34, 184
W. Montgomery 62
W.R. King 62
Wainwright, Lt. Commander 137, 143
Wales, Dr. 78, 148
Walkulla River 72

War Correspondent's Memorial 172
Warley, Lt. 108, 109, 115, 142, 143, 150, 185
Warren, Capt. 58
Warrington and Woolsey 107, 185
Warrior 31, 115, 186
Washington, Mayor John 20
Water Witch 51, 52, 56–58, 60, 61, 67, 179
Watson, Maj. 62, 68
Waud, William 10, 77–79, 84, 87, 88, 151
Weitzel Pioneers 28
Wells, Dr. 60, 79, 88, 105
West Bay 177
Westfield 26, 67, 84, 94, 95, 106, 120, 142, 162, 182
whiskey-skins 11
Whiteman 106, 185
Whittemore, Maj. 97, 165
Whyttle, Lt. 143
Wibels 11
Wild Gazelle 28, 76
Wilder 157
Wilkinson, W. 96, 104, 108, 114
William Bacon 26, 84
Williams, General 26, 28
Wilmington 122
Wilson, Col. Billy 53, 179
Wilson, Capt. 117
Wilson, Vice President Henry 21
Wim, John 148
Winnot, Leonard 148
Winona 26, 57, 76, 95, 96, 101, 136, 147, 148, 162, 180, 187
Winser, Henry 10, 37, 87, 88, 131, 133, 177, 187
Wissahickon 26, 52, 54, 74, 79, 81, 87, 108, 160, 179, 184
Wolcott, General 24, 180
Wood 107
Wood, William 148
Woodhull, Commander 98, 147
Woodward, Mid. 56
Woodworth, Commander 94, 97, 138, 139, 144, 165, 185
Wool, General 44, 178
Worcester and Norwich Railroad 43

Zouave 58

www.ingramcontent.com/pod-product-compliance
Ingram Content Group UK Ltd.
Pitfield, Milton Keynes, MK11 3LW, UK
UKHW040610160426
5217IPUK00034B/1058